Canadian Securities EXAM

Sean Cleary, Ph.D.

JOHN WILEY & SONS CANADA, LTD
Toronto · New York · Chichester · Weinheim · Brisbane · Singapore

John Wiley & Sons Canada, Ltd.
22 Worcester Road
Etobicoke, Ontario M9W 1L1
Visit our Web site at: www.wiley.com/canada

National Library of Canada Cataloguing in Publication Data
Cleary, W. Sean (William Sean), 1962–
    Canadian securities exam fast-track study guide

ISBN 0-471-64517-6

1. Securities—Canada—Examinations—Study guides
2. Investments—Canada—Examinations—Study guides. I. Title.

HG4514.C54 2001   332.63'2'0971   C2001-901059-1

Production Credits
Cover Design and Text: Interrobang Graphic Design Inc.
Printing and Binding: Tri-Graphic Printing Limited

Printed and bound in Canada
10 9 8 7 6 5 4 3 2 1

TABLE OF CONTENTS

ACKNOWLEDGEMENTS

I would like to thank my wife Helen, my children Jason, Brennan, Brigid, and Siobhan, and my parents Bill and Beryl for their support, I would like to thank my assistants, Kim Phillips, Ingrid Kessel, and Morgan Fudge for their capable efforts. I would also like to acknowledge the support and direction provided by the Wiley editorial team, with special acknowledgements to Karen Milner and Elizabeth McCurdy.

HOW TO USE THIS BOOK

DESCRIPTION

This text is designed primarily for students who are enrolled in the Canadian Securities Course (CSC)™ through the Canadian Securities Institute (CSI), and are in their final stages of preparing to write either of their two CSC exams. The CSI does not in any way endorse this product.

One of the most common concerns expressed by my past CSC students has been the abundance of material they need to know (and understand) for the day of the examination. This concern has been alleviated to a certain extent by the reorganization of the CSC, which has resulted in two exams covering approximately half of the course material each. However, there is still a lot of material covered in each of the exams, and it is a daunting task to assimilate such a wide body of knowledge. In fact, many students have been overwhelmed by this task, and have performed below their capabilities as a result of the stress.

This study guide has been conceived and designed in order to help students avoid this problem, and focus on doing their best on the exam. It should be treated as a companion to the CSI materials, not a substitute. It is designed to help students review, digest, and prioritize the vast amount of material they should know. In other words, it provides "quick hits" of the information that's deemed to be need-to-know, in order to do well on the CSC exams.

The focus of this study guide is the review, in abbreviated format, of material that has already been covered previously by students, and provide them with the essential materials required to **pass the exams**.[1]

With this focus in mind, the text includes the following features:

1. The main body of the text provides a clear, succinct summary of the most important topics covered in the CSC textbook.

2. Within the chapter summaries, high priority topics will be noted for students, as indicated by a shaded vertical rule with an exclamation mark.

3. Each chapter will include a number of multiple-choice questions relating to the material in the chapter. The number of questions per chapter will correspond to the suggested guidelines by the CSI regarding the number of questions per chapter to be included on the CSC exams. These guidelines are listed below, and students should keep them in mind as they devote their time and energies to covering the materials included in the course. In other

---

[TM] The Canadian Securities Course (CSC), Canadian Securities, The Canadian Securities Institute, and CSI are all registered trademarks of the Canadian Securities Institute.

[1] This study guide does not serve as a substitute for reading all of the materials covered in the CSC textbooks, but does provide an excellent summary of the most important concepts covered therein.

words, **spend the greatest percentage of your study time reviewing the chapters that will cover materials relating to the largest number of exam questions.**

4. Two practice examinations that cover similar materials that will be included on each of the CSC exams, along with detailed solutions, have been included. Just like the actual CSC exams, these sample exams consist of 100 multiple-choice questions each. In addition, the questions per chapter fall within the CSI recommended guidelines. Each practice exam should be completed after the students have reviewed all the relevant materials, and feel they are "almost" ready to write that particular exam. The exams serve two purposes:

    ◦ they provide feedback regarding areas of strength or weakness, and

    ◦ they help students become more comfortable with the format of the actual CSC exams.

    However, students should be aware that the actual exams may vary substantially from these practice exams, since the CSI makes a conscious effort to change the actual CSC exams on a regular basis.

CSI EXAM QUESTION GUIDELINES

The CSI has provided the following guidelines to students regarding the approximate number of questions that will be included in the exams. While these guidelines are useful in assessing the relative importance of topics, the actual number of questions relating to a particular chapter may vary slightly from one exam to the next.

EXAM #1 (CHAPTERS 1-6)

Chapter	Number of Questions
1	8
2	12
3	15
4	15
5	25
6	25
Total	**100**

EXAM #2 (CHAPTERS 7-13)

Chapter	Number of Questions
7 and 8	30
9	12
10	25
11	8
12 and 13	25
Total	**100**

STUDY SUGGESTIONS

- The CSC exams are two hours in length each and consist of **100 multiple-choice questions (1.2 minutes per question).** They have no essay questions and are designed to test general understanding of a variety of concepts, as well as knowledge of various specific points. It is recommended that students read over the end-of-chapter questions and practice exams included in this study guide in order to get a flavour for the types of questions and concepts that are normally tested. The CSC Workbook also contains about 15 multiple-choice questions per chapter.

- You need to get **60% or better** to pass each of the exams. This means you have to get 60 questions correct. This also means you can afford to get 40 questions wrong. The message is clear—do not get discouraged when you don't know the answer to one question or even a few questions. Remain positive and continue to work your way through the exam with a positive attitude even if you hit a few trouble spots. Maintaining this attitude is also important for your studying schedule. In other words, don't get discouraged if you don't feel comfortable with all of the material. Do your best and devote your greatest effort to those topics that have the highest likelihood of being on the exam (e.g., Chapters 5 and 6 for the first exam, and Chapters 7, 8, and 10 for the second exam).

- You are not penalized for incorrect answers, so even if you don't know the answer or are not 100% certain, **never leave a question blank!** Often, even if you don't know the answer, you may be able to eliminate one or more answers, thus increasing your odds of making an educated guess.

- Cover the relevant material in the CSC textbooks prior to reviewing the material in this study guide. The glossary in the CSC textbook provides a good summary of the major definitions and terms you should know for the exams.

- During the week prior to your scheduled writing of one of the actual CSC exams allow yourself sufficient time for a general **review** of all the material. You should not be seeing any materials for the first time during this week. Past experience indicates that leaving yourself adequate time to prepare during the last week is **essential** for passing the exam, since you are required to know a lot of material on the exam date.

- When you have completed reviewing the material, simulate actual exam conditions and try the appropriate sample examination. This will give you a feeling of how well prepared you are, where your strengths and weaknesses are, and how well you must manage your time during the actual exam. Writing practice exams and reviewing the correct answers is a great way of reviewing essential topics, and simulating actual exam conditions.

- Get a good night's rest and try not to study complex materials the night before your exam, so that your mind will be fresh. Being well rested is especially important for multiple-choice questions, which generally require a great deal of clarity in thought.

- **GOOD LUCK! BE POSITIVE!**

THE CAPITAL MARKETS AND FINANCIAL SERVICES

CSC EXAM SUGGESTED GUIDELINES:

8 questions

INTRODUCTION

The vital function served by financial markets is the transfer of wealth from those who have extra wealth to those who need capital. In other words, *financial markets drive economic growth by transforming savings into investments.*

- The three components of this process of wealth transfer are:

    1. Financial Instruments
    2. Financial Markets
    3. Financial Intermediaries

1. FINANCIAL INSTRUMENTS:

These are legal, formal documents that set out the rights and obligations of the parties involved. The major categories are described below:

DEBT:

- Represents a legal obligation to repay borrowed funds at a specified maturity date, and provide interim interest payments as specified in the agreement.

- Examples include bank loans, commercial paper, treasury bills, mortgages, bonds, debentures, as well as many other instruments.

EQUITY:

- Represents part-ownership of a company.

- Common shares usually provide holders with voting privileges, and may receive dividends (however, they are not obligatory).

- Preferred shareholders typically receive a fixed dividend amount that must be paid before any dividends are paid to common shareholders.

INVESTMENT FUNDS:

- An investment fund is a company that manages investments for its clients. The most common form is the open-end fund, which is known as a mutual fund.

DERIVATIVE PRODUCTS:

- Derivatives are so-called because they derive their value from the price of another underlying asset such as a stock, stock or bond index, commodity price, etc.

- They are suitable for hedging or speculative purposes by more sophisticated investors.

2. FINANCIAL MARKETS:

- The benefits of investment products depend on the existence of efficient markets for buying and selling these instruments. An efficient market should allow for fast and low cost transactions, and maintain a high degree of liquidity. Obviously, proper regulation of these markets is essential.

3. FINANCIAL INTERMEDIARIES:

- Financial intermediaries improve the efficiency of markets by facilitating the trading or movement of the financial instruments which transfer capital between suppliers and users (including corporate, government, private, and global entities).

- Examples of financial intermediaries include the Bank of Canada, chartered banks, trust and mortgage companies, credit unions, insurance companies, pension funds, investment dealers/bankers, venture capital firms, mutual funds, leasing companies, sales finance companies, and factors.

SUPPLIERS AND USERS OF INVESTMENT CAPITAL

INVESTMENT CAPITAL:

Capital incorporates the savings of individuals, corporations, governments, and other entities. It is scarce and valuable; however, it is only economically significant when it is properly utilized.

Capital can be utilized through:

1. **direct investment** in real assets which generate wealth directly (e.g., land, buildings, equipment, human capital);

2. **indirect investment** in financial assets (e.g., stocks, bonds, treasury bills, etc.), which allows issuers of these securities to invest funds directly in wealth generating assets.

Capital is **mobile, scarce, and sensitive**—efficient allocation promotes economic growth, while inefficient allocation can constrain economic growth. As a result of these characteristics, capital is selective and tends to flow toward attractive economic environments.

- Capital tends to flow in and out of countries in response to several variables such as:

  - the political environment;
  - economic trends;
  - fiscal policy;
  - monetary policy;
  - investment opportunities and risk-return opportunities; and
  - labour force characteristics.

- The availability of capital is critical to any nation. It is necessary to promote economic output, improve productivity, encourage innovations, and in general to improve the competitive position of a nation.

SOURCES OF CAPITAL:

Individuals represent a significant source of investment capital in Canada.

- Corporations tend to retain a large portion of their earnings to finance operations and growth, and are not an important source of capital.

- Canadian governments have generally been net borrowers in recent years to fund their deficits.

- Foreign investment has grown in importance in Canada, and has been necessary to fund deficits and growth. The benefit of this fact is that it helps to expand our international trading relationships, while the cost is that this may take long-term cash flows out of the country. It is an issue that will be debated for some time to come.

- Non-residents can invest in Canada through Canadian firms (which may be located at home or abroad), or through bonds or stocks which are listed on foreign exchanges or over-the-counter markets (such as the Nasdaq Stock Market in the United States).

- There are two main categories of international bond issues:

  1. Foreign bonds: offered and denominated in the currency of a country other than the borrower; and,

  2. Eurobonds: which may be denominated in one of several currencies, and are sold in countries other than the currency in which they are denominated.

INVESTMENT OBJECTIVES:

Primary investment objectives include:

1. **safety**
2. **income**
3. **growth** of capital

These objectives are primarily mutually exclusive in the sense that one security can't maximize two or more of these primary objectives. In other words, trade-offs exist. For example, if you wish to maximize safety, you must be willing to sacrifice income and growth potential.

- Secondary investment objectives include marketability or liquidity, and tax minimization. They are secondary in the sense that they should never "override" a primary investment objective.

- The following table shows in general, how well suited bonds, preferred stocks, and common stocks are to satisfying each of these objectives:

	Safety	Income	Growth
Bonds:			
Short-term	best	very steady	very limited
Long-term	next best	very steady	variable
Preferred Stock	good	steady	variable
Common Stocks	often the least	variable	often the most

USERS OF CAPITAL:

- Individuals use capital primarily for consumption purposes, with the funds usually being obtained through personal loans, mortgage loans, or charge accounts.

- Businesses use capital to finance day-to-day operations, to maintain and upgrade plant and equipment, and to finance growth. A large proportion of funds are financed internally (through reinvested earnings), with the remainder coming from bank loans and through the issue of securities such as money market, bond, and equity instruments.

- Canadian governments have a long history of deficits which requires them to borrow to finance their expenditures.

- The federal government finances its debt using:

  1. treasury bills (T-bills);
  2. marketable short and long-term bonds (debentures); and
  3. Canada Savings Bonds (which can only be sold to Canadian residents).

T-bills and marketable bonds may be purchased by foreign investors, and by 1995 approximately 25% of the $593 billion federal debt was owed to foreigners.

- Prior to 1995, the yields on the Government of Canada's debt were generally higher than on U.S. government debt. Since then, our yields have been lower than those in the U.S. This change reflects the improved financial position of the federal government in recent years, as the government reduced, then eliminated its federal budget deficit. The elimination of the federal deficit also contributed to a 30% reduction in the amount of government T-bills outstanding in the market.

- Provincial governments may issue non-marketable bonds to the federal government, or borrow funds from the Canada Pension Plan (CPP) assets (or QPP for Quebec firms). They may also issue marketable bonds, T-bills, or provincial versions of savings bonds.

- Municipal governments borrow to provide local services such as streets, sewers, waterworks, police and fire protection, etc. They often do so in the form of serial or installment debentures (which will be discussed in Chapter 5).

THE ROLE OF FINANCIAL INSTRUMENTS

- The broad categories of financial instruments available were discussed in the introduction at the beginning of this chapter, and they are elaborated upon in subsequent chapters. The role of these instruments is to enable the transfer of capital from suppliers to users. The financial markets provide the environment that allows this transfer to take place, as discussed in the section below.

THE ROLE OF FINANCIAL MARKETS

AUCTION MARKETS (STOCK EXCHANGES):

! **Auction markets** are those where all transactions converge to one location.

! **Restructuring of the Exchanges:**

Prior to 1999, there were five stock exchanges in Canada: the Toronto Stock Exchange (TSE), the Montreal Exchange (ME), the Vancouver Stock Exchange (VSE), the Winnipeg Stock Exchange (WSE), and the Alberta Stock Exchange (ASE). As a result of the restructuring of the Canadian stock exchanges in 1999, there are presently only three exchanges:[1]

1. The Toronto Stock Exchange (TSE): which is now responsible for trading all senior equities in Canada.

2. The Montreal Exchange (ME): which is now the Canadian Derivatives Market, and handles all futures and exchange-traded options activity in Canada, and no longer trades stocks actively.

3. The newly created Canadian Venture Exchange (CDNX): which was formed by merging the Western exchanges and also trades most of the smaller stocks that used to trade on the ME. The CDNX also assumed responsibility for over-the-counter equity trading in Canada when it took over the operations of the Canadian Dealing Network (CDN) in October 2000.

! The TSE accounted for over 91% of the dollar value of stock market transactions in Canada in 1999, while the WSE was extremely small.

- Generally, the exchanges use computerized systems for trading. The TSE closed its floor trading activities and has been fully computerized since April 23, 1997.

- There are over 200 stock exchanges in more than 60 nations around the world, including about 15 in North America. The New York, Nasdaq, Tokyo, London, Paris, and Osaka stock markets are the largest, while the TSE was ranked 15th in terms of trading activity and 9th in terms of market capitalization in 1999.

- Stock exchange memberships (in the form of stock exchange "seats") are sold to individuals, which permits them to trade on the exchange. These seats are valuable assets which may be sold, subject to certain exchange conditions.

- Traditionally, exchanges have been non-profit organizations, and the CDNX continues to be so. The CDNX has two types of ownership shares outstanding: Class A (voting) shares, and Class B (non-voting) shares. The TSE became a "for-profit" private company on April 3, 2000, and the ME followed suit on October 1, 2000.

- Member firms must be publicly owned, maintain capital adequacy requirements, and key personnel must complete required courses of study.

---

[1] The number of Canadian exchanges may be further reduced in the near future, as the TSE made an offer to acquire the CDNX in March 2001.

- Exchanges are governed by bodies that consist of at least one permanent exchange official (e.g., the president), plus Governors selected from member firms, as well as two to six highly qualified Public Governors appointed or elected from outside the brokerage community.

- Exchanges such as the CDNX qualify as non-profit associations and are not subject to corporate income tax.

- Exchanges have the power to suspend the trading or listing privileges of an individual security temporarily or permanently.

Temporary withdrawals of privileges include:

1. **delayed opening** (which may arise if there exist a large number of buy and/or sell orders);

2. **halt in trading** (to allow significant news to be reported, such as merger activity); and

3. **suspension of trading** may occur for more than one session until an identified problem is rectified by the company to the exchange's satisfaction (if the company fails to meet requirements for continued trading or does not comply with listing requirements).

A listed security can be cancelled or delisted for a variety of reasons such as:

1. it no longer exists (e.g., a preferred share issue which has been redeemed);

2. the company has no assets or is bankrupt;

3. public distribution of the security is no longer sufficient; or

4. the company no longer complies with the terms of its listing agreement.

DEALER MARKETS:

Dealer markets or over-the-counter (OTC) markets are comprised of a network of dealers that trade directly with each other over the phone or through a computer network. They are negotiated networks, which maintain bid and ask quotations received from the dealers acting as market makers in given securities. Market makers execute trades from their inventories.

Almost all bonds and debentures are sold through dealer markets (about 31 times the volume that is conducted on exchanges); however, the volume of unlisted equity trading is much smaller than the volume of exchange-traded equity transactions.

- It is important to note that this market does not set listing requirements, nor does it attempt to regulate companies.

- The Canadian Over-The-Counter Automated Trading System (COATS) was introduced in 1986 by the Ontario Securities Commission (OSC) for the purpose of handling electronic quotations and trade reporting for unlisted securities trading in Ontario. Operating authority was transferred to the Canadian Dealing Network Inc. (CDN), a subsidiary of the TSE, in 1991. The CDN consisted of a large network that linked dealers across Canada, and conducted trading beyond exchange hours.

- During October 2000, about 350 of the most actively traded stocks on the CDN were shifted to the CDNX for future trading. The remaining CDN stocks (as many as 800) began trading on the Canadian Unlisted Board (CUB), which is a new Internet-based reporting system owned by CDNX. Most of these stocks are very illiquid and experience very little trading activity (many are inactive). This system is not expected to differ much from the previous one at CDN.

ALTERNATIVE TRADING SYSTEMS:

- **Alternative Trading Systems (ATS)** are computerized systems that execute orders outside traditional exchange facilities by matching orders from their own inventory, or by matching buy and sell orders from outside parties. Sometimes, they permit buyers and sellers to contact each other directly to negotiate trades. These systems are privately owned, often by individual brokerage firms or groups of firms. Most of their customers are institutional investors, who are able to reduce their transactions costs through the use of such a system. In addition, since these systems can operate when exchanges are closed, they are ideal for the trading of securities on a global basis.

- Concern has mounted over the growth of ATS trading because the details of such trades are not available to the general public, there is the ever-present threat of technological problems, and because of the potential issues arising from trading across country borders. In response to such concerns, both Canada and the U.S. have recently introduced legislation to regulate ATS trading activities.

THE ROLE OF FINANCIAL INTERMEDIARIES

- **"Intermediaries"** facilitate the transfer of capital from suppliers to users. There are several categories of intermediaries, and they tend to focus on different aspects of this process. For example, banks and trust companies accept deposits from their customers (capital suppliers) and lend to capital users. Investment funds, pension funds, and insurance companies use the funds collected from their customers to invest in the financial securities (e.g., bonds, equities) of various users of capital. Investment dealers serve a number of functions in the capital transformation process, sometimes acting as agents for their clients, and sometimes acting as principals (on their own behalf). These points are elaborated on in the next section.

- The Canadian financial system is very solid, and has experienced substantial growth in recent years. The total assets of financial institutions has more than doubled over the 1989-99 period from $911 billion to $2.157 trillion. Investment fund assets increased more than ten-fold over this period, from $32 billion to $352 billion. Bank assets also grew dramatically, from $550 billion to $1.397 trillion. This growth has been attributed to increased international activity, changes in the *Bank Act* permitting them to compete in new financial sectors, and the creation of new banks (especially foreign-owned Schedule II banks).

- The distinctions that have traditionally existed between the "four pillars" of the financial services industry (banks, trust companies, the insurance industry, and securities dealers) have become blurred over the past few years. On June 1, 1992, new federal legislation was introduced which removed several of the barriers that existed between these four pillars. The sections below discuss the major types of financial institutions.

THE CANADIAN SECURITIES INDUSTRY

THE SECURITIES INDUSTRY TODAY:

- Some basic characteristics of the Canadian securities industry include:
  1. Capital employed has grown 81% over the 1994 to 1999 period, reaching $8.7 billion (which is still small in comparison to the banks).
  2. The number of new issues brought to market has almost doubled since 1991.
  3. The combined trading activity in money and bond markets has reached approximately $10.2 trillion, down from $11.9 trillion in 1996. Equity trading has increased steadily since 1994, reaching $579 billion in 1999. The decline in overall trading activity is a result of reduced trading in the bond and money markets since 1996.
- There were 188 securities firms in Canada as of March 2000, with seven larger houses which are national in scope. Many of the smaller firms are referred to as "investment boutiques," which reflects the fact that they tend to concentrate on one particular segment of the market.
- In addition to traditional full-service brokers, there is presently a large number of discount brokerage firms in Canada. They provide fewer services, but offer investors much lower fees, and are ideal for more knowledgeable investors.
- One might expect a typical large securities firm to be organized into several departments dealing with sales, underwriting/financing, trading, research and portfolio services, and administration. A number of the smaller dealers specialize in areas such as unlisted stock trading, tax-shelter sales, etc. In addition, the major banks have opened discount brokerage services.
- The industry is highly leveraged, and short-term funding is obtained through a variety of arrangements including:
  1. day-to-day loans by chartered banks which are secured by the dealer's inventory of T-bills and short-term Canada bonds;
  2. call loans by banks which are secured by a wide range of securities and must be liquidated within 24 hours after notice has been given;

3.   purchase and resale agreements with the Bank of Canada; and

4.   free credit balances from customer accounts represent another source of borrowed funds on which interest must be paid.

- Competition in the securities industry has become fierce as a result of the growth of electronic communications and computerized trading, as well as the increased globalization of world financial markets. This increased globalization of markets is evidenced by several developments including the following:

  1.   The increase in the number of "interlisted" securities, which refers to those that are listed on exchanges in more than one country (e.g., Royal Bank is listed on the TSE and the NYSE).

  2.   Most major stock exchanges around the world are linked to one another electronically through exchange trading links.

  3.   Many exchanges around the world are offering extended trading hours, in order to allow response to global events.

  4.   The growth of unregulated markets, such as the Eurobond market.

  5.   There has been a large increase in investment mobility, with investors shifting their funds across borders, much more often, and with less difficulties than in the past.

PRIMARY MARKETS:

An important role for investment dealers (IDs) is to bring together those with surplus capital with entities that require investment capital. This function is performed in the **primary** or **new issue market**, where the *IDs may act as principals or agents.*

Underwriting or **financing** refers to the purchase of new securities from the issuer on a given date at a specified price, which is then to be sold to others. IDs serve as *principals* under this arrangement, and their compensation is the "spread" between the purchase price and the resale price. Under this arrangement, *dealers assume the risk* of the security not selling at adequate prices; however, they take a number of precautions to minimize this risk. Typically, they work closely with the issuers regarding the pricing, timing, and design of the issue so that it will be well received by the market. In addition, *underwriting syndicates* are often formed to spread the financing risk, and enhance marketability of the issue. The issue may also include special clauses which may terminate the agreement under exceptional circumstances.

IDs may also perform this function by assuming the role of *agents* who market the newly issued securities on a "**best efforts**" basis. They receive compensation in the form of a commission, and it is *the issuer which assumes the risk* of the issue not selling. This arrangement is more typical for issues of smaller or more speculative companies, or for "private placements" for large companies with good credit ratings (where the risk of the issue not selling is negligible).

SECONDARY MARKETS:

IDs also serve an important role in **secondary markets**, which facilitate the transfer of existing securities among investors. Secondary markets enhance the effectiveness of the primary market. This function may also be achieved by having **IDs act as principals or agents**.

IDs serve as *principals* by trading securities with clients from their own inventory, and also when they trade for their own account. They earn income in the form of a "spread," and *assume the majority of the risk*.

IDs act as "brokers" (or *agents*) when they execute transactions for customers, and charge them commissions. Minimum commission rates are no longer prescribed by the exchanges, and commissions may be negotiated between clients and their brokers. This has led to the development of several discount brokerage houses in Canada, which eliminate many traditional services offered by full brokerage firms, and pass the savings on to investors in the form of reduced commission fees. They are tailored toward knowledgeable "do-it-yourself" investors.

- A typical "agency transaction" involves clients instructing their IDs to get the best possible price (i.e., a "market order" to be discussed in Chapter 6). Once the transaction is completed on the floor (or electronically), the details of the trade are reported over the exchange's ticker, and the buying and selling firms are provided with specific details of the trade (e.g., price, time, identity of the other party). The firms phone their clients to confirm the transaction, and then mail written confirmation to them that day or the next business day.

- Once the transaction has occurred, the parties must "settle" the transaction. If the buying firm has sufficient funds available in their cash or margin account, these funds will be used to execute the transaction. Otherwise, the buyer must provide sufficient funds by the **settlement date** (three business days after the trade for most securities).

If the certificate is in registered form, the seller must properly endorse and deliver it. Today, in Canada, most stock and bond certificates are held by the **Canadian Depository for Securities (CDS)** clearing corporation, which electronically settles all transactions between members on a daily basis without physically moving the certificates. This system is used by the TSE, the ME, the CDNX, as well as by participating banks and trust companies.

When an ID trades from its own account, the trade occurs at current market value as determined by the exchange. There are detailed regulations which member firms must observe to avoid potential conflicts of interest.

CHARTERED BANKS:

- Banks concentrate on gathering funds through savings deposits and/or certificates of deposit (CDs) and transferring them to users in the form of mortgages and other forms of loans. Their primary source of income is the "spread," which is the difference between the rate they pay to depositors and the rate charged to lenders, although service charges have grown as an important source of income in recent years.

- They are governed by the *Bank Act* which is revised periodically (every 10 years or so).

Schedule I banks must be widely held, with no investor holding more than 10% and foreign ownership is limited to 25%.[2] While there are currently 54 banks in Canada, the Schedule I banks dominate Canada's capital market, with the "Big Six" accounting for more than 90% of the $1.3 trillion in bank assets. The "Big Six" are Royal Bank, Canadian Imperial Bank of Commerce, Bank of Montreal, Scotiabank, Toronto-Dominion Bank, and National Bank. They maintain a network of more than 8,200 retail branches and 15,500 automated banking machines, and are becoming major international participants.

- Banks are generally funded by savings deposits, retained earnings, periodic rights offerings to existing shareholders, debentures (since the 1967 *Bank Act* revision), and preferred share issues (since the 1980 *Bank Act* revision).

- Since most of their liabilities (i.e., savings deposits) are due on "demand," it is important that they maintain an adequate reserve of liquid assets. This used to be a legal requirement; however, it has been removed in recent years.

- In 2000 Canadian banks maintained about 10% of total assets in liquid assets, 34% in personal and business loans, and 30% in residential mortgages.

Schedule II banks may be wholly owned by residents or non-residents. They are generally subsidiaries of foreign banks (42 out of a total of 45 as of May 1999). Until 1980, they were not allowed to accept deposits or call themselves banks, and most restricted their activities to making corporate loans. Non-U.S. banks are restricted to 12% of total assets of the banking system; however, there is no such limit placed on U.S. banks, as a result of the Free Trade Agreement of 1989.

---

[2] These rules will be changed in the near future according to a new legislative policy framework introduced in June of 2000. Under the new rules, there will be three classes of banks, based on the size of their equity base: large (greater than $5 billion); medium ($1 to $5 billion); and small (less than $1 billion). Based on present figures, the $5 billion cut-off point would establish all of the present Schedule I banks as large banks, except the National Bank (although it would be classified as such until deemed otherwise by the Minister of Finance). The large banks will have to remain widely held under new criteria which eliminate the 25% foreign ownership rule; and permit a single investor to own up to 20% of the voting shares of the bank, and up to 30% of non-voting shares, subject to a "fit and proper" test designed to evaluate their character and suitability. Medium banks would be allowed to have a single owner hold up to 65% of shareholdings, and would be required to maintain a public float of at least 35% of voting shares. Small banks would face no ownership restrictions other than the "fit and proper" tests.

- Some of the more significant developments in recent years include:

  1. The movement by banks into the securities business (i.e., all of the big six have acquired investment dealers in the past few years).

  2. Banks are permitted to offer non-banking financial services such as trust and insurance activities through subsidiaries only.

  3. Banks can directly provide investment counseling and portfolio management services.

LIFE INSURANCE COMPANIES:

- Life insurance companies act as trustees for funds they receive from policyholders. Safety of principal is a primary investment objective for these companies. Many of their contracts are long term and, as a result, insurance companies tend to be active in both mortgage and long term bond markets.

- Key 1992 federal legislation (the *Insurance Companies Act*) now permits life insurance companies to own trust and loan companies through subsidiaries. It also maintained the practice of allowing only life insurance companies to offer annuities and segregated funds. Life insurance companies are required to follow investment rules based on a "prudent portfolio approach."

- The insurance industry has been undergoing a significant amount of consolidation in recent years, a trend that has been contributed to by **demutualization**. Demutualization refers to the reorganization of the ownership structure of life insurance companies, from being owned by its policyholders, to being owned by shareholders. This is accomplished by providing the policyholders with the appropriate number of shares to compensate them for the value of their policy holdings.

- Another significant development for life insurance companies has been the growth in segregated funds (to $67.5 billion as of April 2000). These products are similar to mutual funds, and Chapter 8 has been devoted to their discussion.

INVESTMENT FUNDS:

- Investment funds may be set up as a corporation or as a trust. The funds then sell their shares (or trust units) to the public and invest the proceeds in portfolios of securities.

- Closed-end funds normally issue shares only at their initial start-up. Occasionally, they may issue shares at other points in time. They invest the proceeds from the issue in a portfolio of securities in order to earn income and capital gains.

- Open-end funds (or mutual funds) issue and redeem shares on a continuous basis, at the fund's net asset value per share (or unit). These funds account for 95% of aggregate funds invested.

- The objectives of investment funds vary significantly, which is reflected in their portfolio composition. Investment funds are discussed in greater detail in Chapter 7.

OTHER INTERMEDIARIES:

1.   TRUST AND MORTGAGE COMPANIES:

- Many services overlap with those offered by banks including accepting savings, issuing term deposits, making personal and mortgage loans, and selling RRSPs. They remain distinct in that they are the only type of corporations in Canada permitted to act as trustees in charge of corporate or individual financial assets.

- There were approximately 55 of these companies in Canada by the end of 1998, with many of the larger ones now being owned by the chartered banks.[3] For example, the TD Bank acquired Canada's largest trust company, Canada Trust in 1999.

2.   PENSION PLANS:

- Many employees are members of trusteed company pension plans. Pension contributions are made to a trustee who registers the plan, and manages it in accordance with the terms of the plan's trust deed. Typically, the trustee is an independent trust or insurance company.

- The main concerns for these plans focus on safety of principal and income, which results in the plans being large buyers of both government and corporate debt. Since pension benefits typically are paid well into the future, many plans purchase substantial amounts of investment-grade common shares to help protect against inflation. These funds cannot invest more than 20 % of their assets in foreign securities.

- Government-operated pension plans (the Canada Pension Plan (CPP) and the Quebec Pension Plan (QPP)) originated in 1965, and membership by employed persons is mandatory. Both funds provide certain disability, death, widows' and orphans' benefits.

3.   CREDIT UNIONS AND CAISSES POPULAIRES:

- These are cooperative, member-owned businesses which provide basic financial services to their members. They must adhere to the "prudent portfolio approach" to investment.

4.   SALES FINANCE AND CONSUMER LOANS COMPANIES:

- Make direct cash loans to consumers and/or purchase installment sales contracts from retailers and dealers at a discount.

---

[3] In fact, the number of independent trust companies had decreased to 15 as of March 2000, down from 50 in 1990.

5. *PROPERTY AND CASUALTY INSURANCE COMPANIES:*

- Provide property, automobile, health, and accident insurance. They are much smaller than life insurance companies; however, their investment decisions are also governed by the prudent portfolio approach. Liquidity is obviously a primary investment objective, since they must be able to settle claims as they arise.

REGULATORY ORGANIZATIONS

THE OFFICE OF THE SUPERINTENDENT OF FINANCIAL INSTITUTIONS (OSFI):

- The Office of the Superintendent was formed in 1987 by the amalgamation of the Department of Insurance and the Office of the Inspector General of Banks. It regulates and supervises banks, insurance, trust, loan, and investment companies, and cooperative credit associations which are chartered federally. It also supervises federally regulated pension plans. However, it does not regulate the Canadian Securities Industry, which is a provincial responsibility.

- The Financial Supervisory Committee is composed of the Superintendent (the committee chair), the Governor of the Bank of Canada, the Deputy Minister of Finance, and the Chairman of the Canada Deposit Insurance Corporation (CDIC). Its mandate is to facilitate interaction among its members.

THE PROVINCIAL REGULATORS:

Regulation of the securities industry in Canada is a provincial responsibility, which is delegated to securities commissions in most provinces, and is handled by appointed securities administrators in others. The provincial regulators work closely with the Canadian Investor Protection Fund and Self-Regulatory Organizations to maintain high standards.

CANADIAN INVESTOR PROTECTION FUND (CIPF):

- The CIPF is designed to protect investors from loss due to the insolvency of a member of any of the Sponsoring Self-Regulatory Organizations (SSROs), which include the IDA, and the exchanges. It is governed by a 12-member board of governors which includes five representatives from the SSROs, and five governors representing the general investing public. The President and Chief Executive Officer of the Fund, as well as the Chairman, are also governors.

The role of the CIPF is to anticipate and solve financial difficulties of member firms in order to minimize the risk of insolvency, and to attempt to bring about an orderly wind-down of a business if necessary.

- Fund assets are funded by contributions from the securities industry, as well as an operating line which is provided by a chartered bank.

From the moment an investor becomes a customer of any of the SSROs, the accounts are automatically covered by the Fund. The Fund covers separate accounts for individuals provided they are not held for the same purpose. For example, the accounts of a customer maintaining two personal holding corporation accounts would be combined into one. The coverage limit is presently $1 million for losses related to securities holdings and cash balances combined; however, the cash balance coverage cannot exceed $60,000. The Fund does not cover losses that result from changing market values, and rejects claims from parties that are not dealing at arm's length with the insolvent firm, or those whose dealings contributed to the insolvency.

THE SELF-REGULATORY ORGANIZATIONS (SROS):

- SROs deal with member regulation, listing requirements, and trading regulation. These include the TSE, the ME, the CDNX, the Investment Dealers Association (IDA), and it is expected the newly created Mutual Fund Dealers Association (MFDA) will gain approval as an SRO in 2001.[4]

The **IDA** is the national trade association of the investment industry, and is a self-regulatory organization. It represents firms in the securities business across Canada. Its mission is to "foster efficient capital markets by encouraging participation in the savings and investment process, and by ensuring the integrity of the marketplace."

- In addition to being a national trade association, the IDA serves as an industry regulator. These roles complement one another, and its responsibilities include monitoring member firms for capital adequacy and business conduct, as well as regulating the qualifying and registration process of these firms. As the nation's only national SRO, it has the additional responsibility of ensuring that national policies and rules reflect the various perspectives of people in all parts of the country.

In its efforts to foster more efficient capital markets, the IDA serves as a market regulator:

1. playing a key role in formulating policies and standards for primary debt and equity markets; and
2. monitoring activities of member firms, and developing trading and sales practices for fixed-income markets.

---

[4] The MFDA gained approval as an SRO from the Ontario Securities Commission, the British Columbia Securities Commission, and the Saskatchewan Securities Commission in February 2001, and expected to receive a similar endorsement from the Alberta Securities Exchange in March of 2001.

The IDA also serves as an international representative, and as a public policy advocate by striving to provide accurate information and practical advice to government agencies on matters related to the securities industry.

- The IDA strives to ensure the integrity of the marketplace and protection of investors. This requires that member firms maintain financial standards and conduct their business within appropriate guidelines. Financial compliance is monitored by the IDA's Compliance Department, while conduct of business compliance is monitored by their Investigations Department.

- The MFDA was created in 1997 in response to the need for regulation in this rapidly expanding industry. It is responsible for regulating the distribution of mutual fund securities; however, distributors that were previously members of an SRO such as the IDA, will continue to be monitored by that SRO. Regulation of the actual funds will remain the responsibility of the securities commissions.

ARBITRATION:

- While SROs are permitted to discipline their members, they cannot award restitution to parties that may have been wronged by a member of an SRO. The injured party would normally be required to go to court to obtain restitution. In response to this, SROs in all provinces west of New Brunswick have begun offering investors the opportunity to seek compensation through arbitration rather than in court, provided the claim meets certain criteria:[5]

  - attempts were made to resolve the dispute with the investment dealer;
  - the claim amount does not exceed $100,000; and
  - the disputed events must have occurred after certain cut-off dates specific to the province (ranging from January 1, 1996 in Quebec, to June 30, 1999 in the Atlantic provinces).

THE CANADIAN SECURITIES INSTITUTE (CSI):

- The CSI is a not-for-profit organization which was created in 1970, and is the national educator of the Canadian securities industry. Its two goals are to increase the competency levels of people working in the financial services industry, and to promote wider knowledge and appreciation of investing among Canadians. It is overseen by a Board of Governors from the securities industry's SROs.

- Completion of CSI courses is mandatory to meet the requirements for various registration categories and every year, approximately 40,000 industry and non-industry people enroll in CSI courses. Completion of these courses leads to the designations such as the Certified Investment Manager (CIM), Financial Management Advisor (FMA), and Fellow of the Canadian Securities Institute (FCSI).

---

[5] In late 1999, the SROs were working to extend the program to the Atlantic provinces.

Chapter 1: Review Questions

1. The following are all examples of primary investment objectives except for: (   )
   a) safety
   b) liquidity
   c) income
   d) growth

2. Which of the following represent a source of capital?   (   )
   a) individuals
   b) businesses
   c) governments
   d) all of the above

3. When investment dealers market a new security offering on a best-efforts basis, they are acting as _____ in the _____ market.   (   )
   a) principals; primary
   b) agents; primary
   c) principals; secondary
   d) agents; secondary

4. All of the following represent an indirect investment except for: (   )
   a) the purchase of common shares
   b) the purchase of T-bills
   c) the purchase of new land
   d) all of the above are indirect investments

5. When a company calls a news conference to announce a pending merger, the exchange on which its shares are listed is likely to: (   )
   a) delist the security
   b) announce a halt in trading for the company's stock
   c) announce a suspension of trading of the company's stock   (   )
   d) do nothing

6. The _____ was established to protect investors in the event of insolvency of a securities firm. ( )

   a) CDS

   b) IDA

   c) SSRO

   d) CIPF

7. The "four pillars" has traditionally referred to: ( )

   a) banks, trust companies, investment funds, and pension funds

   b) banks, insurance companies, investment funds, and pension funds

   c) banks, investment dealers, trust companies, and insurance companies

   d) banks, insurance companies, trust companies, and pension funds

8. The following are all members of the Financial Institutions Supervisory Committee except for: ( )

   a) the Governor of the Bank of Canada

   b) the Minister of Finance

   c) the Chairman of the Canada Deposit Insurance Corporation

   d) the Superintendent of Financial Institutions

THE CANADIAN ECONOMY

MEASURING THE ECONOMY

Gross Domestic Product (GDP) is the value of all goods and services produced in a country in a given year. It must equal gross domestic income, which will be the same as gross domestic expenditures. Income includes income earned by: labour (wages and salaries); business (corporate profits); lenders (interest); and government (taxes). Total expenditures is comprised of: consumer spending (C); investment in household residences, business investment in inventories, and capital equipment (I); government spending (G); and foreigners' spending on Canadian exports minus Canadians' spending on foreign imports (X-M). Thus, we typically see the following equation used to depict GDP level: **GDP = G + C + I + (X−M).**

Gross National Product (GNP) is the value of all goods and services produced by Canadians at home or abroad. Some countries use this to measure economic activity, rather than GDP.

Growth of GDP generally results from three factors:

1. increases in population;
2. increases in capital stock; and
3. technological innovation.

INTEREST RATES

- **Interest rates** have a very profound affect on securities markets, since they represent the price of credit, as determined by the forces of supply and demand.

Interest rates will differ for a variety of reasons including the **duration** of the borrowing, the terms of the loan, and the **creditworthiness** of the borrower.

High interest rates tend to:

1. **raise the cost of capital** to firms, which reduces business investment;
2. **discourage consumer spending**, particularly for durables; and
3. **reduce disposable income** available for net borrowers due to higher debt servicing charges.

Some **key interest rate determinants** include:

1. **Inflation:** rates rise to compensate lenders for loss in purchasing power as inflation rises.
2. **Foreign developments** and the **exchange rate:** foreign interest rates and domestic exchange rates affect the demand for Canadian debt instruments.
3. **Government deficits** or increases in investment **spending:** these cause an increased demand for capital, which increases rates unless there is a corresponding increase in savings.
4. The **default risk** of the borrower: the greater the risk of default, the greater the rate that must be paid to borrow funds.
5. The **Bank of Canada:** can impact short-term rates directly, and may impact long-term rates less directly through its credibility of commitment to controlling inflation.

- Interest rates are determined based on future expectations, particularly with regards to future levels of inflation. This is because the real interest rate equals the nominal interest rate minus expected inflation. Real rates were historically in the 5%-7% range; however, they have fallen to about 2% in recent years.

MONEY AND INFLATION

- Money includes coins, bank notes and draws on bank accounts. It serves as a unit of account, which establishes the relative values of different goods and services.

Standard **measures of money supply** used by the Bank of Canada include the following:

1. **M1:** currency held outside the bank plus demand deposits less private sector float.
2. **M2:** M1 plus personal savings deposits plus non-personal notice deposits.
3. **M2+:** M2 plus deposits at trusts and mortgage loan companies, credit unions, caisses populaires, plus money market mutual funds plus insurance annuities.

4. **M3:** M2 plus non-personal fixed term deposits plus foreign currency deposits of residents booked in Canada.

The most widely used measure of inflation is the consumer price index (CPI), which tracks the price of a given "typical" basket of goods and services (600 different items included). The cost of this basket is related to a base year cost, which is presently 1992. It may overstate the true level of inflation by failing to capture improved quality of the "basket" and consumers' tendencies to switch to less expensive items.

- **Inflation** refers to a general decline in the value of money due to a sustained trend of rising prices. It is one of the most important factors affecting securities markets, because it erodes the real value of long-term investments.

Inflation has several associated **costs** including the following:

1. It erodes the standard of living for those on fixed income, which may aggravate social inequities.

2. It reduces the real value of investments such as loans, since they are paid back in dollars that are worth less.

3. It distorts signals to economy participants that are normally given through asset prices (since "relative" prices may be harder to establish).

4. Accelerating inflation generally causes increases in interest rates, which may lead to recessionary periods.

- Inflation occurs when demand for goods and services exceeds (or grows faster) than supply. The **output gap** refers to the difference between the potential full capacity level of output from actual output. When actual output is near full capacity, increased demand will lead to inflation.

A number of **indicators** are monitored for signs of changes in inflation including: commodity and wholesale prices; wage settlements; bank credit; and exchange rate movements.

- Monetary economists argue that monetary supply is the main determinant of inflation, while non-monetarists argue that money supply increases in response to changes in demand, and not vice-versa.

LABOUR MARKETS

Three **key labour market indicators** are described below:

1. **Employment** measures the number of individuals that are employed at a given point in time.

2. The **participation rate** measures the percentage of the working age population (15 to 65) that is in the labour force, either working or looking for work. It has risen steadily since World War II, except for a severe decline since the end of the last recessionary period.

3. The **unemployment rate** is measured as the percentage of the labour force that is looking for, but hasn't found employment. It will change in response to changes in the number of people employed, and/or due to changes in the number of people looking for work. There are two general types of unemployment:

   ○ **cyclical**, which arises due to temporary hirings or layoffs which may be attributable to the business cycle; and

   ○ **structural**, which is caused by a variety of factors. It includes normal unemployment caused by people in job "transition" stages, which is often referred to as **frictional unemployment**. Other factors such as regulation and general economic health will contribute to the level of structural unemployment that will exist in an economy even if it is healthy. This level of unemployment is sometimes referred to as the **natural or full employment unemployment rate, or the non-accelerating inflation rate of unemployment (NAIRU)**.

EXTERNAL SECTOR

- Canada's financial interactions with other countries are captured in its **balance of payments**, which is comprised of the current account and the capital account.

The **current account** records all payments between Canadians and foreigners for goods, services, interest, and dividends (i.e., it is similar to an income statement). The most important item is **merchandise trade**. In 1999, Canada exported $360.6 billion of goods and services, and imported $326.8 billion. The U.S. is our major trading partner and accounted for 84% of our exports and 77% of our imports in 1999. Other components of the current account include **investment income, services**, and **transfers of funds** (e.g., through foreign aid and/or wealth brought to Canada by immigrants).

The **capital account** reflects net equity and debt financing by Canada with foreigners (i.e., it is similar to a balance sheet). The major components include: **direct investment** in assets or companies; **portfolio investment** in debt (treasury bills or bonds) or equity; and **international reserves transactions** in currency markets.

- In order to finance current account deficits, a country must issue foreigners an IOU such as a bond or treasury bill, and/or sell domestic assets such as land or companies to foreign interests. This implies that current account deficits require capital account surpluses, since the two accounts must balance.

THE EXCHANGE RATE

The **exchange rate** affects the economy in several ways, most importantly through trade. All else being equal, a higher exchange rate would tend to lower Canada's trade balance. However, there are several other factors at work in determining the impact of a change in the exchange rate on trade. For example, lower inflation rates may offset the impact on foreign trade of a higher exchange rate, due to the lower associated costs.

The **trade-weighted exchange rate** measures the value of the Canadian dollar against ten major currencies, based on the proportion of our trade maintained with each of those countries. In practice, people tend to focus on the Canada-U.S. exchange rate due to its importance to us as a trading partner, and also because of its widespread acceptance as a leading global currency.

Exchange rate systems or regimes are commonly classified as fixed or floating systems. **Floating systems** allow the exchange rate to be freely determined in foreign exchange markets. Under a **fixed exchange rate system**, the central bank "pegs" the domestic currency against another currency or composites of other currencies. This can be achieved by forcing all purchases and sales of the domestic currency to be handled only through its own banks, at its price. This can be costly and distortive to the operation of the economy, and typically leads to the development of black markets. Typically, more advanced countries avoid this approach, and maintain a fixed exchange rate by instructing their central bank to buy and sell the currency in the open market, and adjust interest rates as required to maintain a certain exchange rate range. This approach requires the maintenance of a sizable foreign exchange reserve which must be utilized when the currency faces substantial market pressures. Fixed exchange rates are often used to assist high-inflation countries in "importing" the stability of the country to which it pegs its currency; however, it restricts the local monetary authority's ability to deal with interest rates at the local level.

- The Bretton Woods system was adopted by most major countries from the end of World War II to 1971. It involved pegging currencies to U.S. rates, and the U.S. dollars were freely convertible into gold. Currency devaluations required the approval of the International Monetary Fund (IMF). The U.S. halted the convertibility of its currency into gold in 1971, which led to the end of this system. Canada did not particpate in this system from 1950-62.

The following factors impact on the exchange rate to varying degrees:

1. **Inflation differentials:** countries with lower inflation tend to appreciate through time to reflect their increased purchasing power relative to other countries.

2. **Interest rate differentials:** higher interest rates tend to attract more capital and make a currency value increase, provided the difference is not merely a reflection of higher inflation.

3. **Current account:** countries that continually run deficits will have excess demand for foreign currencies, which puts downward pressure on the domestic currency.

4. **Economic performance:** a strong economy attracts investment capital by offering higher returns, and thus leads to more favourable exchange rates.

5. **Public debt and deficits:** countries with large debts are less attractive to foreign investors because:

    ○ they have higher incentive to allow inflation to grow (and repay in "cheaper" dollars);

    ○ they rely more on foreign investment; and

    ○ debt accumulation affects the country's ability to repay.

6. **Terms of trade:** is the ratio of export prices to import prices, an increase which suggests increased demand for the local currency.

7. **Political stability:** capital tends to exhibit a "flight to quality," particularly in times of increased uncertainty, which implies that instability exerts downward pressure on exchange rates.

Most countries maintain a **foreign exchange reserve**, including Canada, where it is called the Exchange Fund Account. This is a federal government account that is managed by the Bank of Canada, and is comprised of foreign currencies (mainly U.S.$—almost 70% in 2000), gold, and reserves in the IMF.

THE ECONOMY IN THE SHORT RUN

• Although our economy has grown through the years, it has also displayed periods of negative growth. Normal fluctuations in long-term growth, has typically followed a series of patterns referred to as business cycles.

THE BUSINESS CYCLE:

The five major phases of these cycles, described below, are:

1. Expansion
2. Peak
3. Recession
4. Trough
5. Recovery

Expansion: Normal growth stages are typically characterized by: stable inflation; rises in corporate profits; increased job startups, and reduced bankruptcies; increasing inventories and investment by business to deal with increased demand; strong stock market activity; and job creation and falling unemployment.

Peak: Demand has begun to outstrip economic capacity, increasing inflationary pressures, which leads to increasing interest rates and falling bond prices. Investment and sales of "durables" fall, and eventually stock market activity and stock prices decline.

Recession: Often defined as two consecutive quarters of negative growth (although this definition is not used by Statistics Canada (StatsCan) or the U.S. National Bureau of Economic Research). StatsCan judges a recession by the depth, duration, and diffusion of the decline in business activity (i.e., the decline must be of significant magnitude, last longer than two months, and be spread throughout the entire economy).

Trough: Near the end of a recessionary period, falling demand and excess capacity lead to drops in prices and wages. The resulting decline in inflation leads to falling interest rates, which will begin to rally the economy.

Recovery: This phase refers to the period of time it takes for GDP to return to its previous peak. It is generally initiated with an increase in demand for interest rate sensitive items such as houses, cars, and other durable goods, and then spreads throughout the entire economy. Another expansionary phase is said to begin once GDP passes its previous peak.

When economic growth declines substantially, but does not turn negative, and inflation remains in check, it is generally referred to as a "**soft landing**."

BUSINESS CYCLE INDICATORS:

Leading indicators are those that generally change before changes in overall economic activity. They provide useful tools for predicting the future direction of the economy. Some of the more important leading indicators include:

1. housing starts;
2. manufacturers' new orders, especially for durables;
3. changes in profits;
4. spot commodity prices;
5. average hours worked per week;
6. stock prices; and
7. money flows.

Statistics Canada's Composite Leading Indicator is composed of the following 10 items:

1. the TSE 300 Composite Index;
2. Real Money Supply (M1);
3. the United States Composite Leading Index;
4. New Orders for Durable Goods;

5. Shipments to Inventory Ratio-Finished Goods;
6. Average Work Week;
7. Employment in Business and Services;
8. Furniture and Appliance Sales;
9. Sales of Other Retail Durable Goods; and
10. Housing Spending Index.

Coincident indicators change in conjunction with changes in overall economic activity, and are useful for identifying changing points in the business cycle after they have occurred. These include **GDP, industrial production, personal income**, and **retail sales**.

Lagging indicators change after changes in overall economic activity have taken place. These include **business investment spending**, the **unemployment rate**, **labour costs**, **inventory levels**, and **inflation**.

THE ECONOMY IN THE LONG RUN AND ECONOMIC POLICY

- Over the 1950-92 period, real output increased an average of 4.3 times for the G-7 countries, ranging from 2.0 for the U.S. to 10.6 for Japan. Canada's ratio was 2.6.

- Governments throughout the world try to influence both short-term and long-term economic growth through the use of their policies. **Microeconomic policies** focus on the functioning of businesses, workers, and labour and product markets. **Macroeconomic policies** involves the use of monetary policy and fiscal policy, which are described in the next two sections, respectively.

MONETARY POLICY

Monetary policy refers to the use of interest rates, the exchange rate, and the rate of money supply growth to influence demand and inflation. This function is performed in Canada by the **Bank of Canada**, which was founded in 1934.

- The Bank is governed by a Board of Directors that includes: the Governor, the Senior Deputy Governor, and 12 directors (traditionally, there is at least one member from each province). The Minister of Finance appoints Directors for three-year terms. The Directors, with the approval of the Governor-in-Council, appoint the Governor and Senior Deputy Governor for seven-year terms. The Governor is Chairman of the Board and Chief Executive Officer, and is responsible for formulation and execution of monetary policy. The Deputy Minister of Finance also sits on the Board, but cannot vote.

- The responsibilities of the central bank include:

    1. Issuer of the nation's currency.
    2. Banker to the central government.
    3. Operation of monetary policy.

- Its general duties include:

    1. Regulate credit and currency.
    2. Control and protect the external value of the national monetary unit.
    3. Mitigate by its influence, fluctuations in the general level of production.
    4. Promote the economic and financial welfare of Canada.

The major functions of the Bank are:

1. Acting for the government in the issuance and removal of bank notes.
2. Acting as the government's chief fiscal agent and financial advisor. As a fiscal agent, the Bank advises the government on financial matters; administers the deposit and fund accounts; manages international currency reserves and operates for the government in foreign exchange markets; acts as a depository for gold; and acts as the government's debt manager in issuing new debt securities and paying interest on them and retiring them.
3. Acting as controller of the bank's clearing system.
4. Acting as a lender of last resort to chartered banks. The Bank often makes these funds available using purchase and resale agreements (PRAs), where the Bank buys eligible securities from the dealer and simultaneously resells them to the dealer for settlement at a later date. The Bank may also provide assistance to a financial institution that is in serious financial difficulty, only in cooperation with the Superintendent of Financial Institutions.
5. Maintenance of orderly conditions in the financial marketplace. This responsibility is over and above any aims it may have as to target interest rate and exchange rate levels.
6. Conducting monetary policy, which is the Bank's most important function, and is discussed below.

- The Bank is responsible for maintaining stability in the general level of prices, employment, output and trade, and the external value of the Canadian dollar. In recent years, the Bank has focused on price stability, which it sees as the best way **monetary policy** can contribute to stability in employment, output, and the exchange rate.

- Generally, the Bank announces joint targets, in cooperation with the federal government. Since 1961, in the event of a dispute, the finance minister may issue a directive instructing the Bank to follow a certain policy; however, no such directive has ever been issued.

- The Bank attempts to control inflation primarily through raising and lowering interest rates, although its open market transactions do impact money supply as well. The Bank recognizes that monetary conditions are the combined effect of interest rates and exchange rates, and combine the two variables in a "monetary conditions index." Recently the Bank has estimated that a 1% rise in interest rates is equivalent to a 3% increase in the trade-weighted exchange rate. This implies that if rates rose 1%, but the Canadian dollar dropped from $0.71 U.S. to $0.688 U.S. (a 3% drop), monetary conditions would be relatively unaffected.

The Bank influences interest rates in a number of ways, the most important of which are described below:

1. **Cash Management:** This is the Bank's most important tool for influencing interest rates, and involves managing highly liquid reserves in the banking system through its "drawdown" and "redeposit" mechanism. All banks and other financial institutions that clear payments through the Canadian Payments Association (CPA) have accounts with the Bank. Therefore, the Bank can tighten or loosen the supply of cash in the banking system by increasing or decreasing the amount of money in these accounts.

   Generally, the Bank shifts federal funds between accounts at the Bank of Canada, and demand deposits at the clearing banks, in order to give institutions unexpected positive or negative settling balances. If the clearing banks find themselves with a positive balance, they will lend out the excess funds and buy securities, putting downward pressure on interest rates. The Bank achieves this using a "**redeposit**" which moves deposits from its own account to those of the clearing banks.

   The reverse happens if the clearing banks find themselves with a negative balance, which the Bank induces using a "**drawdown**" (which is the reverse of a redeposit). Financial institutions often use this information to make judgments regarding the Bank's short-term stance.

2. **Open Market Operations:** The Bank can also influence rates by trading money market securities in the open market. In recent years, the Bank has targeted the overnight borrowing (lending) rates. The Bank affects overnight rates by:

   - offering to lend overnight money through a **special purchase and resale agreement (or repo or SPRA)** at stated rates below existing market rates in order to **reduce rates**; and

   - offering to borrow overnight from financial institutions through **sale and repurchase agreements (SRA)** (by selling securities to the chartered banks and agreeing to repurchase them the next day) at given rates that are higher than market rates (when it wants to **increase rates**).

   Since 1994, the Bank of Canada establishes a 50-basis point **operating band** for overnight money by conducting repos (or specials) at the ceiling rate and SRAs 50 basis points below the ceiling. The target rate is the mid-point in this range. The bank can also affect three-month treasury bill rates by buying and selling T-bills from its own inventory. When the Bank wants to **lower interest rates** through this mechanism, it **buys T-bills** by offering a price above the present market price, which lowers rates due to the inverse relationship between rates and prices. This action expands the Bank's balance sheet and effectively increases the money supply since the dealer it buys the T-bills from will likely lend out the funds it receives from the Bank. Since the Bank is targeting interest rates and not money supply, it will often "neutralize" the effect on money supply through "drawdowns." When the Bank **sells T-bills**, it exerts pressure designed to **increase interest rates**.

3. **Moral Suasion:** The Bank may simply ask financial institutions to tighten or loosen credit conditions in order to achieve its policy without action in the money market.

The bank rate is the rate at which the Bank of Canada is willing to lend short-term funds to the chartered banks, in its role as lender of last resort. Since 1996, the bank rate is set at the *ceiling of its target range for overnight money rates*. Prior to that, it was set at 25 basis points (one quarter of a percentage point) above the average yield on three-month treasury bills.

FISCAL POLICY

- Fiscal policy is the use of government taxation, spending, and deficits to affect growth. One of the generally accepted duties is to "smooth out" the business cycle by spending more and taxing less when the economy is weak.

- The federal finance minister presents the federal government budget for the upcoming fiscal year (April 1 to March 31) every year, usually in February. The budget includes projections for spending, revenue, deficits (or surpluses), and the level of debt for the upcoming year (and usually at least one additional year).

Fiscal policy affects the economy in several ways:

1. Its **spending** and/or direct transfers to citizens.
2. **Taxes** of various types including direct (income), sales, payroll, capital, and property taxes.
3. **Deficits**, which tend to stimulate the economy, while falling deficits (or surpluses) generally do the opposite.
4. **Automatic stabilizers**, which automatically move counter to the business cycle (e.g., **unemployment insurance** payments increase as unemployment rises, while **income taxes** rise as economic growth increases).

- Canada's failure to address deficits has had several consequences. The cost of interest payments is now the largest single expenditure of the federal government (27.1% of GDP in 1998-99 versus 10.3% in 1974-75). Often fiscal policy has been

unsynchronized with monetary policy, which has increased the cost to the economy. For example, in the late 1980s when there was strong economic growth, governments continued to run deficits, which fueled inflation and led to higher interest rates on borrowed funds. In the end, large debts restrict government's ability to run countercyclical policies, since it has become costly (if not impossible) to continue to run large deficits to generate spending.[1]

Chapter 2: Review Questions

( )   1. The following are all major determinants of interest rates except for:
  a) inflation
  b) exchange rate
  c) default risk
  d) none of the above

( )   2. The following are all determinants of exchange rates except for:
  a) inflation differentials
  b) current account
  c) political stability
  d) none of the above

( )   3. _____ is the term used when the Bank of Canada asks financial institutions to tighten or loosen credit in order to achieve its policy without action in the money market.
  a) Moral suasion
  b) Indirect cash management
  c) Open market operations
  d) Moral persuasion

( )   4. The index used by the Bank of Canada to measure the combined effect of interest rates and exchange rates on the economy is called the:
  a) nominal rate index
  b) fiscal rate index
  c) monetary conditions index
  d) Bank of Canada index

[1] In recent years, Canada's federal and provincial governments have devoted a great deal of attention to eliminating fiscal deficits and paying down government debt. The 1997-1998 budget was balanced for the first time since 1969-70, while the 1998-99 and 1999-2000 budget were also balanced. This marks the first time in almost 50 years that the federal government balanced its books for three or more consecutive years. The budgets 2000-2001 and 2001-2002 were also projected to balance.

5. Which of the following are business cycle leading indicators?   (   )

    I. Housing starts

    II. Business investment spending

    III. GDP

    IV. Stock prices

    V. Inflation

    a) I, IV, and V

    b) II and V

    c) II and III

    d) I and IV

6. Which of the following are business cycle lagging indicators?   (   )

    I. Retail sales

    II. Business investment spending

    III. GDP

    IV. Personal income

    V. Inflation

    a) I, IV, and V

    b) II and V

    c) II and III

    d) I and IV

7. The following are components of the capital account except for: (   )

    a) direct investment

    b) investment income

    c) international reserves transaction

    d) all of the above are components of the capital account

8. The measure of real money supply that is included in Statistics Canada's   (   )
   Composite Leading Indicator is:

    a) M1

    b) M2

    c) M2+

    d) M3

9. _____ is an example of an automatic stabilizer.   (   )

    a) The bank rate

    b) The use of open market operations

    c) Unemployment insurance

    d) A deficit

( )　　10. The Bank of Canada may use _____ when it wants to increase interest rates.

a) redeposits

b) drawdowns

c) T-bill purchases

d) SPRAs

( )　　11. The Bank of Canada may use _____ when it wants to decrease interest rates.

a) drawdowns

b) SRAs

c) neither (a) nor (b)

d) either (a) or (b)

( )　　12. _____ unemployment refers to unemployment caused by people in job transition stages.

a) Cyclical

b) Frictional

c) Structural

d) Natural

FINANCING, LISTING, AND REGULATION

chapter 3

CSC EXAM SUGGESTED GUIDELINES:
15 questions

- This chapter deals with the sources of financing available to governments and corporations. It also describes the listing procedures for companies that wish to be publicly traded, as well as the regulations they must adhere to.

GOVERNMENT AND CORPORATE FINANCING

- Governments need financing for many reasons, such as:
    1. to finance deficits;
    2. to finance infrastructure projects (e.g., roads and bridges);
    3. to fund services (e.g., schools and hospitals); and
    4. to develop income-producing services.

- Most investment firms have seperate government finance departments to act as intermediaries and advisors to the government regarding the issue of new securities. The investment advisor tries to reach a deal that is acceptable to the government issuer and prospective investors. The issue must be structured to accommodate the investors' interest of trying to ensure an adequate return and acceptable level of risk, as well as the issuers' interest in trying to obtain the cheapest source of financing.

- The investment dealer advises the government regarding several matters including:
    - the size of the issue, the interest rate offered, and the currency in which the issue is to be denominated;

- the timing of the issue;
- whether it should be a foreign or domestic issue;
- what possible impact the issue may have on the market; and
- whether it should be a new maturity issue, or if a previous issue should be re-opened.

- The premarketing phase involves soliciting informal advice from market participants and potential investors regarding how the market would react to a particular issue. It occurs before all of the final details of the issue are specified.

The auction or **competitive tender system** is used for most issues by the federal government. **Primary distributors** which are eligible to tender include: Schedule I and II banks (who may only tender for trading accounts and client orders and not for head office accounts such as pension funds); investment dealers; and active foreign dealers. **Competitive bids** may consist of one or more bids in multiples of $50,000 (minimum $250,000 per individual bid) which are submitted (usually electronically) by 12:30 p.m. on the date of the auction. The bid must state the yield to maturity to three decimal places. Primary distributors may also submit one non-competitive tender, in multiples of $5,000, with a minimum bid of $25,000, and a $3 million limit on non-competitive bids per customer. These bids are executed at the average price of the accepted competitive bids.

Generally the coupon rate is set to *within 25 basis points of the average yield* of the accepted competitive tenders, producing an average issue price at (or slightly below) par. When existing issues are being supplemented by additional offerings, bonds are sold at the price equivalents of the bid yields, plus accrued interest if applicable.

- The Bank of Canada may bid to meet its own requirements. It also stands ready to absorb the entire tender if required, which implies the Bank could theoretically set the yield at each tender. Around 2:00 p.m. on the day of the auction, the Bank releases all pertinent information about the tender so that bidders can determine their net position. The dealers who purchase the bonds receive no commissions, and there are no selling price restrictions for the successful bidders.

- Thirty-year bonds are auctioned semi-annually while two-, five-, and 10-year government bonds are offered separately by quarterly auctions in denominations of $1,000, $5,000, $100,000, and $1 million. Treasury bills are offered every other Tuesday by the Bank through a competitive tender in maturities of 91, 182, and 364 days, and in denominations of $1,000, $5,000, $25,000, $100,000, and $1 million.

- Canada Savings Bonds are sold every year, beginning in October, through investment dealers, banks, trusts, and on a commission basis. There is no set limit on the size of the issue; however, investors are restricted in the number they can purchase. Since these instruments are medium-term maturity but are cashable at any time, the rates are generally set in accordance with prevailing short-term rates.

New issues of provincial direct and guaranteed bonds are usually sold at a negotiated price through a fiscal agent (underwriting syndicate).

Direct bonds are issued directly by the government (e.g., Province of Ontario bonds), while **guaranteed bonds** are issued in the name of a crown corporation, but are guaranteed by the provincial government (e.g., Hydro-Quebec). Similar to corporate issues, there may be an exempt list (which is discussed later in this chapter).

- Municipal bond and debenture issues are generally purchased by institutional portfolio managers and pension funds. Non-market sources of funding include:

    1. the CPP (and QPP) which commits a pro-rata portion of each province's obligation to the purchase of municipal securities;

    2. provincial and municipal pension funds, which directly invest in municipal securities; and

    3. the federal government often loans funds to municipalities for specific projects.

Corporations need new financing for many reasons including:

    1. to increase working capital;

    2. to fund bank loans;

    3. to purchase fixed assets; and

    4. to expand production.

Financing may also be required to purchase other companies or for restructuring purposes.

- A competitive tender is an auction by a number of dealers to buy an issuer's new securities. **Negotiated offerings** are more commonly used for corporate issues. They involve negotiations between the investment dealer (ID) and the issuing company regarding the type of security, price, interest or dividend rate, special features, and protective provisions.

THE FINANCING PROCEDURE

- Before entering into a formal arrangement to market a corporation's securities, an investment dealer will undertake a thorough investigation of the corporation including: an extensive industry analysis; an analysis of the corporation's position within that industry; and an analysis of the financial record and financial structure of the corporation.

The dealer advises the issuer regarding the amount, timing, pricing, and attributes of the issue. The dealer also will advise the clients regarding the method of distribution (discussed below) and how the issue is to be marketed. Close relationships often develop, and sometimes a dealer or broker may become the "**broker of record**," which provides it with the right of first refusal on new financing.

- A "**private placement**" is an arrangement with private investors (usually institutional investors) and does not require a full prospectus, only a specific contract (**offering memorandum**). Under these conditions, the dealer usually acts as an agent for the issuer. These will be marketed to exempt institutions in Canada, and/or the U.S.

"Public offerings" are regulated by the CBCA and provincial securities regulations. They require that prospectuses be prepared which include "*full, true and plain disclosure of all material facts relating to the securities offered.*" A material fact is one that significantly affects, or has the potential to have a significant impact on the securities' market price.

Public issues can be classified as one of the following:

1. **Initial public offerings (IPO's):** These occur when a growing firm or crown corporation decides to "go public."

2. **Primary or treasury issues:** These are additional issues of securities that are already held by the public.

3. **Secondary issues:** These are follow-up issues or redistribution of previously issued stock (typically large blocks which have been held by institutional investors).

- The dealer will consider the corporation's existing financing structure, the stability of earnings, and prospects for the future, as well as current market conditions, before recommending an appropriate financing alternative, as well as appropriate protective provisions (for debt and preferred shares) and voting restrictions (for common shares).

Some of the advantages of debt financing include:

1. Interest payments are tax deductible for corporations.
2. Debt is not a permanent commitment.
3. It does not dilute equity ownership.
4. Some or all of the issuing discount may be tax deductible.
5. It is generally the lowest cost financing alternative to a company.

Some of the advantages of equity financing include:

1. There is no obligation to pay any portion of earnings as dividends.
2. Repayment of capital is not required.
3. Assets are not encumbered nor are management's actions restricted.
4. It provides a greater cushion against insolvency and can improve the company's credit rating.

Prospectuses are lengthy, legal documents that contains relevant financial statements, proposed use of funds from the issue, future growth plans, and the relevant information regarding the share issue. Normally, before a final prospectus may be issued, it is necessary to prepare and distribute copies of a **preliminary prospectus**, or **red herring**, to the securities commission and prospective investors. This contains most of the information to be included in the final prospectus except the price to the dealers and public, and sometimes the auditor's report. A statement, in red, must be displayed on the front page to the effect that it is not final and is subject to completion or an amendment before shares can be issued. The dealer may also prepare a **greensheet**, which is an information circular, for in-house use only. It highlights the most important features of the issue, and can be used by the sales department to solicit interest in the new issue.

- During the **waiting period** (between the issuance of red herrings and the receipt of final prospectuses), dealers are prohibited from entering into purchase and sale agreements; however, they can solicit expressions of interest. Meanwhile, the dealer typically proceeds along other lines, attempting to formalize the details of items such as: the Trust Deed or Indenture (for debt issues); the underwriting or agency agreement between issuer and distributor; the Banking Group Agreement; the Selling Group Agreement; and final price to the public and to the dealer.

- Once completed, the prospectus is filed with the relevant securities commissions, and approval generally takes three weeks. If the issuers agree to any proposed changes, the issue is said to be "blue skied" and may then be distributed to the public. It must be accompanied by the consent of all experts whose opinions are referred to in the prospectus. The prospectus is required to be mailed or delivered to all purchasers of the securities, not later than midnight on the second business day after the trade.

The **Prompt Offering Qualification (POP) System** allows senior reporting issuers, who have made public distributions, and who are subject to continuous disclosure requirements, to issue short-form prospectuses. The rationale is that there is already a great deal of information available on the company that would normally be included in a prospectus. These short-form prospectuses save issuers a great deal of time and money, and generally focus on details of the securities being issued such as price, distribution spread, use of proceeds, and security attributes.

Issuers under the POP System:

1. Have been filing annual and interim statements for 12 months (36 in Quebec) prior to the issue.

2. Have filed or will file an Annual Information Form (AIF) with the appropriate administrator.

3. Are not in default of any requirements under the relevant securities legislation.

4. Have a large public float (equity shares listed on an exchange and held by non-insiders with a market value of at least $75 million).

Short-form prospectuses are commonly used for "**bought deals**," and have contributed to the growth of these arrangements, which are a popular form of underwriting in Canada. The issuer sells the entire issue to one investment dealer or to a group that attempts to resell it and accepts all of the price risk. Generally, the dealer has premarketed the issue to a few large institutional investors. Issuers are usually large, well-known firms that qualify for the use of POP; therefore, bought deals are generally executed very swiftly.

- The first step in the **underwriting process** has the issuing company selling the securities to the **Financing Group** (also known as managing underwriters or syndicate managers) which consists of one or two firms. The Financing Group accepts the liability of the issue on behalf of the **Banking Group** members, which includes themselves, as well as other dealers who have agreed to participate based on certain terms.

- Secondly, the Financing Group sells the securities to the **Marketing Group** at a "draw down" price that is slightly above the price paid by the Financing Group in order to provide that group with a differential. At this point "tombstone advertisements" may begin in newspapers which indicate all members of the banking group selling the issue.

- Thirdly, the securities are distributed for sale to the public, with a certain proportion being allocated to:

  1. the **Banking Group** (the largest proportion);
  2. the **exempt list**, which usually includes only large professional buyers, mostly financial institutions, who are exempt from prospectus requirements;
  3. the **Selling Group**, which consists of other dealers who are not part of the Banking Group;
  4. **casual dealers**, who are not members of the Banking or Selling Groups, and may be brokers, broker dealers, foreign dealers, banks, etc.; and
  5. **special groups**, which may include the issuer's banker or dealer, etc.

- In 1999, the first internet prospectus offering was made in Ontario; however, it is still not possible to conduct a public offering over the Internet without the appropriate registered body.

- Lead underwriters generally provide **after-market stabilization** of the issuer's market price. If they intend to do so, it must be disclosed on the first page of the prospectus, with additional details provided within the prospectus. Three possible types of stabilization activities are:

  1. Initially sell more than the original amount of securities offered by the issuer, then buy shares back if the price drops below a certain value. If the price does not fall below this value, the firm can cover their short position by exercising an **over-allotment** (or **green shoe**) option. This option allows the dealer to obtain additional securities from the issuer. The OSC limits the amount of overallotments to 15% of the maximum number of securities permitted to be distributed. The terms of the over-allotment option must be disclosed in the prospectus, and the option may be added or deleted during the period between the filing of the preliminary and final prospectus. The exercise period for these options is 60 days for IPOs, and 30 days for secondary offerings.
  2. Penalize members of the selling group by reducing the proportion of shares they are allocated in future offerings, if their customers sell their shares in weak issues in the period immediately following the issue.
  3. Establishing a "stabilizing bid" to purchase shares at a price less than or equal to the offer price if the issue is not complete. This is the least common type of support.

- Unlisted companies can issue securities to the public using a prospectus, or through the exchanges by filing an exchange offering prospectus or a statement of material facts. This form of distribution is unique to Canada, and is used primarily by junior mining and oil companies. These treasury share underwritings are usually priced below the prevailing market price (but discounts are restricted to be less than 10% to 25% depending on the market price). They must also be used to raise minimum amounts of new capital (from $100,000 to $350,000). Often these shares are required to be held "in escrow" (by a trustee) until certain provisions have been met. **Escrowed shares** typically maintain associated voting and dividend privileges; however, they are not transferable during the period of escrow.

- The **capital pool company (CPC)** program offers businesses an opportunity to raise early-stage financing. It permits an IPO by a newly formed company that has no present business, operations, or assets, other than cash. The funds raised by these IPOs can be used to identify and acquire businesses that would qualify for a regular Tier 1 or Tier 2 exchange listing. The directors and officers of the CPC must contribute at least $100,000 in seed capital, and the issuer must raise between $200,000 and $500,000 in the IPO, and the offering price must be between $0.15 to $0.30. The total amount of capital raised from director and officer contributions plus the IPO cannot exceed $700,000. The shares may have their trading suspended, or be delisted from the exchange, if the CPC does not identify businesses that can be acquired with the funds through a Qualifying Transaction (QT).

THE LISTING PROCESS

New share issues are usually traded OTC initially, and are considered for listing on an exchange only after proof of satisfactory distribution becomes available. Often, the underwriting agreement requires the underwriters to provide some market support for the new security issue for a specified time period.

Sometimes a market develops for new issues prior to their actual listing, and trading is handled by dealers in what is known as the "**grey market**," which is an unofficial OTC market that surfaces until official listing occurs.

Advantages of listing include:

1. prestige and goodwill;
2. better trade credit;
3. established value in mergers and acquisitions;
4. facilitating subsequent debt financing;
5. excellent market visibility;
6. employee stock options have a visible value;
7. more information is available;
8. established collateral value;
9. facilitates valuation for tax purposes; and
10. increased marketability and attention of investors.

Disadvantages of listing include:

1. additional controls on management;
2. additional costs to the company; and
3. market indifference (i.e., if trading volumes turn out to be very low).

- Companies wishing to become listed must apply to the appropriate exchange. The application requires disclosure of detailed company information including:

1. The full details of company officers and directors.
2. The company's charter and any current prospectus.
3. The financial statements for the past three to five years.
4. A written opinion from the company's legal counsel, verifying the organizational matters as presented.

- Once the application has been approved, the company enters into a a formal **Listing Agreement.** The agreement specifies regulations and reporting requirements that the company must follow to maintain its listing. Some of these requirements include:

1. The submission of annual and interim financial statements and other corporate reports.
2. Prompt notification to the exchange(s) about dividends and other distributions.
3. The company's proposed stock options for employees only, underwritings, sale or issue of treasury shares.
4. Notification of proposed material changes in the business or affairs of a listed non-exempt company.

REGULATION AND INVESTOR PROTECTION

- The securities industry is governed by extensive legislation and regulation that is designed to protect investors and ensure high ethical standards. The details are established by provincial securities regulators, in cooperation with the self-regulatory organizations (SROs) since there is no federal regulatory body in Canada. Generally, the provincial securities commissions work closely together to maintain uniform standards. The fundamental principle is to provide potential investors with *full, true and plain disclosure of all material facts* relating to the securities offered. It must be recognized that no laws are infallible, so investors should follow the general rule: "investigate before you invest, and after."

The three basic methods used to protect investors are:

1. Registration of securities dealers and advisors.
2. Disclosure of material facts.
3. Enforcement of the laws and policies.

- Sellers of securities or investment advisors must be registered. Administrators have the power to grant, suspend, or cancel registration. New investment advisors must pass the CSC course, as well as the Conduct and Practices Handbook for Securities Industry Professionals (CPH) exam. In addition, they must:

  1. complete a 90-day training program before they can deal with the public;[1]

  2. be subject to a six-month period of supervision by his or her branch manager; and

  3. complete Part 1 of the Canadian Investment Management (CIM) course within 30 months of becoming a licensed IA (or they may choose to be registered as Investment Representatives, which does not require the CIM course).

- The Uniform Application for Registration/Approval is a standardized application form, signed by the employing firm and the applicant, in which both parties agree to be bound by the regulations of the governing body. It requires applicants to certify details about their personal and educational background. In addition, members must notify administrators of the termination of an IA (providing reasons if they were dismissed), and applicants must notify administrators of any material changes (including address).

- SROs are responsible for ensuring compliance with securities legislation. Some of the required practices and policies include:

  1. Know your client, the first step of which is completion of the Client Application Form.

  2. No employee of a member firm can maintain or control an account at another firm that might benefit them without the consent of an officer of the employing firm.

  3. Full details of every transaction must be forwarded to the client in writing (or sometimes electronically).

  4. Confidential or numbered accounts may be maintained, provided that full client information is maintained at the principal office and is available at all time to the administrators.

  5. Every director of a public corporation has a fiduciary duty not to reveal privileged or inside information to outsiders, particularly if it is likely to impact market price of the corporation's securities.

  In addition, IAs have a fiduciary duty when advising clients, to advise fully, honestly, and in good faith, and to follow the client's instructions or intentions during investment transactions.

- Ethical trading is critical to the proper functioning of capital markets, since without assurances regarding the behaviour of market participants, it would be hard to attract investors. Unethical practices are punishable by fines, suspensions, expulsion, and/or criminal charges. Unethical conduct includes any omission, conduct, or manner of doing business which, in the opinion of the disciplinary body, is not in the public interest nor in the interest of the exchange.

---

[1] This course has been reduced in length and is now referred to as the 30-day course.

- Some examples of unethical practices are:
  1. any conduct that deceives the public;
  2. creating false appearances of trades (e.g., fictitious orders);
  3. price manipulation schemes;
  4. deliberately causing the last sale of the day to be higher than warranted by market conditions (high saling);
  5. misleading any board of governors or committee;
  6. confirming a transaction that never occurred (bucketing);
  7. improper solicitation of orders by phone or otherwise;
  8. high-pressure or other undesirable selling techniques;
  9. violation of any applicable statutes;
  10. attempting to sell a dividend;
  11. assurances of no risk;
  12. taking the opposite side of client trades;
  13. rebating commissions; and
  14. conduct that brings the securities business, exchanges, or IDA into disrepute.

- Regulation prohibits unethical, dishonest, or high-pressure sale tactics including:
  1. calling at residences;
  2. sales made to parties in other provinces (or countries) without appropriate authorizations; and
  3. deliberately or recklessly making illegal representations to assist in obtaining a trade (i.e., fraud).

- Securities legislation requires disclosure of: periodic financial statements (including management discussion and analysis); insider trading reports; information circulars required in proxy solicitation; an annual information form (AIF); press releases; and material change reports.

Security purchasers are provided with the following statutory rights:
  1. **Right of withdrawal**: within two business days of receipt of prospectus, or if a distribution occurs without the required prospectus;
  2. **Right of rescission**: if the prospectus or other related documents contain a misrepresentation (i.e., an untrue statement or omission of a material fact); and
  3. **Right of action for damages**: against the issuer, directors of the issuer, the security seller or underwriter, or any other party (including experts, who are liable only for their statements) who signs a prospectus without exhibiting "due diligence."

Typically there are time limits and maximum liabilities associated with claims for damage. A misrepresentation in a prospectus may also be a criminal offense.

- Corporations are required to provide continuous and timely disclosure including: comparative audited annual financial statements within 140 days of fiscal year-end; and comparative unaudited financial statements within 60 days of the first three fiscal quarters.

- Most provinces require management to solicit proxies from shareholders whenever it calls a shareholders' meeting, and supply such holders with an information circular, including among other things: whether the proxy is revocable or not; whether the solicitation is made on behalf of management; information on the directors to be elected; remuneration of management; matters to come before the meeting; and, any interest of management in such matters. When shares are registered in the name of someone other than the true beneficial holder of the shares (e.g., by a bank or investment dealer), the nominees must mail the appropriate documentation to the true owners.

- Take-over bid legislation is designed to protect the interests of the shareholders of the target company. Provincial legislation requires that take-over bids, which would push the acquiring firm's controlling interest in the target company above 20% of voting securities (10% for federal legislation), must comply with several requirements including:

  1. The bid must be sent to all security holders in that class (or holders of convertibles) within the province.
  2. The offeror shall deliver a take-over bid circular, describing material facts of the take-over, as part of the bid.
  3. A directors' circular, including a recommendation and reasons (or reasons for providing no recommendation), must be sent to security holders within ten days of the bid.
  4. Any securities taken up must be paid for within three days (if more securities are offered than the offeror was willing or able to purchase, the offers would be settled on a pro rata basis, disregarding fractional shares).

Shareholders have the right of rescission or right to damages for any misrepresentations.

- A take-over bid is exempt from the above requirements in any of the following cases:

  1. It is made through the TSE, ME, or VSE in accordance with appropriate regulations.
  2. It involves acquisitions, at market prices, which do not aggregate more than 5% of the securities in a class within twelve months.
  3. It is a private agreement with five or fewer security holders at a price not exceeding 115% of market value.
  4. It is an offer to purchase shares in a private company.
  5. In Ontario only, if there are less than 50 security holders of that class, and the aggregate holdings of the offeror would be less than 2% of total outstanding.

Shareholders have the rights of rescission or right to damages for any misrepresentations. In addition, every person or company acquiring more than 10% of voting shares (or equivalent convertibles) of another company must provide early warning disclosure in the form of a press release which must be filed with the administrator.

Insiders of a reporting issuer are required to file reports of their trading activities in its securities. Insiders are generally defined to include:

1. a director or senior officer of the company, or a subsidiary;

2. a person or company, or director or senior officer of a company, which controls more than 10% of the voting control; and

3. a reporting issuer that has acquired any of its securities.

- Administrators can undertake investigations and subsequent prosecutions to enforce the appropriate laws. While they do not have the power to refund investments or settle internal disputes among shareholders of a corporation, they can: suspend, cancel or revoke registration; order trading in a security to cease; and deny the right to trade securities in a province.

Chapter 3: Review Questions

( )   1. Which of the following is not a basic method used by administrators to protect investors?

a) registration of securities dealers and advisors

b) enforcement of the laws and policies

c) disclosure of material facts

d) none of the above

( )   2. Which of the following types of information must listed companies disclose?

I. Insider trading reports

II. Block trading activity

III. Annual information form

IV. Monthly profit statements

a) I and II

b) I and III

c) II and III

d) II and IV

3. The risk assumed by investment dealers when they act as agents is generally lower than when they act as _____ . ( )

a) brokers

b) fiscal agents

c) principals

d) investment dealers cannot act as agents

4. Bought deals are typically offered in conjunction with companies that: ( )

a) trade in the OTC market

b) wish to issue new securities through a private placement

c) issue full prospectuses

d) issue short-form prospectuses

5. The second step in the underwriting process involves: ( )

a) the issuing of securities to the Financing Group

b) the selling of securities to the Marketing Group

c) the selling of securities to the general public

d) the waiting period

6. The following are all advantages to issuing debt except for: ( )

a) it is generally the lowest cost financing alternative

b) it provides greater financing flexibility

c) some or all of the issuing discount may be tax deductible

d) none of the above

7. The following are all disadvantages of listing shares for trading on a public exchange, except for: ( )

a) additional costs

b) additional controls

c) established collateral value

d) market indifference

8. The following would not be considered corporate insiders. ( )

I. Directors of a company.

II. A shareholder owning 5.5% of a company's shares.

III. The CEO of a company.

IV. The CEO of a subsidiary.

a) I and IV

b) II and III

c) II

d) IV

( ) 9. Shareholders have the following rights associated with the purchase of newly issued shares:

 a) rescission

 b) withdrawal

 c) both (a) and (b)

 d) neither (a) nor (b)

( ) 10. Competitive bids for government bond issues must be:

 a) in multiples of $5,000 subject to a maximum bid of $500,000

 b) in multiples of $5,000 subject to a minimum bid of $25,000

 c) in multiples of $50,000 subject to a maximum bid of $500,000

 d) in multiples of $50,000 subject to a minimum bid of $250,000

( ) 11. Companies that qualify under the POP system do so in order that they can issue shares through:

 a) a greensheet circular

 b) a private placement

 c) a public offering

 d) an initial public offering

( ) 12. Which of the following methods are used to protect investors?

 a) registration of dealers

 b) disclosure of material facts

 c) neither (a) nor (b)

 d) both (a) and (b)

( ) 13. Municipal governments may obtain funding from the following sources except:

 a) the CPP

 b) provincial pension funds

 c) federal government loans

 d) municipal savings bonds

( ) 14. The following are eligible to tender for government bond issues except for:

 a) investment funds

 b) investment dealers

 c) Schedule II banks

 d) Schedule I banks

( ) 15. Which of the following is not an advantage to listing?

 a) prestige and goodwill

 b) market indifference

 c) increased marketability

 d) all of the above are advantages

CORPORATIONS AND THEIR FINANCIAL STATEMENTS

BASIC FORMS OF BUSINESS ORGANIZATION

1. PROPRIETORSHIP:

- Proprietor is owner and operator of business.

- NOT recognized as a separate legal entity.

- Income is taxed as personal income.

- Owner/operator has complete control and claim to profits.

- Owner faces **unlimited liability**, which means that he/she is personally liable for all debts, losses, and obligations arising from business activity.

- This form of business faces capital generation restrictions.

2. PARTNERSHIP:

- Very similar to proprietorship, except that two or more owners are involved.

- There must be at least one general partner who is involved in the day-to-day operations of the business, and who is personally liable for all business debts and obligations.

- Partners in **general partnerships** face unlimited liability and usually joint and several liability (this means that all partners are "jointly" liable for all obligations, but also that each general partner is severally liable for all obligations on his or her own).

- **Limited partnerships** must include at least one general partner who faces unlimited liability and is involved in running the business. Limited partners can not be involved in the daily business activity, and liability is limited to the partner's investment.

3. CORPORATION:

- This is the "dominant" form in terms of dollar volumes of sales.

- Corporations are recognized as **separate legal entities**.

- The business structure allows for **separation of ownership from management**.

- Corporate tax rates are applicable.

- Corporations have an **unlimited life**.

- Owners (shareholders) face **limited liability**, and can personally sue the corporation.

- Shareholders can easily **transfer ownership** by selling their shares.

- The characteristics above suggest that corporations have greater **access to capital** than other forms of business organizations.

THE INCORPORATION PROCESS

The incorporation process begins when one or more persons file documents with the appropriate federal or provincial department. The corporation comes into existence when it is issued a **charter** by the government. Charters may be issued as:

1. **letters patent;**
2. **memorandums of association;** or
3. **articles of incorporation.**

The charter includes the corporate name, the date of incorporation, maximum authorized capital, and other pertinent data. The name of a corporation must identify the business as a corporation through the use of the words limited, corporation, or incorporated (or abbreviations).

- The decision to incorporate federally or provincially will depend primarily on where the business activities will take place. A provincially incorporated corporation may need further licensing or registration to carry on business in other provinces. A federally incorporated corporation is subject to general provincial laws, provided they do not deprive it of the rights associated with being federally incorporated.

Private corporations restrict the right of shareholders to transfer shares, limits the number of shareholders to less than 50, and prohibits inviting members of the public to subscribe for their securities. **Public corporations** face no such restrictions. While the *Canada Business Corporations Act (CBCA)* and many provincial acts no longer distinguish between the two, some securities regulations provide exemptions for private corporations (i.e., those whose shares do not trade on a stock exchange or over-the-counter).

- A corporation is regulated by:
    1. the government act under which it was incorporated;
    2. its own charter; and
    3. its by-laws.

- By-laws are passed by directors and approved by shareholders. They deal with items such as: determining the specifics of shareholders' and directors' meetings; qualification, election and removal of directors; appointment, duties, and remuneration of officers; declaration and payment of dividends; date of fiscal year-end; and signing authority for documents.

SHAREHOLDER RIGHTS:

- Significant events such as the acquisition or liquidation of businesses, or those requiring amendments to the corporate charter require shareholder approval. Usually each common share entitles the holder to one vote, which implies any parties owning more than 50% of outstanding shares could elect every board director. However, sometimes different classes of shares may vote separately for a certain number of directors, while other shares have no voting privileges, and others may have multiple voting rights.

- All shareholders have the right to attend shareholders meetings, and must receive related materials such as proxies and audited financial statements. Some of the important matters dealt with at such meetings include the election of directors, the appointment of independent auditors, and the presentation and discussion of the company's financial statements and auditor's report for the previous year.

A **proxy** represents a power of attorney that allows another party to vote on behalf of the shareholder. It is compulsory for management to solicit proxies by sending a proxy form and information circular to shareholders along with notification of the shareholder meeting. If management obtains a sufficient number of proxies it can control the board of directors. "**Proxy fights**" occur when challengers attempt to solicit proxies before a meeting. These are rare, but can lead to the removal of management if the challengers obtain sufficient support.

During a period of restructuring due to financial difficulties, a corporation may establish a **voting trust**. This involves having shareholders deposit their shares with a trustee to transfer voting control to a few individuals under the terms of a voting trust agreement. These are generally in effect for a limited period of time, or until given objectives have been accomplished.

CORPORATION STRUCTURE:

- Usually, corporations are required to have a minimum number of outside directors that are not officers of the corporation or related companies. Directors are required to attend periodic meetings, where they are normally responsible for:
  - appointing and supervising officers;
  - appointing signing authorities for banking;
  - authorizing important contracts;
  - approving budgets, financing, and expansion plans; and
  - the declaration of dividends.

- Many corporate statutes require that directors *exercise care, diligence, and skill that a reasonably prudent person would exercise* in comparable circumstances. They may be liable under securities statutes for misrepresentations contained in prospectuses and other statutory filings, as well as for violations of insider trading provisions.

- The board elects a chairman, who may also be a senior officer of the company. In addition to presiding over board meetings, the chairman is influential regarding the management policies followed by the corporation. Typically, either the chairman or the president will be the chief executive officer.

- The president is appointed by, and responsible to, the board of directors, and may serve as chairman if necessary.

- An executive vice-president is often the next in line below the president, and may sometimes be the chief operating officer. In addition, companies generally have a number of vice-presidents in charge of specific functional areas such as marketing, production, or finance.

The maximum number of common (or preferred) shares which the corporation may issue under the terms of its charter is referred to as the number of **authorized shares**. Changes in this amount require revisions to the charter. **Issued shares** refer to the number of shares issued by the corporation, while **outstanding shares** are those that are held by investors. If no shares are redeemed and the company does not repurchase any shares, the number of issued shares will equal the number of outstanding shares.

Par value shares have a stated face value which may be misleading, since it has no relationship to either market value or entitlement to some amount of corporate assets. Under the current federal act, shares must be without par value.

- Mortgage bonds are secured by real property, while debentures are not.

Advantages of incorporation include:

1. a corporation is recognized as a separate legal entity that can sue and be sued;
2. limited liability of shareholders;
3. continuity of existence;

4. ease of ownership transfer;

5. professional management;

6. possible tax benefits;

7. a general enhanced capability of accessing capital; and

8. growth potential, due to the ability to obtain large amounts of capital.

Disadvantages of incorporation include:

1. a loss of flexibility;

2. the possibility of double taxation (of corporate profits and dividend income to shareholders);

3. additional administrative costs; and

4. complications involving withdrawal of capital.

UNDERSTANDING FINANCIAL STATEMENTS

- Financial statements demonstrate what a firm owns and what it owes, as well as how profitable it has been in the past. A firm's past performance is important to potential investors since it may provide insight into the company's future prospects which are difficult to predict accurately.

BALANCE SHEET

- The **balance sheet** is divided into two sections: (1) **assets**, which shows what the firm owns and is owed; and (2) **liabilities**, which shows what the firm owes, and **shareholders' equity** or net worth, which represents the shareholders' interest in the company. Shareholders' equity is often referred to as the "book value" of the company, which in general does not correspond to its market value.

ASSETS:

- Assets are generally presented in order of increasing liquidity, with the most liquid assets appearing at the top of the balance sheet, and the least liquid assets appearing at the bottom.

- **Current assets** include cash, marketable securities, accounts or notes receivable (net of an allowance for doubtful accounts), inventories, and prepaid expenses (which represent payments made by the company for services to be received in the near future).

Inventories are generally in the form of raw materials, work-in-process, or finished goods. They are valued at the lower of original cost or current market value. Three common methods for valuing inventory are:

1. **average cost** of all items in inventory;

2. **first-in-first-out (FIFO)** which is the most commonly used method in Canada; and

3. **last-in-first-out (LIFO)** which is acceptable for accounting, but not for income tax purposes.

During periods of increasing prices FIFO will produce higher inventory value and higher profits, LIFO will produce lower inventory values and lower profits, while the average cost method will fall somewhere in between. This is illustrated in the example below.

Example 1

A firm currently has three inventory items on hand which were purchased in the following order for the following prices: $10; $15; and $20. If the firm sells one item today for $30, determine the ending inventory value and profit using each of the three inventory valuation approaches.

	Inventory Value	Profit
FIFO:	15+20 = $35	30−10 = $20
LIFO:	10+15 = $25	30−20 = $10
Average Cost:	[(10+15+20)/3]×2 = $30	30−15 = $15

- **Miscellaneous items** are neither current nor fixed and commonly include the cash surrender value of life insurance policies; amounts due from company employees, officers, or directors; investments of a long-term nature; and investments and advances to subsidiary and affiliated companies.

- **Fixed assets** consist of land, buildings, machinery, and equipment which are long-term in nature. Their value lies in their contribution to producing goods and services, rather than their resale value. The proportion of fixed to total assets varies widely across companies.

Depreciation is a *non-cash expense* charged against fixed assets to reflect their decline in value through time. Depreciation allocates the net cost of assets through time to provide better "matching" of the revenues they generate with the initial cost of said assets. Depreciation is generally charged using:

1. the "**straight line method,**" which charges an equal amount each period based on the initial cost of the asset and its estimated useful life; or

2. the "**declining balance method,**" which applies a fixed percentage (usually double the straight line rate) to the outstanding undepreciated balance.

As a result, the timing of the depreciation charged differs from each of these methods, as illustrated in the example below.

Example 2

A company purchased a $100,000 piece of equipment which has an estimated useful life of 10 years. Determine the depreciation charge and book value for this asset for the first three years using: (a) straight line depreciation; and (b) using the declining balance method.

Year-End	Straight Line		Declining Balance (@20%)	
	Depreciation	Book Value	Depreciation	Book Value
1	10,000	90,000	20,000	80,000
2	10,000	80,000	16,000	64,000
3	10,000	70,000	12,800	51,200

Depletion is similar to depreciation and is used by mining, oil, natural resource, and timber companies to reflect the fact that as these assets are developed and sold, the company loses part of its assets with each sale. An allowance for depletion recognizes the fact that companies must recover their initial costs of acquiring these assets in addition to extraction costs.

Amortization is similar to depreciation and depletion; however, it is applied against deferred charges and intangible assets, which are described below.

- When a company records an expenditure as an asset, rather than expensing it on the income statement, it is referred to as "**capitalizing**" the expenditure. This procedure spreads the associated expense claim over more than one period.

- Capitalized leases are those which are viewed as another means of financing the acquisition of an asset. Consequently, these leases are recorded as if the company had assumed ownership of the asset (which is recorded like any other fixed asset), and assumed a liability, which is recorded at the present value of future lease payments.

- Capitalizing interest occurs when interest costs are capitalized and added to the cost of the asset, rather than expensed. This process is sometimes used by oil and gas companies that are active in exploration, or by utilities companies during periods of construction. This policy should not be changed once adopted, since it effectively increases current income and asset value, and lowers future income amounts.

- **Deferred charges** are similar to prepaid expenses, except that the benefits will extend over a period of years. The cost of such items is spread out over several years by gradually writing off the asset (i.e., amortization).

- **Intangible assets** include goodwill, patents, copyrights, franchises, and trademarks. While they are not tangible in the typical sense, they have the potential to create value by enhancing earnings capability. Creditors often assume these assets will be worth nothing if a company is liquidated. While it is common to think of goodwill as the probability of obtaining repeat customers, from an accounting perspective, it arises when a purchaser pays a price for a company above the value of the company's assets (i.e., is willing to pay for its "good name").

LIABILITIES AND SHAREHOLDERS' EQUITY:

- **Current liabilities** typically include bank advances (short-term loans from financial institutions); accounts payable; dividends payable; income taxes payable; long-term debt obligations that are due within one year; and many other items such as wages payable, legal fees, pension payments, etc.

- **Deferred tax** occurs when the tax figure on a company's income statement differs from tax reported in its tax return. These instances usually result from **"timing" differences** due to the use of different procedures for Canadian Institute of Chartered Accountants (CICA) reporting purposes, versus those used for income tax purposes. The major source of these timing differences is the use of straight line depreciation for accounting purposes, and declining balance depreciation which is used for income tax purposes (capital cost allowances or CCA). The net effect is that assets are "written off" or expensed faster for tax purposes, which causes the taxes payable figure on tax returns to be lower than the tax expense figure in the financial statements. This gives rise to a deferred tax credit (liability) on the balance sheet.

- Some analysts treat deferred taxes as a liability, since it represents taxes that must be repaid in the future. Others view it as equity, because the company is unlikely to have to repay such taxes as long as they are continually purchasing assets for given CCA asset classes. Others disregard this account, treating it as neither debt nor equity in determining net worth or debt ratios.

- **Permanent differences** also exist between income statement and tax return reporting such as:

    1. dividend income received by a Canadian corporation from another Canadian corporation is not taxable for filing purposes; however, it is considered income for accounting purposes; and

    2. interest and penalties on taxes are not deductible for tax purposes; however, they are considered accounting expenses.

These differences do not show up in the deferred tax account.

Minority Interest in Subsidiary Companies is reported on consolidated balance sheets only. It is calculated as the interest that "outsiders" have in the subsidiary firm, which is viewed as a "quasi-liability," which must be deducted in arriving at the consolidated shareholders' equity position of the parent company.

- Other liabilities typically include provisions for estimated losses (e.g., from a lawsuit). Contingencies based solely on conservative thinking, and not to a specific loss are more properly reported as a note to the financial statements.

- **Deferred Income** is the opposite of a deferred charge, and arises when a company has received payment for goods or services that it has not yet provided (e.g., prepaid magazine subscriptions).

- **Long-Term (or Funded) Debt** typically consists of long-term bank loans, mortgage bonds and/or debentures. These items are usually described in detail in a note, including a description of repayment, maturity, and sinking fund provisions.

Shareholders' Equity consists of:

1. **preferred share capital**;

2. **common share capital** (issued and outstanding);

3. **retained earnings**, which belongs to shareholders and represents reinvested profits;

4. **contributed surplus** (sometimes), which also belongs to shareholders, but originates from a source other than earnings. Any excess received for shares which are issued above par or stated price is shown in contributed surplus; and

5. **foreign currency translation adjustments**, which may appear on consolidated statements of companies that have foreign subsidiaries, and reflects a significant change in the value of the subsidiary due to a favourable (or unfavourable) change in the exchange rate.

Total common equity is comprised of items (2) through (5).

EARNINGS STATEMENT

- The **Earnings Statement (or Income Statement, or Profit and Loss Statement, or Statement of Revenue and Expense)** reveals:

  1. where company income comes from and how it is spent; and

  2. the adequacy of earnings to assure continued successful operation and income generation for its security holders.

In short, it is a "*flow*" statement that provides evidence regarding the company's earning power, which is of primary interest to investors.

- It is generally broken down into four broad categories including:

  1. the **operating section**;

  2. the **non-operating section**;

  3. the **creditors' section**; and

  4. the **owners' section**.

The first two sections show the origin of income, while the other two show its distribution. It is important to distinguish between operating and non-operating sources of income to get a true reflection of the firm's true earning power.

- The operating section shows the source of income and associated expenses, as well as the resulting net operating profit or loss, and includes the following items:

  1. **net sales** (gross sales less excise taxes, returns and allowances, and discounts);

  2. **cost of goods sold** (labour, raw materials, and other associated costs);

3. **gross operating profit** $((1)-(2))$;

4. **operating expenses** (selling, general and administrative expenses, depreciation, and other expenses such as pension fund contributions, directors' fees, legal fees, and management compensation); and

5. the **net operating profit or loss**, which results after deducting the expenses in (4).

- The non-operating section contains income from sources including interest and dividend payments received, rents from no-longer required properties, royalties on patent fees, finance charges earned, etc. It also includes income from:

    1. "**unusual items**" that are typical for the normal business activity of the firm, but were caused by unusual circumstances (e.g., unusual bad debt or inventory losses); and

    2. "**extraordinary items**" which are not likely to re-occur such as a loss due to disposal of an operating division.

- The creditors' section shows distribution of income to creditors in the form of interest or lease payments, which is important since they represent a fixed legal obligation.

- The owners' section shows taxes (both current and deferred), and minority interest amounts.

Minority interest arises from the **consolidation method of accounting**, which is required whenever the parent *owns more than 50%* of the voting shares of a subsidiary. When the parent owns *less than 20%* of the subsidiary, the **cost method** of accounting is utilized, while when the parent owns *between 20% and 50%*, it will use the **equity method**. The equity method may lead to the reporting of equity income (or losses) by the parent company even though no cash was received (or distributed). On the other hand, the parent may receive dividends from the subsidiary, which represents cash received, but is not treated as income. As a result, cash earnings calculations should subtract equity income, and include dividends received from the subsidiary (however, this is not always done in practice).

OTHER COMPONENTS

- The **Retained Earnings Statement** is the link between the earnings statement and balance sheet. It provides a record of the profits kept in the company year after year, and accounts for dividends paid every year. It also accounts for adjustments to retained earnings that may occur from time to time as retained earnings are appropriated as reserve against possible events (e.g., such as a decline in the value of raw materials purchased at a time of high commodity prices). The term "reserve" must be used for federally incorporated companies under such circumstances; however, it does not mean that a cash fund has been set aside for this provision. Rather, it means that a portion of retained earnings has been earmarked as unavailable for distribution to shareholders.

- The **Statement of Changes in Financial Position (or Cash Flow Statement)** provides financial statement users with important information regarding the liquidity and solvency of a company by showing the sources and uses of funds over a certain period. It is broken down into the following three areas:

  1. **operating activities**, which shows cash flows from profits and temporary accounts such as receivables and payables;

  2. **financing activities**, which shows cash flows from debt and equity issues or retirements; and

  3. **investing activities**, which shows cash flows from net investment in fixed assets and/or investment assets.

- The **Notes to Financial Statements** provide users with important information regarding items such as: accounting policies; description of fixed assets, share capital, and long-term debt; and, commitments and contingencies. They should also disclose information regarding significant segments of the company's operations by industry and geographical location (including earnings statements and capital expenditures).

- The **Auditor's Report**, which is required by Canadian corporate law, typically has three paragraphs. The first describes the statements examined, as well as a description of the individual responsibilities of management and the auditors. The second describes the scope of the examination, and usually indicates that the examination was made in accordance with generally accepted accounting principles (GAAP). The third gives the auditor's opinion on whether the statements fairly present the firm's financial position. If the auditor finds discrepancies from GAAP, they may be unable to give an opinion, or may offer a "qualified" opinion which refers to any dubious points. A qualified report can be viewed as a signal that the statements may not fairly represent the company's financial condition, and are not allowed in some provinces.

Chapter 4: Review Questions

( )   1. Three features of corporations that allow them greater access to capital are:

a) limited liability, limited life, and ease of transfer of ownership

b) limited liability, unlimited life, and ease of transfer of ownership

c) unlimited life, separation of ownership from management, and voting privileges for shareholders

d) unlimited liability, separation of ownership from management, and voting privileges for shareholders

( )   2. Corporations may come into existence under any of the following legal documents except:

a) articles of incorporation

b) a memorandum of association

c) a voting trust

d) letters patent

( )   3. A corporation's _____ is responsible for declaring dividends.

a) chief executive officer

b) chief operating officer

c) president

d) board of directors

( )   4. During periods of falling prices, FIFO will produce _____ inventory values and _____ profits than LIFO.

a) higher; lower

b) higher; higher

c) lower; lower

d) lower; higher

( )   5. Minority Interest in Subsidiaries arises due to the use of the _____ method of accounting.

a) consolidated

b) equity

c) cost

d) GAAP

6. A fixed asset is purchased for $50,000. The depreciation expense in year two, if it is depreciated on a declining balance method at a rate of 10%, will be:

    a) $5,000

    b) $10,000

    c) $6,000

    d) $4,500

    ( )

7. _____refers to the expense applied to the gradual write-down of the book value of franchise agreements.

    a) Depreciation

    b) Amortization

    c) Depletion

    d) all of the above

    ( )

8. The equity method of accounting is used:

    a) whenever firms acquire the common shares of another corporation

    b) whenever firms acquire more than 10% of the voting shares of another corporation

    c) whenever firms acquire more than 50% of the voting shares of another corporation

    d) whenever firms acquire between 20% and 50% of the voting shares of another corporation

    ( )

9. _____would appear at the top of the assets side of a company's balance sheet, followed by _____ then _____ and then by _____ .

    a) cash; accounts receivable; prepaid exenses; inventory

    b) cash; inventory; accounts receivable; prepaid expenses

    c) cash; accounts receivable; inventory; prepaid expenses

    d) cash; prepaid expenses; inventory; accounts receivable

    ( )

10. The statement of changes in financial position is broken down into the following headings, except for:

    a) operating activities

    b) non-operating activities

    c) financing activities

    d) investing activities

    ( )

( )   11. Deferred charges and prepaid expenses are similar to one another in that they are both charges that represent payments made by a company for which the benefit will last into the future. The main difference between the two is that:

        a) a deferred charge is recorded as an asset on the balance sheet, while a prepaid expense is recorded under the liability heading

        b) deferred charges are included in current assets while prepaid expenses are included as long-term assets

        c) the benefit of deferred charges will be received in the near future while the benefit of prepaid expenses will extend over a period of years

        d) the benefit of prepaid expenses will be received in the near future while the benefit of deferred charges will extend over a period of years

( )   12. Three disadvantages of incorporation include:

        a) ease of ownership transfer, professional management, and double taxation

        b) loss of flexibility, the possibility of double taxation, and additional administrative costs

        c) limited liability of shareholders, continuity of existence, and ease of ownership transfer

        d) management flexibility, complications involving withdrawal of capital, and possible tax benefits

( )   13. What is the difference between "extraordinary items" and "unusual items" on the earnings statement?

        a) Unusual items are typical for the normal business activity of the firm, but were caused by unusual circumstances while extraordinary items are not likely to re-occur such as a loss due to disposal of an operating division.

        b) Extraordinary items are typical for the normal business activity of the firm, but were caused by unusual circumstances while unusual items are not likely to re-occur such as a loss due to disposal of an operating division.

        c) Extraordinary items are always reported "above" unusual items.

        d) There is no difference; they refer to the same thing.

( )   14. Private corporations _____, while public corporations _____.

        a) are owned by private investors; are owned by a government agency

        b) can be either sole proprietorships or partnerships; are always incorporated

        c) restrict the right of shareholders to transfer shares and prohibit inviting members of the public to subscribe for their securities; face no such restrictions

        d) may only issue preferred equity; face no such restrictions

15. Advantages of incorporation include: ( )

    a) management flexibility and possible tax benefits

    b) limited liability of shareholders, continuity of existence, and ease of ownership transfer

    c) accessing capital, professional management

    d) all of the above

FIXED INCOME SECURITIES

OVERVIEW AND TERMINOLOGY

A **fixed income security** provides a known income stream to the holder, and has a known maturity date.

- A traditional fixed income security provides interim payments of interest or dividends. Examples include bonds, debentures, mortgages, swaps, and preferred shares. Discounted fixed income securities are sold at a discount from their face value, with the face value being the amount that is repaid at maturity. The return is the increase in principal value which is treated as income, not capital gains, for tax purposes. Examples include strip (or zero-coupon) bonds, and most money market instruments (e.g., treasury bills, commercial paper, and bankers acceptances).

- **Bonds** are debt instruments that are secured by real assets and are often called mortgage bonds. Details of the bond issue including payment, maturity, security, and bond covenants are included in the **bond trust indenture**, which represents a legal contract between the bondholders and the bond issuers. **Debentures** are similar to bonds, but are generally unsecured, or else secured by a general floating charge over the company's unencumbered assets (i.e., those that have not been pledged as security for other debt obligations).

- Bond prices are quoted based on an index with a base value of 100. When bonds trade at 100, they are trading at par or face value. When they trade above this, they are said to be trading at a **premium**, and when they trade below this they are trading at a **discount**.

- The face value or denomination (e.g., $1,000 or $10,000) represents the amount the issuer contracts to pay at maturity. The **term to maturity** is the remaining life of the bond. Canada Savings Bonds have minimum denominations of $100, while the minimum for most corporate bonds is $1,000.

Short-term bonds have maturities of three years or less. **Medium-term bonds** have maturities ranging from three to ten years, while **long-term bonds** have maturities beyond ten years.

Liquid bonds have significant trading volumes. **Negotiable bonds** are in deliverable form, and **marketable bonds** are those for which there is a ready market.

- Three main reasons for borrowing money is to match the term of assets with the term of liabilities; benefit from the use of financial leverage; and to fund deficits.

- Secondary market trading of debt instruments in Canada is much larger than trading in equities, with 1998 figures of $10.7 trillion for debt and $554 billion for equities. However, the value of debt outstanding in 1998 was about $1 trillion, while the market capitalization on the Toronto Stock Exchange alone was $1.35 trillion.

The following depicts a typical bond quote for a regular bond:

Issue	Coupon	Maturity Date	Bid	Ask	Yield
XYZ Co.	7.0%	1 June/10	100.75	101.25	6.95%

The quote highlights the issuer (XYZ Co.), the associated coupon rate (7.0%), the date the bond matures (June 1, 2010), the highest bid price (100.75), the lowest ask price (101.25), and the associated yield to maturity of the bond (6.95%). The ask price represents the price the bond could be bought for, while the bid price is the price the bond could be sold for, based on $100 of face value. For example, if the face value of the bond was $10,000, you would have to pay $10,125 ($10,000 × 101.25) plus accrued interest (discussed later in this chapter) to purchase the bond.

The quote for an extendible bond that is extendible at the holder's option, would be similar to the one above except that the maturity date would be expressed differently. For example, if an extendible bond matured on June 1, 2007, but was extendible to June 1, 2012, the maturity date would be expressed as: 1 June 07/12.

The quote for a retractable bond that allows the bond holder to sell the bonds back to the issuer prior to the stated maturity date would also have the maturity date expressed differently. For example, if a retractable bond matured on June 1, 2012, but could be redeemed by the holder on June 1, 2007, the maturity date would be expressed as: 1 June 12/07. *Notice the difference between extendibles and retractables: with retractables the more distant maturity date is presented first, while for extendibles it is expressed last.*

GOVERNMENT OF CANADA SECURITIES

Marketable Bonds: These have specified interest payments and maturity date and are **transferable**. Typically, they are non-callable (which will be discussed shortly). Government of Canada **Real Return Bonds** were introduced in 1991 to provide investors with a real yield of about 4.25%. This is achieved by pegging the face value to the CPI, and having the coupon rate of 4.25% apply to the inflation-adjusted face value.

Treasury Bills: These are short-term government obligations that are sold at a discount from face value. Traditionally, they were held by large investors, due to the large issue denominations. However, in recent years, financial intermediaries have repackaged larger offerings into smaller amounts (as low as $1,000) to make them available to retail investors.

Canada Savings Bonds (CSBs): Unlike other bonds, CSBs can be cashed out by the owner, at their full par value plus eligible accrued interest, at any bank in Canada at any time. They are **not transferable**, and their prices do not change over time. They are sold in **registered form** to provide protection against loss, theft, or destruction. In recent years, only individuals, estates of deceased persons, and trusts governed by certain types of deferred savings and income plans have been allowed to acquire CSBs.

- The rates of return on CSBs may be allowed to vary in order to avoid having holders "cash out" in times of rising interest rates. An effective program for selling CSBs is through the payroll savings plans of over 18,000 organizations, which reaches close to 1.25 million employees. Since 1977 they have been available in two forms:

    1. regular interest, which pays annual interest to the holder; and
    2. compound interest, which reinvests the interest, so that interest is also earned on accumulated interest.

- Two additional variations of CSBs have emerged in recent years:

    1. Canada Premium Bonds (CPBs): these are similar to CSBs, but can only be redeemed once a year (on their anniversary date and for the 30 days following that). They usually provide a higher rate than CSBs when issued.
    2. Canada RRSP Bonds: These have been available since 1997. They are similar to CSBs, but provide less flexibility, requiring a minimum purchase of $500, and being redeemable only on their anniversary date, after having provided prior notice.

OTHER TYPES OF BONDS

Mortgage bonds are secured by real property such as land, buildings or equipment. **First mortgage bonds** have first claim to such assets, and as such, they are referred to as "senior securities."

! **Collateral trust bonds** are secured by a pledge of other financial assets such as common shares, bonds, or treasury bills.

! **Equipment trust certificates** are secured by equipment, such as the rolling stock of a railway. The assets pledged as security are owned by investors through a lease agreement with the railway until the loan has been retired. The certificates have serial numbers that dictate their maturity date, with a certain amount maturing every year.

! **Corporate Debentures** are similar to bonds, but are generally unsecured, or else secured by a general floating charge over the company's unencumbered assets (i.e., those that have not been pledged as security for other debt obligations).

Subordinated debentures are junior to some other security, in a manner which may be ascertained from the prospectus.

- **Corporate notes** are unsecured promises to pay interest and repay principal, and rank behind all other fixed obligations of the borrower. **Secured notes** or **collateral trust notes** are secured by notes pledging assets purchased with the loan proceeds, such as automobiles. **Secured term notes** are secured by a written promise to pay regular installments, and these notes trade in the money market.

! Bonds may be:

1. **Domestic:** issued in the currency and country of the issuer (e.g., a Canadian company that issues bonds in Canada in Canadian dollars).

2. **Foreign:** issued in a country other than the issuer's, in the currency of the country in which it is issued (e.g., a Canadian company that issues bonds in the U.S. in U.S. dollars).

3. **Eurobonds:** issued in a country other than the issuer's, but not in the currency of that country (e.g., a Canadian company that issues bonds in Germany in U.S. or Canadian dollars). If the bonds are issued in Canadian dollars, they would be called EuroCanadian bonds, if issued in U.S. dollars, they would be called Eurodollar bonds.

- Warrants are sometimes attached to bonds or debentures (or preferred shares).

! A **unit** refers to a package of two or more securities that are bundled together and sold to the public. A unit typically consists of a bond or preferred share plus a stated number of common shares.

- **Real estate bonds** are those issued to finance real estate projects. They typically involve one or more of the following features which limit the investors' risk:

1. lender owns the development outright, or has shares in it;

2. income participation deals;

3. "rolling over" short-term loans;

4. long-term mortgage based loan with rates revised periodically; or

5. mortgage bonds are combined with share purchase warrants.

Strip (or zero-coupon) bonds are formed when financial intermediaries "strip" coupons off bonds and sell the cashflows separately, creating zero-coupon bonds that pay no coupons, but repay maturity value at the maturity date.

- Subordinated debentures with very long maturities are sometimes referred to as **preferred debentures**. This reflects the fact that their characteristics fall somewhere between preferred shares and regular debentures. Their characteristics include:
  - terms to maturity of 25-99 years;
  - they are ranked below all other debt, but rank ahead of preferred shares;
  - management often has the option to delay interest payments for up to five years; and
  - they trade on exchanges in many instances.

BOND FEATURES

- Interest payments on bonds are based on the stated coupon rate, and are generally paid semi-annually.

Foreign-pay bonds are those whose payments are made in a foreign currency. Some offer the choice of payment in more than one currency, while others may provide interest payments in one currency and principal repayment in another.

Floating rate bonds or debentures (floaters) have "adjustable" coupons which are typically tied to Treasury bill rates, or some other short-term interest rate. They are attractive for the protection offered in times of volatile interest rates, and behave like money market securities in an investment portfolio.

Callable bonds give the issuer the option to "call" or repurchase outstanding bonds at predetermined **call prices** (generally at a premium over par) at specified times. This feature is detrimental to the bondholders who are willing to pay less for them (i.e., they demand a higher return) than for similar non-callable bonds. Generally, the issuer agrees to give 30 or more days notice that the issue will be redeemed. **Call protection** refers to the period of time prior to the first call date during which callable bonds cannot be called. The **redemption price** is often based on a graduated scale, reflecting the fact that the hardship to the investor of having an issue called, is reduced as the time to maturity declines. Provincial bonds are usually callable at face value plus accrued interest. Usually corporate issues have a mandatory call feature for sinking fund purposes.

Sinking fund provisions require the issuer to repurchase a certain amount of debt per year. **Sinking funds** represent the funds set aside by the company for this purpose. Sinking fund provisions benefit the issuer, because it helps them avoid having to come up with the entire face value of the issue at the maturity date. However, they are not always advantageous to debt holders, who may have their securities repurchased by the issuer, even if they had been planning on holding the security to maturity date. In addition, there is often no premium provided in the repurchase price.

Purchase fund provisions are similar to sinking fund provisions; however, they require the repurchase of a certain amount of debt only if the debt can be repurchased at or below a given price. These provisions are generally advantageous to debt holders, since they provide some liquidity and downward price support for the market price of the debt instruments.

Retractable bonds allow the bondholder to sell the bonds back to the issuer at predetermined prices at specified times. **Extendible bonds** allow the bondholder to extend the maturity date of the bond. Both of these bonds offer investors an additional privilege, which implies they will pay more for these bonds (i.e., accept a lower return). In other words, the market prices of retractables and extendibles is normally higher than those for similar bonds lacking these features. They both tend to trade similar to short-term bonds during periods of rising interest rates, as it is likely that they will be redeemed (or not extended). Similarly, they tend to behave like long-term bonds during periods of decreasing interest rates. The holders generally must state their intentions to extend or redeem during the **election period,** which occurs six to 12 months prior to the extendible or retractable dates.

Convertible bonds may be converted into common shares at predetermined conversion prices. This privilege is afforded to the investor in order to make the issue more saleable, and to reduce the interest rate that must be offered to purchasers. Most convertibles increase the conversion price through time to increase the chances of early conversion. Most convertibles are callable. Certain convertibles include a forced conversion clause, which forces conversion by affording the issuer the right to redeem the issue once the common share price goes above prespecified levels.

Convertibles typically trade similar to straight debentures when the conversion price is well below the market price of the common shares. A **premium** appears as market price approaches conversion price, and it is said to "sell off the stock" once market price exceeds the conversion price. The payback period for a convertible measures how long it would take to recover its premium through the difference between its dividend yield versus the lower yield provided by the underlying stock (this will be discussed in depth in the next chapter). As a general rule of thumb, payback periods beyond two years are unattractive.

PROTECTIVE PROVISIONS

Protective covenants are clauses in the trust indenture that restrict actions of the issuer. Negative covenants prohibit certain actions (e.g., restrict dividend payments or prevent pledging of any assets to lenders). Positive covenants specify actions that the firm agrees to undertake (e.g., furnish quarterly financial statements or maintain certain working capital levels). Some common examples are described below.

Prohibition of a prior lien prohibits the issue of securities that would rank senior to first mortgage bond payments. Debentures typically include **negative pledge provisions**, which preclude the issue of additional bonds that are secured by company properties unless the debentures receive similar collateral.

Additional borrowing restrictions may be imposed through two mechanisms. The use of **closed end mortgages** prevents the issue of additional bonds that would be backed by the same assets as the original bonds. An even stronger restriction is given if the mortgage includes an **after-acquired clause**, which implies that subsequent asset purchases would be covered by the original mortgage. It is customary to permit the assumption of **purchase money mortgages**, which are liens attached to new properties subsequently acquired that do not affect the original bondholders security position. **Open end mortgages** typically include general provisions limiting the issue of new bonds to provide a proper margin of safety.

- Covenants may also require that the issuer maintain certain working capital requirements, and/or put restrictions on dividend payments. A **sinking fund clause** requires an issuer to set aside cash in a sinking fund for the purpose of repayment of future debt obligations.

- Covenants often prohibit companies from entering into sale and leaseback arrangements for certain assets, selling assets by sale or merger, disposing of shares of a subsidiary, issuing debt or shares by a subsidiary, disposing of debt or shares of a subsidiary, and merger of a subsidiary with an outside company.

Rating services perform detailed analysis of bond issuers to determine their ability to maintain uninterrupted payments of interest and repayment of principal. Investment grade bonds are those with bond ratings of BBB (Dominion Bond Rating Service (DBRS) and Standard & Poor's), B++ (Canadian Bond Rating Service (CBRS)), or Baa (Moody's) or higher. Junk (or high yield or low-grade) bonds have bond ratings below these. The following are the debt ratings categories for the two Canadian debt rating agencies:

CBRS		DBRS	
A++:	highest quality	AAA:	highest credit quality
A+:	very good quality	AA:	superior credit quality
A:	good quality	A:	upper medium grade credit quality
B++:	medium quality	BBB:	medium grade credit quality
B+:	lower medium quality	BB:	lower medium grade credit quality
B:	poor quality	B:	speculative credit quality
C:	speculative quality	CCC:	highly speculative credit quality
D:	default	CC:	in default
Suspended: rating suspended		C:	second tier of debt of an entity in defaul

Ratings of both services may also be modified by "high" or "low" to indicate the relative ranking within a category, or the trend within the category.

BOND PRICING PRINCIPLES

Regular coupon bonds pay regular interest payments or **coupons (C)** in semi-annual or annual installments, plus the **face** or **par value (FV)** of the bonds, which is paid at the maturity date.[1] The amount of the coupons is determined when the bonds are originally issued and is calculated by multiplying the coupon rate by the face value.

Bonds are valued by determining the **present value** of the cash stream provided by the bonds (which consists of an ordinary annuity of interest payments, and one lump sum repayment). To determine the bond price (B_0) of a bond with an n period term to maturity, we determine the present value of all future cashflows when discounted by the appropriate discount rate (i.e., the market required rate of return denoted as (r) using the following equation:

$$B_0 = C \times \left[\frac{1 - \frac{1}{(1+r)^n}}{r} \right] + FV \times \left[\frac{1}{(1+r)^n} \right]$$

Example 1:

(a) Determine the bond price of a $1,000 face value bond with four years to maturity, that pays interest semi-annually at a coupon rate of 12%. Assume the appropriate discount rate is 10% (this will almost always be stated on an annual basis).

Solution:

C = coupon rate / 2 × face value = .12/2 × $1,000 = $60;
n = term to maturity = 4 years × 2 = 8 (*semi-annual periods*);
r = 0.10/2 = 0.05 (*semi-annual rate*)

$$B_0 = 60 \times \left[\frac{1 - \frac{1}{(1.05)^8}}{.05} \right] + 1,000 \times \left[\frac{1}{(1.05)^8} \right]$$

$$= 60(6.46321) + 1,000(0.6784) = \$1,064.63$$

Note: These bonds sell at a "premium" over par since market rates (10%) are less than the coupon rate (12%). If market rates were above the coupon rate of 12%, the bonds would sell at a discount.

This illustrates the basic "inverse" relationship between bond prices and interest rates:

As rates increase bond prices decrease, and vice-versa.

---

[1] For the actual CSC exam, unless you are told otherwise you should assume the coupons are paid **semi-annually**.

(b) Repeat (a) assuming six years to maturity, and nothing else changes.

Everything else is the same as in (a) except that n = 6 years $\times$ 2 = 12,

$$B_0 = 60 \times \left[\frac{1 - \frac{1}{(1.05)^{12}}}{.05} \right] + 1,000 \times \left[\frac{1}{(1.05)^{12}} \right]$$

$$= 60(8.86325) + 1,000(0.55684) = \$1,088.64$$

These bonds sell at a greater premium over par than the four-year bonds, which illustrates another important bond relationship: the prices of *longer term bonds are more sensitive to interest rate changes* than shorter term bonds (all else being equal).

The required market rate of return on bonds is determined by market activity and is generally referred to as the yield, effective yield, **yield to maturity (YTM)** or the **average purchase/redemption yield**. The YTM is the discount rate that equates the present value of all future expected payments on the bond if held to maturity to its present market price. It can be found by solving the equation below for YTM, given the bond price, coupon rate, maturity value, and term to maturity:

$$B_0 = C \times \left[\frac{1 - \frac{1}{(1 + YTM)^n}}{YTM} \right] + FV \times \left[\frac{1}{(1 + YTM)^n} \right]$$

It may be solved by a financial calculator, by using bond tables, or approximated using the following formula:

$$YTM = \frac{Annual\ Coupons + \frac{(FV - B_0)}{n}}{\frac{(FV + B_0)}{2}}$$

This is an approximation, based on the notion of dividing the average annual cash flows (as measured by the annual interest payments + average annual capital gain or loss) by the average investment in the bond.

Example 2:

Determine the approximate yield to maturity or average purchase/redemption yield for a six-year $1,000 face value bond that pays semi-annual coupons at an annual coupon rate of 12%, if it is presently selling for $980.

Solution:

$$YTM = \frac{120 + \dfrac{(1000 - 980)}{6}}{\dfrac{(1000 + 980)}{2}} = \frac{120 + 3.33}{990} = 12.45\%$$

The yield on treasury bills is determined in Canada using the following equation:

$$T\text{-bill yield} = \frac{Face - P}{P} \times \frac{365}{n} \times 100\%$$

where *Face* is the face value of the T-bill, *P* is its price, and *n* is the number of days to maturity.

Example 3:

Determine the yield on 89-day Government of Canada treasury bills that are presently selling at a price (P) of 98 per 100 of face value:

Solution:

$$T\text{-bill yield} = \frac{100 - 98}{98} \times \frac{365}{89} \times 100\% = 8.37\%$$

The required market rate of return on bonds is determined by supply and demand. Fisher's Law suggests that nominal rates of return will change in accordance with changes in inflation rates, which implies that **nominal rates = real rates + expected inflation rates**. Real rates are determined by the forces of supply and demand for loanable funds. They tend to rise and fall during expansionary and recessionary phases of the business cycle.

The required market return on any bond will equal the riskless rate (i.e., 91-day Government of Canada T-bills) plus a risk premium. The **risk premium** compensates the investor for the assumption of additional risks and may include some or all of the following:

1. **default** or credit risk premium;
2. **maturity** premium;
3. **liquidity** premium; and
4. **issue-specific** premium (for items such as convertible, callable, retractable features).

Some important properties of fixed-income securities are:[2]

1. Prices are inversely related to interest rates.

2. Prices exhibit greater interest rate risk (sensitivity to changes in interest rates) the longer their term to maturity.

3. The smaller the coupon rate (all else remaining equal), the greater the interest rate risk.

4. Special features such as call provisions or convertible privileges lead to special pricing considerations (as previously discussed).

5. Prices are more volatile when interest rates are low, since the relative change of a 1% change in rates is more significant.

6. The current price is the net effect of all of these factors.

Duration is a calculation which equates coupon risk and term risk into a single measure of interest rate risk. It is calculated as the present value weighted average of all cash flows from a bond and measures the responsiveness of bond prices to changes in interest rates over relatively small intervals of interest rate changes.

Duration will always be *less* than the bond's term to maturity for coupon bonds. It will always *equal* the term to maturity for zero-coupon (strip) bonds.

THE TERM STRUCTURE OF INTEREST RATES

The term structure of interest rates or **yield curve** demonstrates the relationship between long- and short-term rates on similar debt instruments (e.g. Government of Canada bonds).

The three major explanations offered for the shapes of term structures include:

1. **Liquidity Preference Theory:** Suggests that investors prefer short-term bonds because they exhibit less interest rate risk; therefore, they must be provided with premiums to induce them to invest in longer term bonds. As a result, yield curves will generally be upward sloping since long-term rates will be higher than short-term rates.

2. **Expectations Theory:** Argues that the yield curve reflects investor expectations about future interest rates. Therefore, an upward sloping yield curve reflects expectations of interest rate increases in the future, and a downward sloping curve reflects expectations of interest rate decreases in the future.

---

[2] Properties (1) and (2) were demonstrated in Example 1 and are the most important ones to remember, along with property (3).

3. **Market Segmentations Theory:** Argues that there exist distinct markets (or segments) for interest rate securities of differing maturities, and rates are determined within these independent markets by the forces of supply and demand. When we aggregate these rates we end up with a given term structure.

- **Bond switches** occur when an investor sells one bond and replaces it with another. Potential benefits include:

   1. an improvement in net yield (e.g., a high tax investor may switch to bonds with lower coupons to reduce the interest income and increase the capital gains portion of income);

   2. term extension or reduction (e.g., switch to longer term bonds if you believe that rates will fall);

   3. improvement in credit (i.e., a flight to quality occurs, particularly during periods of higher market volatility);

   4. portfolio diversification benefits; and

   5. cash take-outs (i.e., if you are able to exchange bonds and pocket some cash in the process).

- Successful bond switching (i.e., achieving the desired results) requires success in forecasting the bond market, which is no easy task. One must be careful to take into account the following considerations: (1) longer term bonds with lower coupon rates are the most volatile; and (2) transactions costs may be significant, particularly for less liquid issues.

DELIVERY, REGULATION, AND SETTLEMENT

Some typical settlement requirements for debt instruments are:

   1. G of C Treasury bills: same day.

   2. G of C Bonds and Guarantees with term <= 3 years (or to earliest call date if the transaction occurs at a premium): second clearing day after transaction.

   3. G of C Bonds and Guarantees with term > 3 years (or to earliest call date if the transaction occurs at a premium) and all provincial, municipal, corporate, and other bonds or debentures; stock; and other certificates of indebtedness (including mortgage backed securities (MBS) except as described below): third clearing day after transaction.

   4. An MBS trade from the third clearing day before month end to the first clearing day before the seventh calendar day of the next month: first clearing day on or after the 15th calendar day of the month.

Bond certificates may be in one of two forms:

1. **Bearer Bonds:** These are presumed to be owned by the party holding the bonds. Coupons are numbered and dated, and may be clipped and redeemed for cash.

2 **Registered Bonds:** The name of the owner is on the face of these bonds, and interest is paid to the registered owner by the issuer. This protects the holder in the event the bond is lost or stolen, because it is difficult for anyone else to redeem them.

- Today settlement for most bonds, in both bearer or registered form, is handled by the Canadian Depository for Securities Limited (CDS) through a computerized settlement procedure called a Book Based System. If a buyer wishes to receive a certificate, the settlement procedure is handled through a certificate based system.

- Bond trading is regulated by the IDA in conjunction with the Toronto Bond Traders Association and Montreal Bond Traders Association. These associations are open to any member of the IDA, the bond departments of any chartered bank, and any other financial house whose application is acceptable to the Board of Governors. The IDA is the senior member and reserves the right of final decision. Trading and delivery regulations cover all major aspects of trading including trading and delivery practices, and general regulations.

Accrued interest refers to the amount of interest earned, but not yet received, by the holder of a bond prior to selling it, and this amount must be paid from the buyer to the previous holder. This amount must be paid to the previous holders above the quoted bond price, the sum of which is referred to as the bond's cash price. Accrued interest is calculated using the following calculation:

Accrued Interest = Par Amount $\times$ Coupon Rate $\times$ (Time Period/365).

Example 4:

Determine the accrued interest on $250,000 face value as of June 12, 2001, if the bonds mature on August 31, 2020, and the coupon rate is 6%. Assume it is not a leap year.

Solution:

We assume these bonds pay semi-annual coupons, since it is not stated otherwise. Since they mature on August 31, coupons must be paid on August 31 and February 28 every non-leap year (February 29 in a leap year). This means the last coupon payment was made on February 28. Therefore, they have 104 days of accrued interest (31 days in March + 30 days in April + 31 days in May + 12 days in June)—in other words, it has been 104 days since the last interest payment. Thus,

Accrued Interest = $250,000 $\times$ .06 $\times$ (104/365) = $4,273.97

- Interest payments received from debt investments are taxed at the taxpayer's full marginal tax rate, unlike dividends and capital gains that receive preferential tax treatment. Interest income must be declared when accrued (earned), whether the payment is actually made or not. For example, while CSBs do not pay interest until they are cashed out, the accrued interest must be claimed every year. The returns earned on debt instruments such as T-bills, which are sold at a discount from face value and then repay the face value at maturity, are considered interest income and are taxed accordingly.

- Other fixed income instruments are offered by intermediaries. Most of them focus on safety. Two of the most common instruments are Term Deposits and Guaranteed Investment Certificates (GICs), which are described below.

Term Deposits offer guaranteed rates for short-term deposits (usually up to one year), and usually levy penalties for early withdrawals.

Guaranteed Investment Certificates (GICs) offer fixed rates for specified periods of time, which may exceed one year. The interest and principal payments are both guaranteed. Non-redeemable GICs cannot be cashed prior to maturity except in the case of death or severe financial hardship. Redeemable GICs can be cashed before maturity, and typically provide lower returns than non-redeemable GICs.

- GICs are currently available with terms up to 10 years, with a variety of payment intervals (e.g., monthly, quarterly, etc.), and many provide compound interest. They may be used as collateral for loans, may be automatically renewed at maturity, and may be sold through an intermediary. Canada Deposit Insurance Corporation (CDIC) does not offer coverage for GICs with maturities beyond five years, and not all GICs are RRSP eligible.

- Some special features available with GICs include the following:
  1. **Escalating-Rate GICs:** the interest rates increase through time.
  2. **Laddered GICs:** the GIC is broken into equal terms to reduce interest rate risk (e.g., a three-year $6,000 GIC is divided into a one-year $2,000 GIC, a two-year $2,000 GIC, and a three-year $2,000 GIC).
  3. **Instalment GICs:** the initial contribution is followed by regular periodic minimum deposits.
  4. **Index-Linked GICs:** the returns are linked to equity returns based on a particular domestic or global index.
  5. **Interest-Rate-Linked GICs:** the returns are linked to changes in other interest rates such as the prime rate, or money market rates.

Chapter 5: Review Questions

1. The _____ suggests that the yield curve represents the supply of ( )
and demand for bonds of various terms, which are primarily influenced by
the bigger players in each sector.

   a) Liquidity Preference Theory

   b) Expectations Theory

   c) Market Segmentation Theory

   d) Term Extension Theory

2. What is the yield to maturity on a 10% bond that pays out coupons semi- ( )
annually and has 10 years to maturity if the bond is selling at $113.40?

   a) 10.0%

   b) 8.54%

   c) 8.12%

   d) none of the above

3. What is the yield on a 90-day T-bill purchased for $96,000 with a maturity ( )
value of $100,000?

   a) 16.9%

   b) 16.2%

   c) 16.4%

   d) 16.6%

4. In the case of zero-coupon bonds, duration is: ( )

   a) less than its term to maturity

   b) equal to its term to maturity

   c) greater than its term to maturity

   d) equal to zero

5. Yield differences result from all of the following, except differences in: ( )

   a) credit quality

   b) maturity

   c) liquidity

   d) inflation rates

( )   6. What would be the market price of a 10% non-callable corporate bond with a face value of $1,000 and 14 years to maturity, if it pays interest semi-annually, and the required rate of return on similar bonds is presently 8.4%?

        a) $1,129

        b) $1,130

        c) $1,000

        d) $985

( )   7. If the bonds in Question 6 were callable bonds, we would expect they would sell for _____ the price determined in Question 6.

        a) the same as

        b) higher than

        c) lower than

        d) cannot say

( )   8. How much accrued interest would have to be paid if you purchased the bond in Question 6 on February 8, 2001, if the bond matures on June 30, 2020?

        a) $5.34

        b) $10.41

        c) $10.68

        d) insufficient information

( )   9. For risk-free securities, the nominal interest rate is the sum of:

        a) actual and expected inflation rates

        b) expected inflation and expected return

        c) the real rate of interest and expected inflation rate

        d) the market rate of return and real rate of interest

( )   10. If the yield to maturity is greater than the coupon rate, a bond must be:

        a) selling at a discount

        b) selling at a premium

        c) selling at face value

        d) a zero-coupon bond

11. Which of the following statements regarding bond prices is true? ( )

   a) Short-term bond prices will increase more than long-term bond prices if market yields increase.

   b) Short-term bond prices will increase more than long-term bond prices if market yields decrease.

   c) Short-term bond prices will increase less than long-term bond prices if market yields increase.

   d) Short-term bond prices will increase less than long-term bond prices if market yields decrease.

12. Which of the following bonds should have the least price volatility? ( )

   a) 9%, 10-year bond

   b) 9%, 3-year bond

   c) 6%, 10-year bond

   d) 6%, 3-year bond

13. Which of the following statements regarding Canada Savings Bonds is true? ( )

   a) They are non-transferable.

   b) They are issued in bearer form.

   c) They may only be issued as compound interest bonds.

   d) all of the above are false

14. A bond that is issued by a Japanese company in Canada that is denominated in U.S. dollars is an example of a: ( )

   a) domestic bond

   b) foreign bond

   c) eurobond

   d) foreign pay bond

15. _____ are debt securities that are secured by financial assets. ( )

   a) Collateral trust bonds

   b) Equipment trust certificates

   c) Financial bonds

   d) Income bonds

16. Government of Canada Real Return Bonds provide holders with real return of: ( )

   a) 3.25%

   b) 3.50%

   c) 4.25%

   d) 5.25%

( )   17. A trade in a bond with two-and-a-half years to maturity settles:

a) the same day

b) the next business day

c) in two business days

d) in three business days

( )   18. _____ bonds are those that are in deliverable form.

a) Marketable

b) Negotiable

c) Liquid

d) Registered

( )   19. Bonds with a 10% coupon rate will trade at the following price when the appropriate market interest rates are 10%.

a) 100

b) 105

c) 95

d) insufficient information

( )   20. A(n)_____ prevents the issue of additional bonds against property that was pledged under a previous debt agreement.

a) open end mortgage

b) closed end mortgage

c) after-acquired clause

d) both (b) and (c) are true

( )   21. Sinking fund provisions _____ .

a) are the same as purchase fund provisions

b) are generally advantageous to the bond holder

c) neither (a) nor (b) is true

d) both (a) and (b) are true

( )   22. GICs _____ .

a) cannot have maturities greater than five years

b) cannot be used as collateral for loans

c) can be automatically renewed at maturity

d) cannot be contributed to an RRSP

23. Duration will always be _____ the bond's term to maturity for coupon bonds.

   a) more than

   b) less than

   c) equal to

   d) unrelated to

Refer to the following bond quote to answer Questions 24-25:

XYZ Company   7.50%   1 June 09/04   102.10   103.50   8.21

24. Which of the following statements regarding this bond are false?

   a) It is a retractable bond.

   b) It is an extendible bond.

   c) It has an associated coupon rate of 7.50%.

   d) It pays coupons on June 1st and December 1st every year.

25. If you were to purchase this bond on the date this quote was available, and the date was January 1, how much would you have to pay the seller for the bond?

   a) $1,021

   b) $1,035

   c) $1,041.37

   d) $1,027.37

EQUITIES

INTRODUCTION

- A **common share** provides proportionate ownership in the company's equity value, the value of which will change in response to changes in the value of the firm's equity and the number of shares outstanding. These shares will be attractive to investors looking to profit from the future accomplishments of the issuer.

- A **preferred share** provides the owner with a claim to a fixed amount of equity that is established when the share is first issued. These will be more attractive to investors who desire steady income and a more secure position with respect to claims on the assets and income of the company than common shareholders hold.

PREFERRED SHARE CHARACTERISTICS

- Most preferred shares have an associated "preference as to assets" clause and pay fixed dividend amounts (either as a fixed dollar amount or as a stated percentage of par value). While payment of preferred dividends is not obligatory like interest payments, payments to common shareholders are prohibited until preferred shareholders have been paid in entirety. Failure to pay anticipated preferred dividends will weaken investor confidence in the issuer, and affect its' general credit and borrowing power.

- Preferred dividends are paid from after-tax earnings, and, unlike interest payments, they do not provide the issuer with a tax-deductible expense. Shareholders receive some relief in the form of a dividend tax credit, which implies they will pay lower taxes on a dollar of dividend income than on a dollar of interest income.

- Preferred shares are primarily fixed income instruments which offer limited opportunity for capital gains in comparison to common shares. Interest rates have a larger impact on their value than do the earnings of the issuer, and their value tends to go up (or down) as interest rates decline (or increase).

Companies issue preferred shares as a compromise between the demands created by debt, and the dilution of equity caused by the issuance of additional common shares, or when market conditions are unfavourable for new common share issues.

Investors may be attracted to preferred shares when they desire dividend income, which offers tax advantages over interest income. In addition, sometimes there are special features which make preferred shares attractive to investors (which are discussed below).

TYPES OF PREFERRED SHARES

Straight Preferreds: May have some or all of the features discussed in the section on page 91 entitled "Preferred Features." Generally, they have a stated par value and pay a fixed dividend rate.

- Investors should consider the following questions before purchasing straight preferreds:

  1. Does it pass the four tests cited at the end of this chapter?
  2. Is the dividend cumulative?
  3. Are there adequate protective provisions?
  4. Are there purchase fund or sinking fund provisions?
  5. What is the relationship between call and market price?
  6. Are they eligible for dividend tax credits?
  7. Is their yield comparable to similar investments?
  8. Are they listed on an exchange?
  9. What is their marketability (average monthly trading volume)?
  10. Do they have a rating by services or internal ratings?

Advantages and disadvantages of straight preferreds include:

  1. tax advantage of dividends;
  2. less safety than debt;
  3. "fixed" income;
  4. no voting privileges;
  5. no maturity date;
  6. less marketable than common shares; and
  7. less appreciation potential than common.

Similar to bonds, straight preferred shares can be valued according to the present value of their future dividends. Since the dividends are for a fixed amount and there is no maturity date, the future dividends represent a perpetual annuity (or perpetuity). Denoting P_{ps} as the market price, D_p as the dividend amount, and k_p as the market required rate of return on the preferred shares, they can be valued according to the following equation:

$$\mathbf{P_{ps} = D_p / k_p}$$

This equation can be rearranged to determine the required rate of return on the preferred shares as:

$$\mathbf{k_p = D_p / P_{ps}}$$

Example 1:

(a) Determine the market price of a preferred share that pays an annual dividend of $2, when market rates are 10%.

Solution:

P_{ps} = $2 / .10 = $20

(b) Repeat (a) assuming market rates are 12%.

Solution:

P_{ps} = $2 / .12 = $16.67 (notice that the price falls as rates rise just like with bonds)

(c) Repeat (a) assuming market rates are 8%.

Solution:

P_{ps} = $2 / .08 = $25 (notice that the price rises as rates fall just like with bonds)

Example 2:

Determine the market yield on preferred shares that provide a $5 annual dividend and are presently selling for $60.

Solution:

k_p = $5 / $60 = 0.0833 or 8.33%

Convertible Preferreds: Are convertible into common shares at a conversion price that is generally set at a modest premium above its converted value to discourage early conversion.

! The **conversion "premium"** may be calculated as the cost of purchasing the required amount of convertible preferreds that could be converted into common shares, over and above the cost of purchasing the common shares directly in the market.

Example 3:

Determine the premium of a convertible preferred share that is presently selling for $50 and is convertible into two shares of common shares which are presently selling for $23.

Solution:

It would cost $50 to buy two common shares using the convertible versus $2 \times \$23 = \$46$ to purchase them directly. Therefore,

Dollar premium = $50 − $46 = $4

Percentage premium = premium / cost of purchasing common = 4 / 46 = 8.70%

! The **payback** is the number of years to pay back the premium from the convertible's higher dividend stream. In other words:

Payback = (%premium) ÷ (convertible yield − common yield)

Example 4:

Determine the payback for the preferred share in Example 3 if the annual dividends are $2.00 for the preferred shares, and $0.80 for the common shares.

Solution:

The dividend yield for the preferred shares = 2 / 50 = 4.0%

The dividend yield for the common shares = 0.80 / 23 = 3.48%

Therefore, payback = (8.70%) / (4.0% − 3.48%) = 16.73 years

! Generally investors prefer convertibles with *lower premiums* and *shorter paybacks;* however, this will be dependent on the circumstances (which should be investigated).

- No commission is charged on conversion, and a capital gain or loss is not recorded until the common shares are actually sold.

- Investors must consider:
    1. the outlook for the common stock;
    2. the life of the conversion privilege;
    3. the reasonableness of the premium; and
    4. the selling price in relation to the call price.

- Advantages and disadvantages of convertible preferreds include:

  1. they are two-way securities;
  2. they generally provide higher yield than the underlying common shares;
  3. they provide the right to obtain common shares without paying commission;
  4. they provide lower yields than straight preferreds;
  5. they may provide for less than "board lots" of common shares which makes them harder to sell; and
  6. they revert to straight preferreds after conversion period if not converted.

Retractable Preferreds: Can be tendered by holder to the issuer for redemption. Investors must consider:

  1. the life of the retraction privilege; and
  2. the relationship of the market price to the retraction price.

- Advantages and disadvantages of retractable preferreds include:

  1. they are less vulnerable to interest rate changes (short maturity potential);
  2. there exists the potential for capital gains if bought at a discount from retraction price;
  3. they sell above retraction price and at least as high as call price when rates drop;
  4. they do not retract automatically; and
  5. they become straight preferreds if not retracted.

- The yield on a retractable may be calculated as follows:

  (1) when selling above retraction price:

  Yield = annual dividend / market price

  (2) when selling below retraction price:

  Yield = (annual dividend + annualized capital gain) ÷ ([market price + retraction price] / 2)

Example 5: ———————————————————————————

(a) Calculate the yield for a 7% $100 par value preferred share that is retractable at $100 in six years and six months time when it sells for $103.

   Solution:

   Yield = $7 / $103 = 6.79%

(b) Repeat (a) when the preferred share is selling for $97.

   Solution:

   Yield = ($7 + [100 − 97] / 6.5) ÷ ([97 + 100] / 2) = 7.462 / 98.5 = 0.07576 or 7.58%

! **Variable or Floating Rate Preferreds:** Dividend payments vary with interest rates over certain time periods.

- Investor considerations:
    1. lower dividends must be acceptable if rates drop; and
    2. does it compare favourably with similar investments.

- Advantages and disadvantages of variable or floating rate preferreds include:
    1. higher income if rates rise;
    2. variable income amounts which may be difficult to predict; and
    3. prices will be relatively unresponsive to changes in rates.

! **Preferreds with Warrants:** Often warrants are sold along with preferreds in a unit, to provide a *sweetener* for investors.

- Investors should consider:
    1. the outlook for common stock;
    2. the length of the warrant's life;
    3. the relationship between the exercise price and the market price;
    4. are odd lots involved;
    5. any protection provided against dilution;
    6. how many warrants will be outstanding; and
    7. are the warrants listed on an exchange.

OTHER PREFERREDS

! **Participating Preferreds:** Have certain prespecified rights to share in company earnings over and above their specified rate.

- Investors should consider:
    1. limited or full participation;
    2. trade-off versus yields of similar preferreds; and
    3. likelihood of higher dividends.

- Advantages and disadvantages of participating preferreds include:
    1. possibility of higher dividends; and
    2. limited advantage over common for limited participating feature.

- **Foreign-Pay Preferreds:** Pay dividends in foreign currencies. Benefits or costs depend on the resulting exchange rates, and beliefs regarding future exchange rates is a key factor in assessing the desirability of holding such instruments.

- **Auction Preferreds:** Their dividend rate is determined by an auction between the holder and the issuer, and they usually offer minimum and maximum reset dividend rates.

- **Deferred Preferreds:** Do not pay dividends until some specified future maturity date, at which time the accrued dividends are treated as interest income. If they are sold prior to the maturity date, the income is treated as a capital gain (or loss). These provide investors with an opportunity to defer taxes paid on income earned until a later date.

- **Split Shares:** Also known as **structured preferreds** or **equity dividend shares**. These represent common shares that have been split into two different shares: the *equity dividend share* that receives the dividends, and the capital share that receives the greatest potential for capital gains. Most of these are redeemable; however, if redeemed prior to maturity, the investor foregoes dividend income.

PREFERRED FEATURES

Preferred shares usually have a **cumulative** feature associated with their dividends. This requires the firm to pay all preferred dividends (current and arrears), before paying any dividends to common shareholders, which makes the preferred less risky than common shares from the investor's point of view.

- **Callable preferred shares** are generally callable at a premium over par value, similar to callable debt, which benefits the issuer.

Generally, preferred shares are **non-voting**. However, if a pre-specified number of dividend payments are not made, they may receive voting privileges.

- Some preferreds have **purchase funds** that require the company to purchase a specified amount of preferreds in the open market, if they are available at or below the stipulated price. This provides built-in market support for these shares.

- Sinking fund provisions are less common for preferred share issues. They have the potential disadvantage to investors that the required purchases may be called in by lot at the sinking fund price plus accrued and unpaid dividends, if the fund's open market operations are unsuccessful.

- Generally, both purchase and sinking funds improve the position of remaining preferred shareholders, by reducing the number of shares outstanding.

- **Protective provisions** generally include:
  1. restriction of common dividends unless working capital and/or purchase or sinking fund requirements are met;
  2. the right to vote is provided in event of arrears beyond a stipulated amount; and
  3. restrictions on further preferred issues, sale of assets, or changes in the terms of the original issue.

ASSESSING PREFERRED SHARE INVESTMENT QUALITY

The following **four tests** are employed to assess the investment quality of preferred shares:

1. **Preferred Dividend Coverage:**

   Preferred Dividend Coverage = (net earnings before extraordinary items − equity income + minority interest in earnings of subsidiary companies + all income taxes + total interest charges) ÷ (total interest charges + before-tax preferred dividend payments).

   This ratio is discussed in depth in Chapter 10. Rules of thumb are for utilities and industrials to maintain coverage above 2.0 and 3.0 for each of the past five years. The trend is also very important. Before-tax dividend payments may be calculated by multiplying actual payments (which come from after-tax earnings) by (100) (100 − tax rate).

2. **Record of Continuous Dividend Payments:** This information can be obtained for Canadian companies from *The Dividend Record*, which is published by the Financial Post Datagroup.

3. **Adequate Equity Behind Each Preferred Share:** Equity (or book value) per preferred share (as calculated below) should be at least two times the dollar value of assets to which the preferred share is entitled over each of the past five years, and exhibit a stable or rising five-year trend. This ratio is discussed in detail in Chapter 10.

   Equity per Preferred Share = (preferred equity + total common equity) ÷ (number of preferred shares outstanding)

4. **An Independent Credit Assessment:** In Canada, both DBRS and CBRS provide ratings for preferred shares. The CBRS ratings are:
   - P-1+ (securitized preferred shares);
   - P-1 (highest quality);
   - P-2 (good quality);
   - P-3 (medium quality);
   - P-4 (lower quality); and
   - P-5 (poor quality).

   DBRS ratings range from Pfd-1 (high) for highest quality, to Pfd-3 (low) for the lowest quality.

- In addition to these four tests, investors should also consider other relevant economic, industry, and financial factors; examine the most recent quarterly results available; and confirm that the shares were underwritten by an established securities firm.

- Top quality straight preferreds would fit into a conservative investor's portfolio, while medium- to high-quality preferreds would be appropriate for moderately aggressive investors, and low-quality to speculative preferreds would only be appropriate for aggressive, experienced investors and speculators.

- Assuming high-quality preferreds, the following special types would be most appropriate for the following types of individual investment portfolios:

    1. Convertible: aggressive and moderately aggressive

    2. Retractable: conservative

    3. Variable dividend: aggressive and sophisticated

    4. Warrants attached: aggressive and moderately aggressive

    5. Participating: conservative and moderately aggressive

    6. Foreign-pay: aggressive and sophisticated

COMMON SHARES

- Common share capital is sometimes referred to as risk capital to reflect the possibility of total loss of investment if the issuer fails. Today, most share certificates are in "street" form which makes them easily transferable.

The following rights are associated with common share ownership:

1. **Potential for Capital Appreciation:** As earnings are reinvested in the firm, the asset base and common equity base grow.

    Stock splits have little effect on existing shareholders. For example, a two-for-one split doubles the number of shares authorized, issued, and outstanding, and will likely cause the market price to fall to half of the previous market price. They are typically used to obtain a price in a target range which will entice investors, and prevent odd-lot problems that may be associated with high-priced shares. **Reverse splits** (or **consolidations**) occur when shares are trading at a value that may be unattractive to investors because they are too low.

2. **Right to Receive Common Dividends:** The firm's dividend policy is established by the Board of Directors, and dividend payout ratios vary across firms and industries. The Board of Directors decides whether to pay dividends, the amount of the dividend, and the payment date. Reductions or omissions occur sometimes, and reflect the risks of common share investment. Sometimes these payments are restricted by provisions in outstanding bond and/or preferred share issues.

    Regular dividends are those which investors can reasonably expect will be maintained in the future. **Extra** (or **special**) **dividends** are those which may arise due to unusually favourable circumstances, and cannot be assumed to persist into the future. Extra dividends should only be included in the calculation of a firm's dividend yield if there is strong evidence that they will be paid again.

Payments are made to shareholders of record on the **dividend record date**. The **ex dividend date** is set at the second business day before the record date, and shares trade without the right to the associated dividend on and after this date. This ensures that a purchaser of the share three days before the record date would settle by the record date (since common share trades settle on the third business day after a trade). Shares are said to trade **cum dividend** up to the ex dividend date, and trade **ex dividend** thereafter. This will be reflected in the share price, which typically falls by an amount close to the dividend amount on the ex dividend date.

- **Dividend reinvestment plans (DRIPs)** reinvest shareholders' dividends to purchase additional shares for them; although the shareholder is taxed as if they had received the actual cash dividends. In effect, these plans provide investors with an automatic savings plan which has the advantage of using dollar cost averaging. The shares are typically purchased through the open market by trustees, and the plan permits the purchase equivalent of fractional shares. Variations allow investors to contribute additional cash amounts to the plan and/or provide for the purchase of treasury shares at pre-specified discounts from the open market prices.

- **Stock dividends** may be offered when the firm wishes to preserve cash. They give the shareholder ownership of additional shares, and are taxed the same as cash dividends.

3. **Voting Privileges:** Shares may be normal voting, multiple-voting, non-voting, subordinate voting, or restricted voting. Restricted voting shares are protected by certain rights and regulations designed to ensure their position is not abused.

4. **Tax Treatment:** Income from common shares is afforded favourable tax treatment through:[1]

   ○ the federal tax dividend credit, which reduces the effective tax rate on dividend income;

   ○ capital gains exemptions, which exempt 50% of capital gains from taxation; and

   ○ stock savings plans which entitle residents of several provinces to deduct up to specified annual amounts from (or obtain a tax credit for) the cost of certain stocks purchased in the respective provinces.

5. **Marketability:** Investors can buy or sell shares in the open market at any time. Occasionally, share trading may be suspended by securities commissions as a result of a material change in affairs. In addition, foreign ownership in certain companies (e.g., banks, trust and insurance companies, broadcasting and communications companies) is restricted.

- Other rights and advantages include the right to elect directors, receive copies of annual and quarterly reports, examine certain company documents such as the by-laws, question management at shareholder meetings, and limited liability.

---

[1] The effect of the dividend tax credit and the capital gains exemptions on taxes is discussed in detail in Chapter 11.

Stock quotations are provided in financial publications. They typically provide information regarding the following:

1. **High or low:** the highest (or lowest) trading price during the previous day (or week, or 52-week period);

2. **Close:** the last trading price of the day;

3. **Change:** the change from the previous day's closing price;

4. **Volume:** the number of shares changing hands during the day;

5. **Div.:** the total dividends per share paid over the past 52 weeks; and

6. **Bid (ask):** the highest (lowest) price a potential buyer (seller) is offering

CASH AND MARGIN ACCOUNTS

Clients who open **cash accounts** are not granted credit by the securities firm, and are expected to make full payment for purchases by the settlement date. The **settlement date** is:

1. the same day for Government T-bills;

2. two business days after for other Government of Canada direct and guarantees up to three years; and

3. three business days after for all other securities (including preferred and common shares).

Margin accounts are established for clients to enable them to buy (or short sell) securities by initially contributing only part of the full price of the transaction, with the remainder being borrowed from the member (with interest being charged on the borrowed amount).

- Investment firms are allowed the use of customers' free credit balances, but must give them written notice to this effect.

- The term "margin" refers to the amount of funds the investor must contribute to the margin account.

Maximum loan values by exchange and IDA members for securities other than bonds and debentures, expressed as maximum percentages of market value, are:[2]

- 70% for securities eligible for reduced margin;
- 50% for prices of $2 and over that are not eligible for reduced margin;
- 40% for prices of $1.75 to $1.99;
- 20% for prices of $1.50 to $1.74; and
- no loan value for prices under $1.50.

---

[2] Member firms may establish more stringent margin criteria if they so choose.

- When the margin falls below the specified level (due to a decline in market value of the underlying security), the client receives a "**margin call**" from the member firm requiring the client to deposit additional funds (or securities) to the account, or else shares will be sold to bring the account within margin. If the security rises in value, the account may have excess margin in the account which may be utilized by the client.

Example 6:

(a) Determine your margin requirement if you purchase 1,000 common shares of company A on margin when it is trading at $2.00 and is not eligible for special margin.

Solution:

Total cost A = $2 × 1,000	= $2,000
Less: ID max. loan (@**50%**)	= $1,000
Equals: Margin requirement	= $1,000

(b) If the price of A immediately decreases to $1.50, how much (if any) will you be required to deposit in your margin account?

Solution:

Notice the new percentage limit on the maximum loan is now 20%.

Original cost A	= $2,000
Less: Revised ID max. loan A (@**20%**)	
= 0.20 × $1.50 × 1,000	= $300
Gross Margin Requirement	= $1,700
Margin deficit (surplus)	= deficit $700
(since there was only $1,000 in the account)	

Therefore, the required deposit is $700, which will increase the margin contribution to $1,700 and reduce the loan amount to $300 (the allowable amount).

(c) What if, instead of falling, the price had risen to $3? In other words, repeat (b) assuming the new price was $3.

Solution:

Original cost A	= $2,000
Less: Revised ID max. loan A (@**50%**)	
= 0.50 × $3.00 × 1,000	= $1,500
Gross Margin Requirement	= $500
Margin deficit (surplus)	= surplus $500

(since there was already $1,000 in the account)

Therefore, you may withdraw $500, which will reduce the margin contribution to $500 and increase the loan amount to $1,500 (the allowable amount).

SHORT SALES

Short sales occur when an investor sells securities they do not own. The investor is said to be in a "short" position since he or she must repay it in the future (hopefully it can be repurchased after prices have fallen). The investor must leave the proceeds of the short sale with the dealer (who then has free use of these funds), and deposit a certain portion of the market value in addition to the proceeds. It is, in essence, the reverse of buying a stock on margin.

Required account balances, expressed as percentages of market value are:

- 130% for securities eligible for reduced margin;
- 150% for prices of $2 and over that are not eligible for reduced margin;
- $3.00 per share for prices of $1.50 to $1.99;
- 200% of market value for prices of $0.25 to $1.49; and
- 100% of market plus $0.25 per share for prices under $0.25.

Example 7:

(a) Determine the amount that an investor must deposit in their account, if they short sell 1,000 shares of a stock that is eligible for reduced margin and is trading for $10.

Solution:

Minimum account balance (@**130%**)	= 1.30 × $10 × 1,000	= $13,000
Less: Proceeds from short sale	= $10 × 1,000	= $10,000
Equals: Minimum margin requirement		= $3,000

(b) What will happen if the price of the shares which were sold short immediately increases to $12?

Solution:

Minimum account balance (@**130%**)	= 1.30 × $12 × 1,000	= $15,600
Less: Proceeds from short sale	= $10 × 1,000	= $10,000
Equals: Minimum margin requirement		= $5,600
Required deposit = margin deficit = 5,600 − 3,000		= $2,600

(c) Instead of (b) what would happen if the price of the shares had immediately decreased to $8?

Solution:

Minimum account balance (@**130%**)	= 1.30 × $8 × 1,000	= $10,400
Less: Proceeds from short sale	= $10 × 1,000	= $10,000
Equals: Minimum margin requirement		= $400
Required deposit (surplus) = margin surplus = 400 − 3,000		= ($2,600)

The $2,600 represent surplus funds, which may be withdrawn.

> Profits and losses are calculated based on the difference between the initial selling price and the subsequent purchase price. For example, if you short sold 100 shares for a price of $5 per share and repurchased the shares when the price was $4 per share, you would gain $1 per share, for a total of $100.

- There is **no time limit** on the maintenance of a short position; however, the client must buy the necessary shares to cover the position if the broker is unable to borrow sufficient shares to do so. Because of this potential problem, many experienced traders confine short sales activities to stocks that are actively traded. Members are required to disclose which trades are short sales, and the TSE compiles and publicly reports total short positions twice a month.

- Difficulties and hazards of short selling include:

  - difficulties in borrowing a sufficient number of shares;
  - responsibility of maintaining an adequate margin;
  - liability for any dividends paid;
  - threat of buy-in requirements if margin is not maintained and/or if originally borrowed stock is called by its owners and cannot be replaced;
  - difficulty in obtaining up-to-date information on total short sales;
  - possibility of volatile prices should a "rush" to cover occur; and
  - the unlimited potential loss.

EQUITY TRANSACTIONS

- Traditional equity transactions involve a buyer, who is represented by an investment advisor (IA) as their agent, and a seller, who is also represented by an IA as their agent. The respective IAs report the current bid and ask prices to their clients. Assuming that the bid price is $20, and the ask price is $21, the buyer knows he can purchase at least one board lot (100 shares) if he is willing to pay the current ask price of $21 per share. Similarly, the seller can sell at least one board lot if she is willing to accept the current bid price of $20 per share. The clients may then decide to inform their IA to obtain the best possible price for the stock, which is referred to as a market order (discussed in the next section). A transaction occurs if the buyer is willing to accept a seller's price, or vice-versa.

- After a transaction has occurred, both the buyer and the seller must receive a confirmation of the transaction, which describes the transaction details, as well as the amount of commissions due and payable. The parties involved are then required to "settle" the transaction (within three business days if it is an equity trade).

- An alternative transaction format that is very common is to have one IA act as an agent for both the buyer and seller.

- IAs can also act as principals in an equity transaction, when they fill a customer's order from their own inventory in a security. In this situation, the trade is executed at the market price as determined by the exchange, which is based on detailed procedures designed to protect the investor.

BUY AND SELL ORDERS:

1. **Market orders** are executed at the best available price.
2. **Limit orders** are executed only if a specific price or better can be obtained.
3. **Day orders** are limit orders that are valid only for the day.
4. **Open** or **good till cancelled (GTC) orders** are limit orders that remain open until executed. Usually they are held open for 30, 60, or 90 days.
5. **All or none (AON) orders** are only executed if the total number of shares specified in the order can be obtained or sold. Alternatively, the investor may specify a minimum number of shares that is acceptable.
6. **Any part orders** are the opposite of AON orders. They will accept any amount of shares, whether in round or odd lots, up to the total amount of the order.
7. **Good through orders** remain valid orders for a specified period of time, after which they are automatically cancelled if not yet filled.
8. **Stop loss orders** are orders that generate *market orders* to sell if the price drops below a certain level. They are used to limit losses on long positions.
9. **Stop buy orders** are the opposite of stop loss orders. A *market buy order* is generated if the price rises above a certain level to limit losses on short positions.
10. **Professional (Pro) orders** are transactions involving partners, directors, officers, shareholders, IAs, or specified employees. These orders must be appropriately labelled as **Pro** or **N-C** (non-client) or **Emp** (employee).

- The **preferential trading rule** requires IAs to give priority to client orders over those of non-clients, which may include professional orders from partners, directors, officers, shareholders, IAs, and in some cases, specified employees.

Chapter 6: Review Questions

(   )   1. The settlement date for convertible preferred shares is the _____ the transaction.

a) second clearing day after

b) third clearing day after

c) same day as

d) next clearing day after

(   )   2. The minimum required margin deposit as a percentage of the market value of securities that are purchased of shares with a market price of $1.91 per share is:

a) 30%

b) 40%

c) 50%

d) 60%

(   )   3. You purchase five board lots of the common shares of company A on margin. The share is presently trading for $1.50. How much cash must you deposit with your broker?

a) $375

b) $450

c) $600

d) $750

(   )   4. Refer to the information given in Question 3. If the price of A dropped immediately to $1.40, how much will you be required to deposit into your margin account?

a) $10

b) $50

c) $100

d) $150

(   )   5. A friend of yours decides to short sell 1,000 shares of security B that is eligible for reduced margin and is trading at $8. What amount must she deposit into a margin account?

a) $2,400

b) $4,000

c) $4,800

d) $6,400

6. Refer to the information given in Question 5. If the price of B dropped immediately to $7, how much would your friend be required to deposit into her account?

( )

   a) $1,500

   b) she can withdraw $1,500

   c) $1,300

   d) she can withdraw $1,300

7. Refer to the information given in Question 5. What profit (loss) does your friend realize if she closes her short position when the price of the underlying share is $5?

( )

   a) profit of $3,000

   b) loss of $3,000

   c) profit of $5,000

   d) loss of $5,000

8. Which of the following statements regarding stop loss orders and stop buy orders are true?

( )

   I. A stop loss order is used to reduce losses on a short sale, while a stop buy order is used to limit losses on long positions.

   II. A stop loss order is used to limit losses on long positions, while a stop buy is used to reduce losses on a short sale.

   III. Both involve margin deposits.

   IV. Both generate market orders.

   a) I and II

   b) I and III

   c) II and III

   d) II and IV

9. If you call up your broker and tell her to sell 100 shares at the best available price, she will execute a:

( )

   a) good through order

   b) market sell order

   c) limit sell order

   d) GTC order

Refer to the following information to answer Questions 10-12:

A convertible preferred share is presently selling for $35 and is convertible into three shares of common shares which are presently selling for $11. The annual dividends are $2.00 for the preferred shares, and $0.22 for the common shares.

( )   10. What is the conversion premium percentage?

        a) 5.7%

        b) 6.1%

        c) 6.3%

        d) insufficient information

( )   11. What is the dividend yield on the common shares?

        a) 0.7%

        b) 1.0%

        c) 2.0%

        d) 5.0%

( )   12. What is the payback for these convertibles?

        a) 0.6 years

        b) 1.1 years

        c) 2.3 years

        d) none of the above

( )   13. The cumulative feature, associated with some preferred shares, requires the company to do which of the following?

        a) pay all current dividends on preferred shares prior to paying dividends to common shareholders

        b) pay all dividends, both current and arrears, on preferred shares prior to paying dividends to common shareholders

        c) accumulate and set aside funds in order to pay preferred share dividends

        d) none of the above

( )   14. Participating preferred shares would be most appropriate for which of the following types of investors?

        a) speculators

        b) aggressive and sophisticated

        c) conservative and moderately aggressive

        d) none of the above

( )   15. What would be the market rate of return on 8% preferred shares with a par value of $50 that are trading for $65?

        a) 5.5%

        b) 6.2%

        c) 8.0%

        d) insufficient information

16. The following suggest that a preferred share of an industrial company is high quality except for: (   )

    a) it has a preferred dividend coverage ratio of 2.5

    b) it has an equity per preferred share ratio that is 2.5 times the par value of the shares

    c) it is rated P-1 by CBRS

    d) none of the above

17. Which of the following are examples of protective provisions associated with preferred shares?   (   )

    I. The right to vote if a specified number of dividends are omitted.

    II. Restrictions placed on the sale of assets.

    III. The callable feature.

    IV. The issue of Class A shares.

    a) I and II

    b) I and III

    c) II and III

    d) II and IV

18. A company has 1 million shares outstanding before it undergoes a 1 for 4 consolidation. After the consolidation, the number of shares outstanding will be: (   )

    a) unchanged

    b) 0.25 million

    c) 2 million

    d) 4 million

19. A company declares a dividend that is payable on January 25 to holders of record on Friday, December 8. In order to be entitled to receive this dividend, you must buy the shares prior to: (   )

    a) January 25

    b) December 7

    c) December 6

    d) December 5

20. The minimum required account balance, relative to the market value of securities, for a short sale transaction involving a share that is trading for $0.90 is: (   )

    a) 150% of market value

    b) $2.00 per share

    c) 200% of market value

    d) this security may not be sold short

Refer to the following information to answer Questions 21-22:

Morgan decides that Protec Wireless Inc. shares are undervalued given their new wireless technology. He decides to buy 2,000 shares on margin (eligible for reduced margin) at $9.

( )   21. How much money will Morgan have to deposit into his margin account to meet the margin requirement in order purchase the shares?

a) $12,600

b) $9,000

c) $5,400

d) none of the above

( )   22. One week later Protec's shares are trading at $13. How much money can Morgan withdraw or use to margin another stock purchase?

a) $12,600

b) $5,200

c) $5,400

d) none of the above

( )   23. What is the difference between a market order and a day order?

a) Market orders are executed at the best immediately available price, while day orders are executed at the best price available during the entire day.

b) Market orders are where the client sets a specific price at which the transaction can be executed, while day orders have certain restrictions placed upon them before they can be executed.

c) Market orders are executed at the best available price, while day orders are executed only if a specific price or better can be obtained.

d) Market orders are where the client sets a specific price at which the transaction can be executed, while day orders are executed only if a specific price or better can be obtained.

( )   24. What difficulties and hazards are associated with short selling a stock?

I. There can be difficulties borrowing the required quantity of the security sold short to cover the short sale.

II. The short seller is not liable for any dividends paid during the period the account is short.

III. There are difficulties in obtaining up-to-date information on total short sales on a security.

IV. The short seller is responsible for maintaining adequate margin in the short account.

a) I, II, III, IV

b) I, II, IV

c) II, III

d) I, III, IV

25. A "traditional" equity transaction involves a buyer, a seller, and _____.   (   )

a) one IA acting on behalf of both the buyer and the seller

b) one IA acting on behalf of the buyer, and one IA acting on behalf of the seller

c) neither (a) nor (b)

d) either (a) or (b)

MANAGED PRODUCTS

INTRODUCTION

- There are a wide variety of mutual fund products available to investors. Many funds are part of fund groups, which are responsible for their management and distribution to the public. Distribution may be accomplished using internal sales representatives, through stockbrokers, through independent mutual fund salespeople, or through combinations of these approaches. Proprietary funds are alternative fund groups, whose funds are managed and sold using internal resources only, such as those offered by banks, trust companies, life insurance companies, and credit unions.

- The total asset value of Canadian mutual funds has grown dramatically in recent years, increasing 834% from $45.7 billion in October 1991 to $427 billion in October 2000.

- The fund's investment objectives are stated in its prospectus, which also specifies what represents an acceptable level of risk for the fund.

The **advantages** of mutual funds include:

1. professional management;
2. diversification;
3. variety of types of funds;
4. variety of purchase plans;
5. various special options;
6. liquidity;

7. transferability;

8. ease of estate planning;

9. loan collateral; and

10. eligibility for margin;

The **disadvantages** of mutual funds include:

1. costs such as sales fees and management fees detract from the investor's returns;

2. unsuitable for short-term investment (except for money market funds which are so tailored);

3. unsuitable for emergency reserve;

4. professional management is not infallible; and

5. tax complications may arise if the investor's tax preferences are not consistent with the objectives of the fund.

THE STRUCTURE OF MUTUAL FUNDS

Investment funds are companies (or trusts) that sell their shares (or units) to the public and invest the proceeds in a diverse securities portfolio. The funds earn income in the form of interest, dividends, and/or capital gains, and they may be organized as a trust or as a corporation.

Open-end funds (or **mutual funds**) continually issue and redeem their units on demand at a value that is very close to the net asset or "break-up" value per unit of the fund's portfolio. This right of redemption is the most distinguishing feature of open-end funds.

- In Canada, the most common form of mutual fund is in the form of an **open-end trust**, which issues units (usually only one class of units) in the trust to investors. Some of these provide unit holders with voting privileges, but not all of them.

- The trust itself is not taxable: the income earned by the fund, net any fees and expenses, is attributed to the unit holders. The fund is established in the form of a **trust deed**, which describes:

    - the fund's investment objectives;
    - the fund's investment policy;
    - any investment restrictions; and
    - details regarding the fund manager, distributors, and custodians.

- Some funds are set up as federal or provincial corporations, and investors in these funds receive shares in the fund rather than units. As corporations, the funds are taxable, although they are generally eligible for special rates. In addition, they can virtually eliminate any taxes by declaring dividends that are equivalent to their net income over a given year, thus passing the tax consequences on to shareholders in the form of the dividends they receive.

ORGANIZATIONAL STRUCTURE:

• Mutual fund organizations consist of four parts:

1. **Directors or trustees:** directors (for corporations) or trustees (for trusts) are ultimately responsible for fund activities; although they often hire independent managers, distributors, and/or custodians to operate the fund on their behalf.

2. **Fund managers:** they must observe guidelines in the fund's charter, as well as constraints imposed by securities commissions such as owning less than 10% of one firm's total securities or voting stock, no purchases of other non-related mutual funds, no borrowing for leverage purposes, limitations regarding percentage of illiquid securities such as unlisted stocks, and prohibitions regarding commodity or commodity futures purchases.

3. **Fund distributors:** parties that sell shares or units in the fund.

4. **Custodians:** collect and distribute cash for the fund as required (usually they are trust companies).

THE PRICING OF MUTUAL FUND SECURITIES:

The **offering price** refers to the price an investor pays for a share or unit in a mutual fund.

The **redemption price** refers to the price investors receive when they sell shares or units back to the fund.

Mutual funds shares or units can be purchased or redeemed at a price that equals or is very close to the fund's **net asset value per share (NAVPS)**, which may be calculated as follows:

NAVPS = (total assets [including portfolio at market value] − total liabilities) ÷ (total shares or units outstanding)

Example 1: ───

Determine the NAVPS for a mutual fund that holds a portfolio of securities worth $200 million, has liabilities of $2 million, and has 20 million units outstanding.

Solution:

NAVPS = (200m − 2m) / 20m − $9.90

All funds are required to compute the NAVPS at least once a month (once a week for equity funds and once a year for real estate funds). Most do so on a daily basis (quarterly for real estate funds).

MUTUAL FUND CHARGES:

Mutual funds are often classified with respect to the type of sales commission, or "load" they charge. **Load funds** charge a commission on the purchase and/or sale of fund units or shares. Those that charge sales commissions when the units are purchased are called **front-end load** funds, while those that charge a redemption fee (or deferred sales charge) when the units are sold are called **back-end load** funds. The amount of redemption fee often declines through time, and is often completely eliminated after a holding period of six years. Many load funds give the investor the option of front- or back-end loads.

No-load funds do not charge direct selling charges. However, they typically levy modest administration fees, and charge other management fees that may add up. Investors should carefully read the prospectus to determine the net cost of these services. Some funds charge a distribution charge to pay commissioned salespeople, while trailer fees (or service fees) are those paid by a manager to the selling organization.

The **offering or purchase price** for a front-end load fund relates the sales charge to the net asset value (NAV). It is calculated in the following manner:

Offering or Purchase Price = (NAV) ÷ (100% less sales charge)

Example 2:

Determine the offering price for a fund that has a NAV of $10 and a 5% up-front sales charge.

Solution:

Offering price = $10 / (1.0 − .05) = $10.52

- Notice in Example 2 that $0.52 is 5.2% of the NAV (or net amount invested).

The **redemption or selling price** for back-end load funds, relates the sales charge to the net asset value (NAV). It is calculated in the following manner:

Redemption or Selling Price = (NAV) × (100% less sales charge)

Example 3:

Determine the selling price for a fund that has a NAV of $10 and a 5% back-end redemption charge.

Solution:

Selling price = $10 × (1.0 − .05) = $9.50

- Notice in Example 3 that $0.50 is 5.3% (0.50 / 9.50) of the net amount received.

- **Trailer** (or **service**) **fees** are paid by the fund manager to the distributor of the fund, and are usually paid out of the management fee. The rationale for the payment of trailer fees is that salespeople provide an ongoing service for investors. However, their use is criticized because they provide salespeople with the incentive to keep customers in funds, even when it may not be in their best interests. In addition, the higher management fees detract from the wealth of the investor.

- Some funds charge a set up fee in addition to any load fees. In addition, some funds charge **early redemption fees**, if the funds are redeemed within a certain period of time. For example, some no-load funds charge a 2% early redemption fee if fund units are sold within 90 days of purchase.

- Some fund companies permit investors an unlimited number of "switches" between funds managed by the same company, at no cost. Other funds charge for every switch or permit a specified number of free switches, with any additional switches being subject to a "**switching fee**." These fees may often be negotiated with the investment advisor, and sometimes they can be waived.

- Management fees represent the amount of compensation paid to mutual fund managers. These vary, depending on the nature of the fund (from 1% for some money market and index funds to 3% for some equity funds). It is typically expressed as a percentage of net fund assets.

In addition to management fees, other fund expenses such as trading costs, audit, legal, informational, and safekeeping and custodial fees are also included in the calculation of a measure called the **management expense ratio (MER)**. These expenses decrease the returns to fund holders. It is calculated in the following manner:

MER = [(Aggregate Fees and Expenses Payable During the Year)] / (Average Net Asset Value for the Year) × 100%

The expenses are charged directly to the fund and not to the investor, and reduce the return to investors. For example, a fund that earned a gross return of 20% and had an MER of 2% would report a compound annual return of 18%. Published rates of return for funds are those resulting after deducting the MER.

- The management fees and management expense ratios must be included in the fund prospectus for the past five years.

MUTUAL FUND RESTRICITONS:

Mutual funds are subject to many restrictions. Some are subject to all of the restrictions below, while others are subject to only some of them. These restrictions do not permit funds to:

1. purchase more than 10% of the total securities or 10% of the voting stock of a company;

2. buy shares in their own company;

3. purchase more than 10% of the net assets of one company, or 20% of the net assets of companies in the same industry (except for specialty funds);

4. borrow for the purpose of creating leverage;

5. buy on margin or short sell;

6. purchase commodities or commodity futures; and

7. hold beyond certain percentages of illiquid securities, such as those sold through private placements or unlisted stocks.

The use of derivative securities such as options, futures, forwards, rights, warrants, and combination products by mutual funds is permissible for specific purposes only. In particular, derivatives should not be used for speculative purposes, but may be used for the following reasons, provided their permitted use is specified in the fund's simplified prospectus:

- ○ to hedge against risk;

- ○ to facilitate market entry and exit; and

- ○ to create clone funds.

- For example, a manager may use options in an index fund such as put options on i60 units (discussed at the end of this chapter) to provide price protection for their portfolio against changes in aggregate stock market values. Alternatively, a fund manager holding foreign securities may use currency futures to hedge themselves against changes in exchange rates.

- National Instrument 81-102 regulates the use of derivatives by mutual funds, specifying restrictions on holdings (no more than 10% of the fund's assets, except for clone funds), acceptable hedge positions, terms to expiry, and regarding which advisors are permitted to trade in these securities.

Unacceptable sales practices for fund salespeople include:

1. quoting a future price;

2. offer to repurchase securities;

3. selling without a license (i.e., not being registered in the appropriate province);

4. advertising the fact that they are registered;

5. promising a future price;

6. selling to an individual in another province (or country) where the salesperson is not registered; and

7. sale of unqualified securities.

- Fund managers and distributors also face sales restrictions including:

1. managers may not provide distributors with "rewards;"

2. commissions can only be changed through a change in the prospectus;

3. managers may not provide funds for general marketing expenses of the distributor;

4. managers may not subsidize courses designed to enhance selling skills; and

5. non-monetary benefits cannot be provided beyond a nominal value for sales-people.

- NI 81-102 and NI 81-105 (discussed in the next section) provide specific guidelines regarding sales communications, and it is the salesperson's responsibility to know the relevant guidelines. The overriding concern is that such communications are not misleading in any way. The following items can be included in sales communications:

  ○ fund characteristics;

  ○ fund comparisons with similar funds or appropriate indexes;

  ○ performance details, which are subject to specific guidelines;

  ○ advertise the fact that a fund is no-load; and

  ○ any information or comparisons must disclose all relevant facts.

REGULATION OF MUTUAL FUNDS

Most Canadian mutual funds are regulated by the securities acts of the provinces within which they operate. As discussed in Chapter 1, securities regulations are based upon the principles of personal trust, disclosure, and regulation.

The **code of ethics** for registered salespeople in the securities industry applies to mutual fund salespeople. The code requires mutual fund salespeople to:

1. use proper care and exercise professional judgement;

2. display integrity and trustworthiness, and be fair and honest in dealings with the public, clients, employers, and employees;

3. conduct business in a professional manner and encourage others to do so;

4. act in a competent manner and improve their professional knowledge towards this end; and

5. maintain client confidentiality.

- While mutual funds are regulated by provincial securities commissions they also deal with the Canadian self-regulatory organizations (SROs) such as the stock exchanges and the Investment Dealers Association (IDA), which were discussed in Chapter 1. The provincial regulators have more power and have greater latitude in imposing penalties on mutual fund companies.

- As discussed in Chapter 1, the Mutual Fund Dealers Association (MFDA) is a newly created SRO that regulates the distribution of mutual funds, but not their management.

- Securities regulators have issued several national and provincial policy statements to govern the activities of mutual funds. The most comprehensive and influential policy statement until February 1, 2000 was National Policy Statement No. 39 (NP 39), at which time it was replaced by **National Instrument 81-102 (NI 81-102)**, and a companion policy (NI 81-105).

- Since most funds continually issue new shares, they are in a *continuous state of primary distribution*, and must annually file a prospectus or simplified prospectus.

- Funds file simplified prospectuses if they comply with the appropriate regulations (i.e., NI 81-102). These regulations concern restrictions on investments, changes that require security holder and/or securities' authority approval, custodianship of a fund's portfolio securities, commingling of money, and calculating net asset values. The simplified prospectus system also requires funds to file annual information forms (AIFs), annual audited or unaudited financial statements, as well as other information such as material change reports and information circulars.

The **simplified prospectuses** must contain all material information and must be amended when material changes occur. Fund buyers must receive copies of this document *no later than two business days after an agreement of purchase* has been made. The simplified prospectus consists of two parts. The first part provides general information about the particular fund and other funds managed by the fund company, and about mutual funds in general. The second part contains specific information about the fund.

- The AIF contains most of the information included in the simplified prospectus, plus additional information regarding:

   ○ significant holdings in other issuers;

   ○ the tax status of the issuer;

   ○ directors, officers and trustees;

   ○ associated persons; and

   ○ details regarding any material contracts outstanding.

- The financial statements should be provided to investors and should be filed with the appropriate securities commission before the specified deadline. The financial statements for the fund should include the:

   ○ balance sheet;

   ○ income statement;

   ○ statement of investment portfolio (i.e., details of the securities the fund is holding);

   ○ statement of changes in net assets (equivalent to a statement of changes in financial position); and

   ○ statement of portfolio transactions, which is generally not included in the financial statements, but the statements should inform investors that this statement is available to them upon request.

REGISTRATION REQUIREMENTS:

- Mutual fund managers, distributors, and their sales personnel must be registered with the securities commissions in which they do business. Educational requirements include that salespeople must complete the Canadian Funds Course, the CSC, or another qualified education program, such as the Investment Funds Institute of Canada (IFIC) mutual fund course.

- In order to become registered under provincial securities laws, salespeople must file the **Uniform Application for Registration Approval**. Once registered, they must inform the provincial administrators of any changes in the information provided in their original application within five business days (10 days in Quebec) including:

  - a change of address;
  - any disciplinary actions by a professional body;
  - a personal bankruptcy (Ontario and Quebec);
  - any criminal charges; and
  - any civil judgements.

- If a registered salesperson no longer works for a registered dealer, their registration is suspended automatically, and the dealer must notify the provincial administrator. The salesperson's registration can be reinstated, only if they go to work for another registered dealer, who must provide written notice to the administrator.

- Financial institutions (FIs) that serve as fund distributors must also comply with several guidelines including:

  1. control of registrant: sales are only permitted through branches or departments of registered dealers;

  2. registration of employees;

  3. dual employment: dual employment is permitted by employees if it is permitted by the laws governing the FI;

  4. conflicts of interest: dealers must have appropriate guidelines in place to prevent and/or deal with such situations;

  5. in-house funds: if a FI wants to sell the funds of a third party, they must obtain the appropriate approvals;

  6. proficiency requirements should be satisfied by officers, directors, and salespeople; and

  7. premises and disclosure: the business must conduct business in a way that makes it clear to clients that the dealer and the FI are distinct, and this point should be disclosed to clients.

REDEEMING MUTUAL FUND UNITS OR SHARES

- Mutual funds shares or units can be redeemed at a price that equals or is very close to the fund's NAVPS less any applicable redemption fees.

- Canadian tax regulations generally treat mutual funds as conduits that pass income flows to its holders. Fund holders receive T3 (or T5) forms that report all income earned through the year including interest, dividends, capital gains, and foreign income.

When fund units are redeemed, this action is considered a disposition for tax purposes, and the proceeds are subject to capital gains or losses. A complication arises due to the reinvestment of interest and dividends. This implies that investors (or their investment advisors) must keep track of the actual purchase prices of all shares (or units) in a fund, and make appropriate adjustments to the **adjusted cost base (ACB)**. The ACB is the value used to estimate the cost of purchasing fund units, and is compared to the selling price (less any selling costs) in order to determine the amounts of any resulting capital gains (or losses).

- Periodic reinvestment of interest and dividends can also cause foreign content of RRSPs to exceed the maximum limit of 30% (as of 2001), which would result in a 1% monthly penalty on the excess amount.

- During the year funds make capital gains and losses when they sell securities. These gains are taxable in the hands of the investor; therefore, investors should determine if a capital gains distribution is pending before purchasing a fund.

- When common stocks pay dividends, the value of the stocks decline by roughly the amount of the dividend on the ex dividend date. However, most funds automatically reinvest dividends to purchase new shares in the fund at the NAVPS. This policy leaves investors with more units in the fund, but the units are worth less (as a result of the decline in the value of the underlying common shares that paid the dividend). The net effect is that the fund holder's wealth is relatively unaffected by the dividend payments.

Systematic withdrawal plans may be arranged to meet investors' cash flow requirements, and can be set up for monthly, quarterly, or other intervals. There are four general types of withdrawal plans:

1. **Ratio withdrawal plan:** a specified percentage of fund shares (usually between 4% and 10%) are redeemed at fixed intervals (amounts will vary according to prevailing market values).

2. **Fixed dollar withdrawal plan:** a specified dollar amount is withdrawn at regular intervals.

3. **Fixed period withdrawal plan:** a specified amount is withdrawn over a predetermined period of time, with the amount determined in a manner such that all the funds should be used up by the end of the time period. For

example, if the time period was established as four years, the investor would withdraw one quarter in the first year, one third in the second year, one half in the third year, and the remaining balance in year four.

4. **Life expectancy adjusted withdrawal plan:** a variation of (3) which is designed to provide as high an income as possible during the holder's expected life, with the amounts withdrawn being adjusted in relation to the amount of capital remaining in the plan and the plan holder's revised life expectancy.

TYPES OF MUTUAL FUNDS

• The **objectives** of investment funds vary significantly, which is reflected in their portfolio composition. The objectives are covered in the fund's offering prospectus and generally cover the degree of safety or risk that is acceptable, whether income or capital gain is the prime objective, and the main types of securities in the fund's investment portfolio. As of October 2000, the breakdown of fund assets in billions of dollars was: Balanced 66.8; Canadian Equity 103.2; Foreign Equity 124.5; U.S. Equity 35.4; Bond and Income 26.7; Foreign Bond and Income 4.3; and Dividend and Income 18.1.

1. Money Market Funds: Their objectives focus on income and liquidity. They invest in short-term money market instruments such as T-bills, commercial paper, and short-term government bonds. These funds will be attractive to investors seeking low risk and high liquidity.

2a. Mortgage Funds: Riskier than money market funds since terms of investments may be five years or greater, so there is more interest rate risk (although it's less than most bond funds which have longer maturities).

2b. Bond Funds: Primary investing objectives are income and safety; however, they are still subject to capital gains and losses due to inherent interest rate risk.

3a. Balanced Funds: Strive to provide a mixture of safety, income, and capital appreciation. Usually, the fund must adhere to minimum and maximum percentages that can be invested in each asset class.

3b. Asset Allocation Funds: Similar objectives to balanced funds, but they are typically not restricted to hold specified minimum percentages in any class of investment.

4. Equity or **Common Stock Funds:** Primary objective is capital gains. The bulk of assets are in common shares, although they maintain limited amounts of other assets for liquidity, income, and diversification purposes. Equity funds may vary greatly in degree of risk and growth objectives.

5. Growth Funds: These funds tend to invest in small capitalization (small-cap) stocks. These companies are smaller and are believed to have greater prospects for growth. Many are young, and most do not pay dividends. As a result, these funds tend to be riskier than traditional equity funds.

6. Specialty Funds: Attempt to obtain superior capital gains, and are less diversified than traditional funds in the hopes of achieving these results. They typically concentrate on companies in one industry, one segment of the capital market, or in one geographical location. **International or Global Funds** represent a type of specialty fund that invest in foreign securities. They carry the additional risk of foreign exchange exposure. Two additional subsets of specialty funds are listed below.

6a. Real Estate Funds: Invest in income-producing properties for long-term growth and capital appreciation. Valuation is necessarily based on external appraisals of properties included in the portfolio, and are, therefore, conducted relatively infrequently (monthly or quarterly). They are less liquid than other funds and investors may be required to give advance notice of their intention to sell fund units.

6b. Ethical Funds: These funds are relatively new and are guided by moral criteria, which may prevent the funds from investing in companies that produce tobacco, etc.

7. Index Funds: Their objective is to mirror the performance of a market index such as the TSE 300, or Scotia McLeod Bond Index. The management fees are generally much lower than for actively managed funds.

8. Dividend Funds: Their objective is to take advantage of the tax advantage afforded by dividends; therefore, they are not that appropriate for RRSPs or RRIFs where the credit cannot be applied. Price changes tend to be driven by changes in interest rates and general market trends.

The fund types above have different risk-return characteristics. Generally higher returns entail higher risk. The following list provides the CSI rankings of most of the fund categories above, from lowest risk-lowest return, to highest risk-highest return:

- Money Market
- Mortgage
- Bond
- Balanced
- Dividend
- Equity
- Real Estate
- Specialty

FUND MANAGEMENT STYLES

EQUITY MANAGEMENT STYLES:

- Fund management styles tend to be **active** or **passive** in nature. Active managers try to outperform benchmarks, while passive managers try to match the benchmark performance, usually by using some manner of indexing. Most equity funds are managed using an active approach, with index funds being an obvious exception. Some of the possible strategies that are pursued by equity fund managers are described below.

1. Value Investing: Value managers look for "bargains" based on intensive research. Portfolios tend to be less volatile than growth portfolios, since prices are already low, which is reflected in low price-earning (P/E) ratios and higher dividend yields than growth portfolios. Investors should be reasonably risk tolerant, with longer term investment horizons. This approach runs the risk of missing out on some companies with substantial growth potential, and may also lead the manager to avoid investing in industries that are experiencing rapid growth, if this growth is reflected in high market prices.

2. Growth Investing: Growth managers invest in stock portfolios that tend to be very volatile, with low dividend yields, and high P/E and market-to-book ratios. Investors should be less risk averse and possess relatively long-term investment horizons. This approach works best during bull markets, when prices are rising. It is also consistent with momentum investing, which involves purchasing stocks that have been doing well in the recent past.

3. Indexing and Closet Indexing: Indexing is a passive strategy that involves the purchase of securities that comprise a market benchmark such as the TSE 300 Index or the S&P 500 Index. There is no need to perform in-depth security analysis, and the costs of this long-term, buy-and-hold strategy are very low, which corresponds to low management expense ratios. This approach is consistent with the belief that markets are efficient, which means it will be difficult to outperform the market. Therefore, it makes sense to "match" the market performance and reduce expenses.

The term **closet indexers** refers to managers that do not index per se, but tend to keep their portfolio weightings (across industry or regional sectors) similar to the weightings in the chosen market index.

4. Theme Investing: Theme managers select securities for their portfolio based on certain economic and/or industry trends that they believe will benefit the chosen stocks. As a result, they tend to be concentrated in particular industries, based on prevailing trends.

5. Sector Rotation: Sector rotators focus on particular sectors (e.g., industries) in accordance with a top-down analysis (discussed in Chapter 10), which may result in higher volatility and greater risk (due to lower diversification).

6. Small-Cap Investing: Small-cap managers invest primarily in small capitalization (small-cap) stocks. These companies are smaller and tend to provide higher return and risk potential than larger ones. Typical cut-off points in terms of market capitalization are $250 million or $500 million for Canadian funds, or $1 billion for U.S. funds. These funds tend to be riskier than traditional equity funds, performing better during bull markets and worse during bear markets.

7. Venture Capital: This style is a high-risk strategy designed to provide maximum growth potential. If the funds are invested using a Labour Sponsored Venture Capital Corporation (LSVCC), tax relief is also provided in the form of federal and provincial tax credits. These investments are suitable for investors with a high tolerance for risk, who are already well-diversified in core asset categories. In addition, investors may lose their tax credits if they withdraw the funds prior to eight years.

8. Yield Investing: These funds concentrate on securities that provide high-income yields, such as preferred shares, high dividend paying common stocks (e.g., utilities and banks), or riskier securities such as Real Estate Investment Trusts (REITs) or resource royalty trusts. They are appropriate for investors who seek income, plus some capital appreciation potential.

9. Multi-Manager: Multi-manager funds are dividend into two or more portfolios that are managed separately. Since these funds may be managed using a combination of styles, they tend to be lower risk than those that adhere to one style only. The downside is that the superior performance of one manager may be offset by the weak performance of another.

10. Specialty: Specialty managers typically concentrate on companies in one industry, one segment of the capital market, or in one geographical location. They are suitable for investors searching for growth, who are well-diversified in core asset categories.

FIXED INCOME MANAGEMENT STYLES:

- Fixed income managers may use several styles, some of which are described below.

1. Interest Rate Anticipation: These managers lengthen the duration of their bond portfolios when they expect interest rates to fall, and shorten the duration when they expect rates to increase. They do so in order to attempt to maximize capital gains on the portfolio. This strategy is active and entails more risk than a typical buy-and-hold bond strategy, since future interest rates are difficult to predict accurately.

2. Indexing: This is a passive strategy that involves buying and holding the bonds held in a bond index such as the Scotia McLeod Bond Index. The objectives are to match the market benchmark performance and reduce management fees.

3. Term to Maturity: This approach limits the manager to invest in bonds with specified terms to maturity (e.g., less than 10 years to maturity). This limits the risk of the fund.

4. Credit Quality: Managers focus on the credit quality of bonds, relative to their yields. In general, corporate bonds provide higher yields than government bonds, and lower rated corporate bonds provide higher yields than higher rated ones. In addition, lower rated bonds may have less liquidity than higher rated corporate bonds, and government bonds, which contributes to the higher yields required by investors. Managers focusing on obtaining higher yields must usually take higher risk, and those seeking safety must accept lower yields. In addition, they may engage in **spread trading** (i.e., trading based on beliefs that spreads between different categories of bonds will narrow or widen in the future).

5. Duration Switching: Managers switch into and out of securities in order to altar the duration of their portfolio to obtain their desired mix of yield and interest rate risk.

COMPARING MUTUAL FUND PERFORMANCE

- Mutual fund performance characteristics are published regularly in the *Financial Post* and *The Globe and Mail.* Items of interest include:
    - the NAVPS;
    - the change in NAVPS;
    - simple rates of return (e.g., for one month or one year);
    - the volatility (as measured by standard deviation, beta, or a simple 1-10 rating);
    - the expense ratio;
    - compound rates of return for longer periods (e.g., three years, five years, and 10 years);
    - how it is distributed;
    - how it is (or isn't) loaded; and
    - whether it is RRSP eligible or not.

  Rates of return include management fees and expenses, but not sales charges.

- Money market funds are reported differently to reflect the fact that earnings are distributed to shareholders, so the NAVPS remains constant and is not reported. Typically for these funds we observe a current yield (which is the rate of return on the fund over the most recent seven-day period), and an effective yield that is the compound return that would arise if the current yield is compounded over a year.

- In order to gain meaningful information about a fund's performance, it must be compared to something: i.e., its peer group, or an appropriate market benchmark, such as the TSE 300 Index (for Canadian equity funds).

> ! The recommended return measure for portfolios is to report a **time-weighted rate of return (TWRR)** as determined using the Modified Dietz method (described below).

- TWRRs are estimated by finding an average return over some interval. The average returns do **not** include the effect of cash flows such as deposits, withdrawals, and reinvestments.

- It is recommended that the TWRR is calculated every day to obtain the most accurate estimate, although this may be difficult for funds that hold less liquid securities whose value is difficult to estimate on a daily basis (such as real estate or mortgage-backed securities portfolios).

- The **Modified Dietz method** approximates the TWRR, reducing the extensive calculations required for determining the TWRR on a daily basis. The formula is:

(MVE − MVB − F) / (MVB + FW)

where,

MVE = the end-of-period market value, including accrued income;

MVB = the beginning-of-period market value, including accrued income from the previous period;

F = the sum of cash flows within the period (contributions are positive, withdrawals and distributions are negative);

FW = the sum of each cash flow multiplied by its weight.

This measure is the one used by the Association of Canadian Pension Management, and the CSI says it is the recommended measure of the Association for Investment Management and Research (AIMR).

- For advertising purposes, funds are required to report three-month, six-month, one-year, three-year, five-year, and 10-year total returns, after deduction of management expenses, when available. Advisors should focus on returns beyond the one-year horizon, although there is no guarantee that history will repeat itself with respect to fund performance.

- One must be careful not to compare apples with oranges when assessing mutual fund performance. In other words, fund performance should be compared to that of funds with similar stated objectives. In addition, one must be aware that the name or class of the fund may not accurately reflect the asset base. For example, one Canadian equity fund may have 90% invested in Canadian equities, and 10% in cash, while another might hold 30% in cash, 20% in foreign equities, 10% in bonds, and only 40% in Canadian equities. Finally, segregated funds may report their performance before the deduction of any expenses charged to the fund.

- Another complication that arises is that there is often no attempt to account for the relative risk of the fund versus similar funds. In order to obtain a true picture of fund performance, the risk of funds should be measured according to measures such as:

  ○ standard deviation of fund returns: which measures the total volatility of the fund's returns;

- beta: which measures the volatility of the fund's returns relative to those in the market portfolio (higher betas imply higher risk);
- the number of years the fund lost money;
- the fund's best and worst 12-month periods; and
- the fund's worst annual, quarterly, or monthly losses

There are several dangers to be avoided when evaluating a mutual fund's performance including:

1. The fund's record is history and there is no guarantee that it will be repeated.
2. The past record of a fund can be misleading if the fund makes fundamental changes in its investment objectives and/or changes the fund manager.
3. The performance of peer group averages will be higher than the appropriate universe because they are "survivorship biased" (i.e., they include the returns of only the funds that survive the period).
4. Funds should be compared against only those with similar objectives.
5. Comparisons should attempt to account for the relative risk of the fund versus similar funds using measures such as beta and/or standard deviation.
6. Avoid short-term comparisons. A minimum of three years is an acceptable comparison period.
7. Avoid selecting comparison periods where there are no comparable figures for peer groups and/or market benchmarks.

OTHER MANAGED PRODUCTS

I. CLOSED-END FUNDS:

Closed-end funds normally issue shares only at start-up or other infrequent periods. They reinvest proceeds and borrowings in a portfolio to earn income and capital gains. The shares or units of these funds trade on stock exchanges.

The market price of these units is typically at a discount from the break-up value of the portfolios to reflect the market's view that the closed-end fund is a going concern, and/or to reflect the lower liquidity that is associated with these funds. In general, the greater the discount, the more attractive these funds are as investments, especially if they are trading below historical discount values.

- The **advantages** of closed-end funds include:
  1. They provide diversification potential.
  2. They may be sold short, unlike open-end funds.
  3. They do not require liquid funds to be available for redeeming shares, unlike open-ended funds.

4. Since the number of units is fixed, capital gains, dividends, and interest income may be paid directly to investors, rather than reinvesting in additional units.

5. They may have lower management expense ratios because they involve the administration of a fixed number of units.

- The possible **disadvantages** of closed-end funds include:

1. They are subject to stock exchange reporting requirements.

2. Performance comparisons are difficult because there are less available, and they are not followed as closely.

3. Discounts from NAV may increase, resulting in capital losses.

4. They are less liquid than open-end funds, since they must be bought and sold in the market.

5. Deferred sales charges are generally not on a declining percentage basis.

6. They do not generally provide for automatic reinvestment of distributions, so the investor must invest these funds themselves.

7. If they trade on foreign exchanges, the dividends do not qualify for the dividend tax credit.

2. LABOUR SPONSORED VENTURE CAPITAL CORPORATIONS (LSVCCS):

LSVCCs are sponsored by labour organizations and their specific mandate is to invest in small- to medium-sized businesses. They offer investors a tax credit and are usually provincially based, although some federally based LSVCCs do exist. There are currently more than 20 available in Canada.

The **advantages** of LSVCCs:

1. They provide investors with the potential for long-term capital appreciation, and enable investors to invest in specific industry sectors.

2. They provide investors with tax credits. Provincial tax credits vary, but are generally between 15% and 20% of the investment for most LSVCCs, although some do not offer provincial credits. There is no maximum amount an investor may invest in an LSVCC; however, the federal tax credit applies up to a maximum investment of $5,000, and provincial tax credits are subject to maximum amounts. In addition, some provinces impose lifetime limits. The maximum allowable credit for federal LSVCCs is 15%, although the total maximum combined credit may not exceed $1,500. Thus, the maximum annual investment eligible for the tax credits is $5,000 (i.e., 15% of $5,000 = $750 (federal) and 15% of $5,000 = $750 (provincial)). The unused portion of the federal credits is not refundable and may not be carried forward or backward to apply to other years.

3. Most LSVCCs are RRSP and RRIF eligible, which implies the potential for a double tax advantage. In addition, the foreign content of RRSPs that include LSVCCs may exceed the allowed maximum.

Example 4:

Determine the net investment for an investor in the 40% marginal tax bracket who purchases $5,000 worth of LSVCCs that qualify for a 15% federal credit and a 15% provincial credit, and contributes them to her RRSP.

Solution:

The investor will receive a federal tax credit of $750 ($5,000 × .15), and a provincial tax credit of $750 ($5,000 × .15). In addition, she can deduct $5,000 from her taxable income, which results in tax savings of $2,000 (40% of $5,000). Thus, her net investment is $5,000 − $750 − $750 − $2,000 = $1,500.

The **disadvantages** of LSVCCs include:

1. They are **highly speculative** investments, which make them suitable only for investors with a high-risk tolerance. This is because they invest primarily in start-up companies, and it is estimated that 80% of these companies do not survive more than five years.

2. The management expense ratios tend to be higher than for mutual funds due to the additional effort that must be devoted to managing these investments.

3. Redeeming LSVCCs is more complicated than for mutual funds and the rules vary across the provinces. Federal tax credits are subject to recapture by tax authorities if they are redeemed before they have been held for eight years. Provincial holding period requirements range from zero, to other predefined periods. This recapture can be avoided under one of the following circumstances:

   ○ redemption occurs within 60 days of acquisition, the shares are not held for RRSP purposes, and they have not been claimed already;

   ○ the original purchaser turns 65, retires, or is no longer a Canadian citizen, and the shares were held for at least two years;

   ○ the original purchaser becomes disabled, permanently unfit for work, or terminally ill; or

   ○ the original purchaser dies.

Unlike mutual funds, LSVCCs:

1. are not restricted to 10% ownership in a given company (in fact, they may exceed 20%);

2. have restrictions on transferability and redemption; and

3. valuation will not be based exclusively on the market, but requires valuation by independent qualified persons which are to be updated by management.

! LSVCCs are only suitable as long-term investments due to their speculative and illiquid nature, as well as to restrictions regarding the provision of tax credit benefits. They are not suitable for investors looking for short-term or income generating investments. Investors must be aware of the highly speculative and illiquid nature of these investments, which make them suitable only for investors with a high-risk tolerance. The track record of the fund manager may be a particularly important factor to consider.

3. INCOME TRUSTS:

- **Income trusts** sell a fixed number of units in the trust and the units trade in the over-the-counter market, similar to closed-end funds. The trust holds income-producing assets, and passes the income through to the unit holders. They often provide for tax deferral since the expenses tend to exceed the cash inflows during the early years of the trust. They differ from fixed income debt instruments such as bonds because their payouts are usually not guaranteed, and the yields are usually higher. Some examples are described below.

! **Real Estate Investment Trusts (REITs)** are pools of funds invested in portfolios of real estate assets (in trust). They usually invest in income producing properties, and provide investors with a fixed income by paying out a high proportion of their income (usually 95%) to unit holders. As a result, their prices tend to be very sensitive to interest rates, rising when interest rates fall, and falling when rates rise. In order to limit the risk of these investments, REITs tend to focus on established, income-generating real estate assets, avoid real estate developments, and limit their leverage ratios to below 50% to 60%. As trusts, they do not provide unit holders with the limited liability feature associated with corporate ownership.

! **Royalty trusts** provide their unit holders with royalties received from the owners of natural resource assets. The income may be eligible for federal or provincial tax credits, and most are eligible for RRSPs, RRIFs, and other registered plans. They provide a hedge against the inflation associated with the underlying assets, since the payments will increase if the value of the underlying commodity increases. They are risky investments due to the volatile nature of commodity prices.

! Similar, to mutual funds, **Unit Investment Trusts (UITs)** are investment companies that hold portfolios of securities. The units in the trust trade in secondary markets, although they usually provide sellers with the option of selling the units in the market or redeeming them to the fund. UITs usually hold the same securities and units are issued infrequently—often they are available for purchase from the issuer for a limited period of time. Many have a maturity date at which time the securities are sold and funds are distributed to unit holders.

! **Funds of funds** are funds that invest in other mutual funds to offer investors a package that best suits their needs.

4. MANAGED ACCOUNTS:

Wrap accounts are products offered by investment dealers that provide investors with discretion in designing their portfolios to satisfy their individual needs. They come in a variety of forms. For example, **pooled wraps** combine an investor's money with that provided by other investors.

- One common form allows clients to invest in a selected number of professionally managed portfolios, for which the clients pay an annual management fee (generally from 1.5% to 3% of the amount invested) rather than paying commission on each transaction. Usually the percentage value of the fee declines as the amount invested increases. The minimum investment is generally $50,000 and the administration fee is a tax-deductible expense (unlike mutual fund management fees). Alternatively, investors can build their own portfolio in conjunction with their investment advisor. Investors are generally charged a fee based on the amount invested and are allowed a certain number of "free" transactions.

- Wrap accounts allow investors to make use of professional money managers within a structured framework that is ideal for implementing asset allocation decisions. It is not suited for investors that wish to play an active role in choosing stocks, and it does not involve a great deal of active trading on the part of the manager.

Wrap accounts offer the following **advantages:**

1. individualized asset allocation;
2. establishing optimal risk-return portfolios; and
3. improved reporting.

They provide the managers with additional flexibility and allow them to customize investors' portfolio holdings to meet specific goals, and in light of specific constraints. Management fees may be lower than for traditional funds depending on the size of the investment. Some arrangements also permit clients to make payments to RRSPs or RRIFs; although the wrap fees are not deductible inside an RRSP.

Wrap accounts have the following possible **disadvantages:**

1. limited range of investment management alternatives;
2. high minimum investment restrictions; and
3. expenses may exceed those of traditional funds, especially since the fees are on top of the MERs of any underlying funds used in the package.

Another alternative to mutual funds is for clients of investment dealers to maintain discretionary or managed accounts. **Managed accounts** are managed on a continuing basis by the member, usually for a management fee. **Discretionary accounts** are similar but are generally opened as a convenience to clients who are unwilling or unable to attend to their own accounts (for example if they are seriously ill or are out of the country). Managed accounts may be solicited, whereas, discretionary accounts may not. Both accounts require written consent of the client, and the authorization must include investment objectives.

5. INDEX-LINKED GUARANTEED INVESTMENT CERTIFICATES (GICS):

Index-Linked GICs link their returns to equity returns based on a particular domestic or global index. They are attractive to conservative investors who desire safety as well as the opportunity to obtain yields above standard deposit instruments.

- The Canada Deposit Insurance Corporation (CDIC) insures the investors against issuer default, and the income earned on these instruments is treated as interest income. One risk faced by investors is that they may not fully participate in gains on the underlying index, since many of the returns are capped at maximum returns that may be short of those actually provided by the index.

6. HEDGE FUNDS:

Hedge funds are professionally managed portfolios that are traditionally sold to "sophisticated," wealthy investors. Minimum investments are usually between $90,000 and $150,000. Hedge fund managers often pursue strategies not available to traditional mutual fund managers, which may involve additional risks. These funds may try to hedge against a variety of factors such as market risks (domestic or foreign), foreign exchange risk, commodity price risk, or inflation. Some of the more aggressive funds may use leverage to magnify gains or losses, further contributing to their risk.

The **advantages** of hedge funds include:

1. the potential to provide protection against inflation, or declines in market returns, commodity prices, or foreign exchange rates;
2. additional diversification; and
3. the potential for magnified capital gains.

The **disadvantages** of hedge funds include:

1. the risk of substantial losses due to high volatility displayed by some of these funds;
2. hedging risks may also limit profits; and
3. liquidity risk may be associated with the use of some derivatives.

7. OFFSHORE FUNDS:

Offshore funds may only be offered through private placements and usually require high minimum investments. They are based outside Canada, but are subject to Canadian regulation.

The **advantages** of offshore funds include:

1. access to unique investment opportunities such as leverage, hedging, or short-selling;

2. denominated in foreign currencies; and

3. usually have lower management fees due to smaller number of contributors, plus the fact that many are located in tax havens.

The **disadvantages** of offshore funds include:

1. not eligible for RRSPs or other registered plans;

2. dividends received are not eligible for dividend tax credit;

3. foreign currency risk may be important;

4. accounting, reporting, and other regulatory requirements may be less stringent than in Canada; and

5. hard to conduct performance comparisons due to lack of available data.

8. INSURANCE PRODUCTS:

- **Segregated funds** differ from traditional funds and are offered by insurance companies. They are legally considered to be insurance products and funds must be separated from other assets of the insurance company. They provide death benefits and must guarantee that a minimum percentage (75% is required, but most funds offer 100%) of the investor's payments into the fund will be returned when the fund matures. They may also be structured so that the assets within the fund cannot be seized by creditors if the investor declares bankruptcy. In addition, upon the death of the owner, the assets within may be transferred to beneficiaries without being subject to probate fees. These products are the topic of Chapter 8.

- **Universal life insurance** includes an investment component that is considered to be separate from the life insurance component. For qualifying plans, growth of the "reserve account" is not taxable until the funds are removed from the policy, which enables investors to defer paying taxes on earned income.

9. MORTGAGE BACKED SECURITIES (MBS):

MBSs are pools of residential mortgages that have been "bundled" or packaged into one big asset pool, with units in the pool sold to investors. They are guaranteed by the Canada Mortgage and Housing Corporation (CMHC), and they pay out the interest to unit holders The most common form includes five-year pools. They usually offer a yield that is higher than that available on T-bills; however, the secondary market may suffer from illiquidity.

10. SCHOLARSHIP TRUSTS:

- **Scholarship trusts** are offered by non-profit companies and have been around since the 1960s. Subscribers (parents or grandparents) to the plan can make contributions all at once or at regular intervals for a predetermined number of years.

These funds may invest in government-guaranteed investments such as T-bills, bonds, federal mortgages, GICs, and term deposits. They are scheduled to mature when the beneficiary (or nominee) is expected to begin post-secondary education. The plans are eligible for Canada Education Savings Grants, since the plans are registered as Registered Education Savings Plans (RESPs), which are discussed in Chapter 11.

- The scholarship is awarded only when the nominee attends a qualifying institution, and they are only given a certain number of years to enroll. Any interest earned on behalf of nominees who do not subsequently qualify for benefits, is owned by the pool and becomes available to other qualifying nominees. Scholarships are available for up to four years, although many permit the nominee to take a year off from their studies in between. When withdrawals begin, the nominee is taxed on the interest income earned within the plan, and the subscriber is able to deduct past membership fees that were paid. Some plans permit a lump sum withdrawal. In these cases, the nominee loses access to other funds in the pool, and the subscriber may not deduct the membership fees.

- If the nominee does not pursue post-secondary education, the subscriber can contribute up to $50,000 from the plan to an RRSP, if they have sufficient contribution room. If the subscriber terminates the plan early, only the principal (minus membership fees) is returned and the interest earned is lost.

11. COMMODITY POOLS:

- **Commodity pools** are specialized, high-risk funds that are designed primarily for wealthy investors. They invest primarily in pools of futures, forwards, and options on a variety of underlying commodities. They also invest in T-bills to offset the leverage associated with the derivative products. They usually have minimum investment requirements, such as $2,000 or higher, and some require that investors have minimum levels of net worth and/or income. They are eligible for registered products, and may enable investors to increase foreign content in such plans since they are not subject to foreign ownership restrictions.

12. INVESTMENT CONTRACTS:

- Investment opportunities that are customized and do not fall into traditional categories may be covered by an **investment contract (IC)** as long as the investor contributes the funds, receives a share of the profits, and is not directly involved in managing the investments. The investor should be provided with a prospectus, and the salesperson should be properly registered.

13. QUEBEC BUSINESS INVESTMENT COMPANY (QBIC):

- **QBICs** permit investors to purchase common shares in qualified, privately controlled, Quebec small businesses (SMB). Investors, including SMB managers and employees, receive a tax deduction up to 150% of their investment, up to 30% of their net income. The shares may be transferred to a self-directed RRSP or RRIF, and must be held at least 24 months.

14. INDEX PARTICIPATION UNITS:

Index participation units (IPUs) are exchange-traded funds. The units of these trusts hold shares of companies in market indices in proportion to their weights in the underlying index.

IPUs differ from traditional mutual funds in several ways including:

1. they are traded throughout the day on exchanges;
2. lower management fees;
3. lower portfolio turnover, which also reduces capital gains income, reducing taxes payable;
4. they permit short selling; and
5. they may be purchased on margin, which varies from dealer to dealer for mutual funds.

Two IPUs that are presently available to Canadian investors are described below:

1. **I-60s:** These came into existence in March of 2000 and represent units in the S&P/TSE 60 Index. They trade on the TSE (ticker symbol XIU), and the units are valued at one-tenth the value of the S&P/TSE 60 Index. For example, if the value of the index is 450, the value of each unit is $45. Dividends are paid every quarter in December, March, June, and September.

2. **DJ40s:** These were created in June of 2000 and represent units in the Dow Jones Canada Index Participation Fund, which holds stocks that mimic those held in the Dow 40 Index. They trade on the TSE (ticker symbol DJF), and their value is set at one-tenth of the index value plus accrued income.

Chapter 7: Review Questions

( )

1. Which of the following is **NOT** a type of withdrawal plan available to mutual fund investors?

    a) Ratio Withdrawal Plan

    b) Fixed Dollar Withdrawal Plan

    c) Life Expectancy Adjusted Withdrawal Plan

    d) none of the above

( )

2. _____ investment funds are riskier than _____ funds, but are generally less risky than _____ funds.

    a) Money market; bond; dividend

    b) Mortgage; money market; bond

    c) Bond; balanced; mortgage

    d) Balanced; equity; dividend

( )

3. The offering price of a fund that has a net asset value (NAV) of $40 per unit and has a 6% sales fee is:

    a) $37.60

    b) $40.60

    c) $42.40

    d) $42.55

( )

4. The following statements regarding LSVCCs are false.

    I. They may exceed 10% ownership in companies.

    II. They are primarily long-term investments.

    III. They are not RRSP eligible.

    IV. They provide most of the return to investors in the form of dividends.

    a) I and II

    b) III and IV

    c) I and III

    d) II and IV

( )

5. _____ accounts are opened for clients as a convenience to clients who are unable or unwilling to attend to their own accounts, while _____ accounts allow investors to tailor portfolios to their individual needs.

    a) Managed; discretionary

    b) Discretionary; managed

    c) Wrap; managed

    d) Discretionary; wrap

6. Advantages of mutual funds include the following except: ( )

    a) the variety of types of funds available

    b) the variety of purchase plans available

    c) management fees are tax deductible

    d) liquidity

7. Which of the following statements regarding segregated funds are true? ( )

    I. They guarantee a fixed return to investors.

    II. They are considered to be insurance products.

    III. They are riskier than mutual funds

    IV. They tend to have higher management fees than mutual funds.

    a) I and II

    b) II and IV

    c) I and III

    d) III and IV

8. The following are components of a mutual fund organization except: ( )

    a) the simplified prospectus

    b) fund managers

    c) distributors

    d) custodians

9. Mutual funds that charge the investor at redemption are known as ( )

    _____ .

    a) open-ended funds

    b) no-load funds

    c) deferred sales charge loads

    d) funds with trailer fees

10. Mutual fund companies charge _____ for running the specific ( )
    funds.

    a) management fees

    b) switching fees

    c) open-end fees

    d) trailer fees

11. The advantage(s) of professionally managed hedge funds include: ( )

    I. Risk reduction.

    II. Anticipation of market trends may protect a unit holder from declines
    in the stock market.

    III. Higher capital gains.

IV. Low management fees.

a) IV

b) I, II, III

c) I, II

d) II, III

( )   12. Index participation units (IPUs) provide investors with a:

a) direct stock market investment with low MERs

b) diversified portfolio representing a proportionate interest in the basket of stocks that make up the underlying index

c) liquid investment that trades throughout the day

d) all of the above

( )   13. _____ are a type of wrap account.

a) Royalty trusts

b) REITs

c) Pooled wraps

d) Segregated wraps

( )   14. The _____ method provides a good approximation method for estimating mutual fund returns by assuming a constant rate through the period.

a) apples and oranges

b) Modified Dietz

c) time-weighted rate of return

d) daily valuation method

( )   15. When portfolio managers recognize and invest based on a prevailing trend in the market this is known as _____ .

a) theme investing

b) sector rotation

c) small-cap investing

d) specialty investing

( )   16. _____ fund managers' objective is to match the performance of the market as represented by a specific benchmark portfolio.

a) Equity

b) Index

c) Growth

d) Asset allocation

17. The use of derivative products by mutual fund managers is: (   )
    a) strictly prohibited
    b) only permitted for market entry and exit
    c) permissible for creating clone funds
    d) none of the above

18. Closed-end funds offer the following advantages except: (   )
    a) they may be sold short
    b) deferred sales charges usually decline through time
    c) they provide diversification potential
    d) they do not require large amounts of liquid funds

19. REITs have which of the following characteristics?   (   )
    a) their prices fall when interest rates rise
    b) they generally have leverage ratios above 60%
    c) they provide their unit holders with limited liability
    d) none of the above

20. The following investments are RRSP-eligible except: (   )
    a) Offshore funds
    b) Commodity pools
    c) Royalty Trusts
    d) QBICs

SEGREGATED FUNDS

KEY FEATURES OF SEGREGATED FUNDS

- Segregated fund contracts, or **segregated funds** (hereafter seg funds), combine investments with certain insurance aspects.

Seg funds have many similarities to investment funds, which were discussed in Chapter 7; however, they also have several important differences. Unlike investment funds, they are exempt from provincial securities laws. In addition, the contract holders of a seg fund do not own the underlying assets in the fund but are protected by provisions in the contract.

Seg fund contracts involve three parties:

1. the **contract holder:** the purchaser;

2. the **annuitant:** the person whose life is insured; and

3. the **beneficiary** (or beneficiaries): the person or entity that receives the benefits payable.

- The contract holder may be someone different than the annuitant as long as it is held outside an RRSP.

- More than one beneficiary may be named, and eligible beneficiaries include the estate of the contract holder and charitable organizations.

- Beneficiaries should be designated at the time the contract is established, and they may be either revocable or irrevocable. In the later case, any changes require the consent of the named beneficiary. An irrevocable beneficiary may be established to control the timing of transferring assets to children. For example, an irrevocable beneficiary could be designated, with the provision that the contract is reassigned to the child when they turn 21.

One of the most distinguishing features of seg funds is that they must guarantee that a minimum percentage (required is 75%, but most funds offer 100%) of the investor's payments into the fund will be returned when the fund matures (usually at the end of 10 years). These maturity guarantees provide insurance against capital losses, which will appeal to risk-averse investors.

Some other important features of seg funds include:

1. They provide death benefits, and if the holder dies, the fund holdings are not subject to the delays or fees associated with probate hearings.

2. They provide business owners with a way to protect assets from being seized by creditors or lawyers.

3. Contract holders generally pay for these additional benefits in the form of higher management fees, and investment advisors should help investors determine if the benefits justify the additional expense.

Since seg funds are insurance products, they provide protection from creditors, unlike mutual funds. The full value of the fund is payable to the plan's beneficiaries, and is not subject to probate fees. In order for "creditor-proofing" to apply the fund must satisfy one of the following conditions:

- For plans with revocable beneficiary status, the beneficiary must be a spouse, child, or parent of the *contract holder* in Quebec.

- For plans with revocable beneficiary status, the beneficiary must be a spouse, child, or parent of the *annuitant* in other provinces.

- All non-registered plans with irrevocable beneficiaries are eligible, with no restrictions regarding who the *beneficiaries* are.

Once a non-registered plan has been pledged as security for a loan, creditor-proofing may be waived. Registered plans may not be used as loan collateral without triggering tax consequences.

Seg funds that qualify for creditor protection are generally exempt from being seized in the event of bankruptcy; although this may be challenged if it can be shown the contributions were made with the intent of evading legal obligations. Creditor protection of these funds may be challenged if:

- it can be shown the purpose was to evade debt obligations;

- the contributions were made within one year of the date of bankruptcy; and

- the contributions were made while the client was legally insolvent, which may cover investments made as far as five years in the past.

Since periodic contributions are often made to seg funds, it is possible that some contributions would be protected, while others would not.

- While insurance products are generally not considered a part of the estate of the contract holder, the surrender value of a seg fund is considered matrimonial property. Hence, the cash surrender value is part of the assets to be divided by two spouses who are divorcing in all provinces except Quebec. In Quebec, the spouses will divide the cash surrender value, less the cash surrender value when the marriage began.

- The use of seg funds provides advantages for individuals in the area of estate planning since the proceeds are passed on to beneficiaries without the time delays and financial costs associated with probate. In addition to eliminating probate fees, they also reduce the beneficiary's legal and other related expenses.

CONVERGENCE WITH MUTUAL FUNDS

- Seg funds have grown dramatically in recent years, with total assets reaching $59.3 billion by the end of 1998, up from $25.8 billion at the end of 1993. They have been around since the 1960s, and have historically been used primarily for pension plans (e.g., 80% of the assets belonged to group plans as late as 1993). They have been increasingly marketed to individuals in recent years. Mutual fund companies have increased their involvement in this area by providing services to seg funds, and also by sponsoring their own seg funds in co-operation with insurance companies.

Guaranteed investment funds (GIFs) were first introduced in 1997 (by Manulife Financial). A GIF is a type of seg fund that holds well-known mutual funds as its underlying assets. GIFs are presently offered by insurers, investment fund companies, and banks.

- Seg funds have evolved in many other ways in recent years, and there is now a wide range of funds, including specialized funds, available for investors. In addition, many mutual funds now offer capital guarantees such as those provided by seg funds.

- The convergence between seg funds and mutual funds has led to concerns by regulators that care must be taken to create a level playing field for the two products. Some progress was made in May of 1999 in the form of a joint study conducted by the Canadian Securities Administrators (CSA), and the Canadian Council of Insurance Regulators (CCIR). This study compared the features of seg funds and mutual funds.

Some of the most notable differences between mutual funds and seg funds are listed below:

Feature	Seg Funds	Mutual Funds
1. Legal status	insurance contract	security
2. Asset ownership	insurance company	the fund
3. Regulation body	insurance regulators (provincial)	securities regulators
4. Maturity guarantees	minimum 75% after 10 years (usually set at 100%)	usually none
5. Death benefits	yes; may be subject to restrictions	usually none
6. Creditor protection	yes; subject to conditions	none
7. Probate bypass	yes	none

REGULATION

- There were more than 40 seg fund issuers by mid-1999, most of which were insurance companies. Issuers must be authorized to conduct life insurance business, and must be licensed by provincial insurance regulators. Seg fund laws and regulations are very similar across all provinces and territories, which have all accepted the Canadian Life and Health Insurance Association (CLHIA) guidelines. The CLHIA is a national industry trade group that represents almost all seg fund issuers. There are some regulatory differences across the provinces however. Quebec is distinct in having adopted a more unified approach to regulating the financial services industry than other provinces.

- Before seg funds may be offered to the public, they require approval from the appropriate provincial insurance regulator. Applications must initially be filed with the CLHIA, which conducts an extensive review. Once CLHIA approval has been obtained, the application package is forwarded to the provincial regulators, who rely heavily upon the CLHIA review, and many will not conduct any additional reviews. Most provinces impose a 30-day waiting period from the date of the CLHIA application.

- Compliance reports must be filed annually by the fund, and are reviewed to ensure that the fund's characteristics comply with the CLHIA guidelines.

- The Office of the Superintendent of Financial Institutions (OSFI) requires that federally regulated insurance companies are adequately capitalized, as dictated by the solvency requirements outlines in the federal *Insurance Companies Act*. The main requirements for seg funds include:

    1. The amount of the maturity guarantee may not exceed 100% of contributed capital (this also applies to those that permit "reset" guarantee features).
    2. The initial term of the contract can not be less than 10 years.
    3. No guarantees prior to maturity or death are permissible.

- In addition to the requirements above, the OSFI requires life insurance companies to maintain "minimum continuing capital and surplus requirements," and federally incorporated companies must have at least $10 million in capital when incorporating. If a company does not properly account for its assets, or if its liabilities are not being paid, the OSFI may take temporary control of their assets, including seg funds.

- Seg fund contract holders are protected against the insolvency of its issuer by the very fact that the funds are segregated from the company's general assets. They also receive additional protection through the Canadian Life and Health Insurance Compensation Corp. (**CompCorp**), which was founded in 1990. CompCorp is a self-financed industry body that provides customers with protection in the event of insolvency of one of its members.

STRUCTURE

The structure of seg funds differs fundamentally from mutual funds. While the latter are set up as trusts or corporations, seg funds represent life insurance contracts, known as **individual variable insurance contracts (IVICs).**

- Seg fund unit holders do not own the underlying assets, and are not participating policy holders, and the fund assets are held separately from the other assets of the insurer. As a result, if the insurer becomes insolvent, the seg fund assets belong to the contract holders. On the other hand, the contract holders do not have voting rights and cannot attend meetings.

- The recent growth in popularity of seg funds, as well the entry of mutual fund companies has led to variations in the basic structure of these funds. Some of the more notable developments in recent years are described below:

  - The recently introduced GIFs have attracted investors who like the combination of investment and insurance provided by these "fund-on-fund" structures.

  - **Portfolio funds** invest in other seg funds in order to provide investors with the chance to hold diversified portfolios of seg funds. The disadvantage of these funds is that they are less flexible than traditional wrap programs offered by investment dealers. In addition, the management expenses usually exceed those for individual seg funds and GIFs, since the asset allocation fees are paid on top of the management fees for the individual funds.

  - **Protected funds** are mutual funds that provide the maturity guarantees similar to those offered by seg funds. Since these funds are not insurance products, they can be sold by mutual fund salespeople, and may change other features that are required for seg funds. For example, one company has offered a five-year maturity guarantee instead of a 10-year one. In addition, traditional death benefits do not apply.

ADMINISTRATION

- Historically, seg funds have been administered by the life insurance companies owning the funds; however, the large number of recent changes have presented challenges to this approach. Some companies have turned to mutual fund companies to provide such services; however, this approach is also limited by the inherent differences between mutual funds and seg funds. In particular, seg funds have unique administrative needs related to the following factors:

  1. **Investment management:** while insurance companies may manage the seg fund investments internally, many have chosen to use portfolio management subsidiaries, or use sub-related advisors.

2. **Trustee services:** Since seg funds are legally treated as insurance products, they are exempt from the trustee requirements associated with mutual funds. In addition, the IDA requires that seg fund contracts sold by securities dealers to investors be held in the name of the IDA member. This has led to concerns regarding creditor protection, which requires that the designated beneficiary has a relationship with the annuitant (except in Quebec).

3. **Custodial services:** Seg fund investors are protected by having the fund assets segregated from the issuer's other assets, and they also have a claim to the other assets of the issuer. As a result of this enhanced protection, seg fund issuers are permitted to act as custodians of the funds, unlike mutual fund sponsors who must appoint a third-party custodian. While many do so, some companies have chosen to designate a custodian or sub-custodian.

4. **Asset valuation:** Seg fund assets must be valued at least on a monthly basis (except for real estate assets, mortgages, or derivatives); although most are done so daily. The net asset value of the fund must be determined weekly; daily if derivatives are used.

5. **Foreign content restrictions:** Seg funds may be contributed to registered retirement or education plans. Prior to January 1, 2001, they were not subject to the 25% foreign content rule. After that date, they have been subject to foreign content restrictions.[1]

- Seg funds must track several features in addition to those normally administered by mutual funds including:

  - the owner or contract holder;
  - the annuitant;
  - the benficiary;
  - the age of the annuitant;
  - maturity guarantees: these require that administrators track the dates and amounts of deposits to the plan. Funds that permit multiple reset guarantees require additional monitoring;
  - death benefit guarantees;
  - market values: market values determine if preset provisions are to be used;
  - withdrawals: withdrawals affect guarantees. Generally, it is assumed that withdrawals are made from the most distant past contributions; and
  - transfers between funds: these may affect the initial values and dates of maturity guarantees, which may be reset.

- Seg funds usually allow holders to make purchases or withdrawals at the fund's most recent net asset value. In order to purchase units, the investor must first establish a contract with the insurer, since they are technically making a deposit or premium payment. Contract holders must receive disclosure documents prior to entering into the contract. The administration of seg fund offerings is processed through FundServ, which also provides clearing and settlement services to the industry.

---

[1] The foreign content limit increased to 30% in 2001.

Money market seg funds settle on *the day following the trade date*, while other funds settle in *three business days* (the same as mutual funds).

- Minimum deposits may be similar to those required for mutual funds; however, some companies require higher minimum investments.

- Seg fund owners can withdraw some or all of their cash value at any time, except for those with locked-in plans, or in rare circumstances where fund liquidity is an urgent concern.

- Most companies permit a certain number of free transfers to other seg funds within the family per year, and charge for additional transfers.

MATURITY GUARANTEES AND BENEFITS

Maturity guarantees altar the normal risk-return relationship for investors by allowing them to participate in potential market gains, while at the same time protecting the value of their investment. The OSFI requires a minimum term of 10 years for these guarantees.

The minimum guarantee amount under provincial legislation is 75%; however, most companies offer a 100% guarantee. This reflects the fact that it is unlikely that investments will lose money over a 10-year holding period, based on historical evidence. Some companies do provide the minimum 75% guarantee, and these funds tend to have lower management expenses to reflect the lower risk associated with the guarantee.

Maturity guarantees are generally set up in one of two forms:

1. **Deposit-based guarantees:** these provide guarantees for each deposit made, with the term being based upon the date of the deposit.
2. **Policy-based guarantees:** these simplify record-keeping by grouping all contributions made within a 12-month period together, and giving them the same maturity date. Insurers also have the option of grouping together payments within a given calendar year.

- The value of maturity guarantees has been subject to debate. Some suggest that the guarantees do not justify the additional expense of ensuring the guarantee, since historical evidence suggests it is very unlikely that investment returns will be negative over a 10-year holding period. For example, the TSE 300 Index has never had a negative return during a 10-year period. Others suggest that the associated insurance premiums are insufficient to cover the potential cost of such guarantees, since the payouts could be very large and widespread, if they ever become necessary. In fact, a 1998 report issued by the Canadian Institute of Actuaries (CIA) characterized the risks associated with seg fund guarantees as "low frequency and high severity."

- There is no maximum age limitation for non-registered seg fund holders; however, many companies enforce their own limits. Those held in RRSPs or locked-in retirement accounts must be terminated before the holder turns 69; while holders of funds in RRIFs or life income funds must be under 90. The minimum age requirement is 16.

! Many seg fund issuers have begun offering investors the option of buying funds with maturity guarantee "**reset dates**." These permit investors to lock-in capital gains, but also extend the maturity date of the guarantee. Some funds provide automatic resets, while others provide investors the option of doing so a certain number of times per year (usually one to four times). Age restrictions may apply.

- A recent innovation offers holders an automatic daily reset feature. The maturity guarantees for these funds are automatically reset every day, at the higher of the most recently established guaranteed value, or the current market value of the fund. The CIA has expressed concern about the additional risk associated with these guarantees. In addition, there are additional expenses associated with providing such flexible reset provisions.

- If seg funds are purchased primarily due to the maturity guarantees and death benefits, the investor should consider what proportion of their funds should be held in seg funds. This will depend on several factors including:

  - The client's level of risk tolerance: the higher the tolerance, the less funds should be contributed to seg funds, due to the costs associated with the maturity guarantee.

  - The proportions of funds held in cash, fixed income, and equity asset classes: the higher the proportion held in cash and fixed income, the lower the need for the guarantee.

  - The investment's time horizon: the shorter the term, the less need for an insured fund.

An alternative strategy would be to invest in seg funds for the long-term investment component, and invest in an annuity product to generate short-term income.

! The **death benefits** provided by seg funds are attractive to investors who desire higher returns, but are concerned with insuring the amount they leave to their heirs. The benefits are set up to ensure the beneficiary receives at least the value of contributions to the fund, less associated fees. If the market value of the fund is below this value, the beneficiary would receive the difference in cash. For example, if the guaranteed amount was $50,000 and the market value of the fund was $60,000 at the time of death, there would be no payout. However, if the market value had been $45,000, the beneficiary would receive a payment of $5,000 on top of the fund's value.

- Age restrictions may apply to death benefits. Beyond a certain age, they may not apply, or the percentage of the guarantee may decline through time.

Example 1:

The percentage of death benefits for a given seg fund declines from 100% to 90% for contributions made after the annuitant reaches age 80, and then to 80% after they reach age 82. If $10,000 is contributed in each of four years, starting when the annuitant is 79, what is the payout to the beneficiary if the annuitant dies at age 83? At the time of death the market value of the fund was $35,000, assuming no deferred sales charges apply.

Solution:

The contribution when the annuitant is 79 would be 100% guaranteed, the next two would be 90% guaranteed, and the fourth payment would be 80% guaranteed. So,

Death benefit amount $= 10,000 + (10,000 \times 0.90) + (10,000 \times 0.90) + (10,000 \times 0.80)$
$= \$36,000$

Death benefit payment $= 36,000 - 35,000$ (market value) $= \$1,000$

Death benefits may also be restricted by the length of time the contract has been held, with the percentage often graduating upwards and reaching 100% after a certain holding period.

• Insurers are permitted to provide death benefits greater than 100% of the invested amount, and a few have opted to do so. For example, Manulife Financial introduced a series of funds providing death benefits that increased an additional 4% per year. The trade-off for this feature was to eliminate the two optional reset dates per year, and replace this feature with an automatic annual reset date on the anniversary of the contract.

CompCorp provides insurance to seg fund holders in the event of default of any of its members, but this does not apply to fraud. Their guarantee applies to death benefits and maturity guarantees only, not to the fund assets. To qualify for protection, the fund contract has to be written in Canada by a member company; however, the contract holder does not need to be a Canadian resident to qualify.

The coverage is limited to $60,000 per insurance company for both individual and group plans. Thus, an investor who has both an individual and group plan set up with the same company would qualify for total coverage of $120,000 ($60,000 coverage for each plan).

• There is no legal requirement for seg fund issuing companies to provide details of their independent credit ratings, as established by agencies such as the Canadian Bond Rating Service (CBRS), or Dominion Bond Rating Service (DBRS). However, these ratings are available for most seg fund providers, and some companies may provide them to customers in promotional materials.

FEES AND EXPENSES

- Similar to mutual funds, seg funds incur many expenses that are deducted from the value of the fund assets including:

  - legal, audit, and registration expenses;
  - administration, record-keeping, and accounting expenses;
  - document preparation, mailing, and filing expenses; and
  - taxes (including income taxes, sales taxes, and capital gains taxes).

- Seg funds face expenses above those of mutual funds, primarily related to death benefits and maturity guarantees. The associated costs rise as the term to maturity declines and/or as the percentage value of the guarantee increases. As a result, there has been a recent movement by some funds to reduce the guarantee amount to 75%. While it is difficult to pinpoint the true cost of maturity guarantees, there is no doubt that seg funds display higher management expense ratios (MERs) than mutual funds. The IVIC guidelines require that funds separate the insurance portion of the expenses from the expenses associated with managing the underlying fund.

- The sales charges for seg funds are similar to those for mutual funds. Sales fees are generally front-end or deferred-load charges, although a few offer issuers no-load funds. Trailer fees and switching fees may also apply.

TAX CONSIDERATIONS

Seg funds are taxed as if they were trusts that are separate from the insurer's other assets. The company that owns the fund is not taxed on its income, which is passed on to the contract holders. Unlike mutual funds, no distributions to contract holders are required, since they do not actually own the fund's assets. Taxes are **allocated** to contract holders based on their percentage share of such income, which is prorated according to the proportion of the year they held the fund. This **time-weighted** allocation of taxes differs from the "distribution" approach used by most mutual funds, and avoids having investors pay an undue amount of taxes if they purchase a fund just prior to a distribution. As a result of this practice, seg funds do not experience the seasonal tax distortions experienced by mutual funds.

- When mutual funds make a distribution (usually done once a year, near year-end), the net asset value (NAV) of each unit will fall by this amount; however, most funds purchase units for the holders with the distributions. This process reduces the NAV of each unit, but the investors' end up with additional units, leaving the value of their holdings relatively unchanged. However, they must pay taxes on the amount of the distribution, whether they held the funds for the entire year, or for only one day.

- In contrast, with seg funds, the income earned on the fund is allocated to contract holders throughout the year, and does not reduce the NAV of the fund. This time-weighted approach ensures that investors are only taxed on their portion of the income earned by the fund while they owned the fund. The example below demonstrates the difference in these approaches.

Example 2:

A seg fund and a mutual fund both have a beginning of year NAV of $9, and both earn income of $1.00 per unit during the year.

(a) What will be the year-end NAVs and the total wealth for a shareholder who owned 100 units of each fund at year-end?

(b) How much income will be charged against the investor in part (a) if he bought the units in each fund six months prior to year-end?

Solution:

(a) Mutual Fund:
NAV prior to distribution = 9 + 1 = $10
Investor wealth (prior to distribution) = 100 units × $10 = $1,000
NAV at year-end (after distribution) = 10 − 1 = $9
Investor wealth (year-end) = [100 units + ($100 / $9) units] × $9 per unit
= [100 units + 11.11 units] × $9 per unit = $1,000

Seg Fund:
NAV at year-end = 9 + 1 = $10
Investor wealth (year-end) = 100 units × $10 = $1,000

(b) Mutual Fund:
The investor will be charged with (and taxed on) income of $1 × 100 units = $100.

Seg Fund:
The investor will be charged with (and taxed on) income of $1 × 6/12 × 100 units = $50.

- Some general principles to remember regarding seg funds are:

    1. Seg fund NAVs are the same for all contract holders at a given point in time.
    2. The NAV will vary depending on the time of purchase.
    3. Income allocations do not reduce seg fund NAVs.
    4. Seg fund allocations are paid throughout the year.

- An additional tax advantage of seg funds is that they are able to pass capital losses on to investors, unlike mutual funds, which must save them to offset future capital gains.

! The payments associated with maturity guarantees are taxable. While the amount of the payment is usually taxed as a capital gain, some tax experts argue that the entire amount should be fully taxable as regular income. The example below depicts three possible scenarios.

! Example 3:

A client invests in a seg fund with a 100% maturity guarantee. Assume the adjusted cost base (ACB) of her investment is $10,000 (which includes all contributions plus sales commissions paid), and that no redemption fees are payable. Also assume that any maturity guarantees are treated as capital gains. Determine the tax consequences under the following scenarios:

(a) She redeems her deposit after 10 years, when its market value is $12,000.

(b) She redeems her deposit after 10 years, when its market value is $9,000.

(c) She redeems her deposit after 12 years, when its market value is $10,000; however, the maturity guarantee had been reset at $12,000 after she had held the fund two years.

Solution:

(a) She will be taxed on $2,000 in capital gains income (12,000 − 10,000).

(b) No taxes are payable. The $1,000 capital gain associated with the maturity benefit (10,000 − 9,000) will be offset by the $1,000 capital loss on her investment (9,000 − 10,000).

(c) No capital gains are taxable when the maturity guarantee is reset. When the fund is redeemed, a taxable capital gain of $2,000 is triggered (12,000 guaranteed amount −10,000 ACB).

- Death benefits are also subject to more than one tax treatment, having been treated as:

  ○ taxable capital gains;
  ○ taxable regular income; and
  ○ non-taxable.

A recent interpretation by Canada Customs and Revenue Agency has suggested that both maturity guarantees and death benefits should be treated as capital gains.

- The *Income Tax Act* requires seg funds to have a December 31 fiscal year-end. Income allocations are reported annually on a T3 slip, which must be reported by the contract holder. Holders are subject to taxes on capital gains that arise from switches from one fund to another, or when they redeem units.

- Unlike mutual funds, which add any commission fees to the adjusted cost base, commission fees for seg fund transactions are reported separately, and may be claimed as capital losses when the contract is redeemed by the contract holder.

The amount that may be claimed is in direct proportion to the proportion of the original shares purchased that have been redeemed. For example, if an investor redeemed 30% of fund units that were originally purchased, and the total commission fee was $100, the investor could claim a $30 capital loss.

- If the contract owner is not the annuitant, the policy remains intact after their death. However, the owner's estate would be subject to a resulting capital gain or loss from the disposition of the fund at its fair market value, unless they named a spouse as the successor owner.

- The government has recently announced that it will attempt to capture GST/HST on insurance premiums received by an insurer to cover the death benefits and maturity guarantees associated with seg funds.

When seg funds are held in registered plans the annuitant must be the contract holder, which is not the case for non-registered plans. Registered plans are non-transferable, unless the annuitant dies. As of January 1, 2001, seg fund contracts held within registered plans must comply with foreign content limitations. Seg fund contracts may be registered as locked-in plans in the form of a locked-in RRSP, a locked in retirement account (LIRA), or a locked-in retirement income fund (LRIF).

- RRSPs must be terminated when the plan holder turns 69. At that time, they may be redeemed, or converted into a registered retirement income fund (RRIF) or annuity. RRIFs may designate spouses, children, or grandchildren as beneficiaries, which allows the fund to be redeemed gradually through time. If not so designated, the sponsor must pay out the entire amount immediately. When these plans are rolled over to a spouse, they become the new annuitant, and the new maturity date will be 10 years hence at that time.

Seg funds may also be contributed to Registered Education Savings Plans (RESPs) in order to provide for post-secondary education for children, which will be discussed in greater detail in Chapter 11. The maturity guarantees may be particularly attractive for these plans, since the contributor can attempt to invest the funds aggressively, but have an assured value available when the funds are required.

- Similar funds borrowed for other types of investments, the interest paid on funds borrowed to contribute to non-registered, and variable income (e.g., equity or balanced funds) seg funds are tax deductible.

DISCLOSURE

- As a result of new disclosure regulations that were established by the CLHIA, seg funds face similar requirements to the ones faced by mutual funds. However, some key differences remain. One of the most important distinctions arises because seg funds are not owned by their contract holders. As a result, contract holders are not permitted to vote on material changes such as changes in management or in investment objectives.

- Seg fund issuers must obtain the approval of provincial regulators. The first step in this process requires the filing of the appropriate documents (application form, draft contract, information folder, and summary fact statement) with the CLHIA. A new information folder must be filed by the earlier of 13 months after the filing of the last statement, or 16 months after the latest audited statements.

The key disclosure documents include:

1. **Application Form:** Prior to signing the application form, which includes pertinent details about the client and the plan being established, clients must receive a copy of the fund's information folder,

2. **Contract:** This must describe the benefits and identify which benefits are guaranteed, and which will vary with the market value of the fund. The contract will indicate how often the fund is valued and describe the associated fees and how they are determined. It should also include a warning to clients that the fund's market value will fluctuate.

3. **Information Folder:** This is the most important disclosure document, similar to the prospectuses that are provided by mutual funds. It describes the salient features of the seg fund with regards to benefits, investment policies, and associated charges and redemption procedures. There are additional requirements for funds held in registered plans, while real estate funds must also include a statement stressing the long-term nature of these funds.

4. **Summary Fact Statement:** Potential contract holders must be provided with this document. It provides a short summary of the fund's past performance, its investment policies, as well as the fund's top three holdings (although many companies exceed this requirement).

5. **Financial Statements:** Contract holders must be provided with audited financial statements, if they are available. The statements must be prepared in accordance with GAAP. In addition to traditional financial statement information, the funds must disclose information regarding management and other fees, as well as the manner in which they are determined.

6. **Client Statements:** Clients are sent a number of reports including:

   ○ trade confirmations;

   ○ the value of their holdings and changes in the value of their holdings;

   ○ the unit value of the fund; and

   ○ annual reports reporting performance details.

- Public information providers of mutual fund performance usually include seg fund unit values and performance statistics in these reports.

- All sales communications are guided by regulations that satisfy CLHIA guidelines, which were recently revised in order to bring them in line with mutual fund advertising guidelines. Many items fall into the category of sales communications, including reports to contract holders and, any verbal or written communications with prospective customers.

- The representations of seg fund salespeople or sponsors are restricted. They may not:

  - make claims regarding future values that do not pertain to the maturity value or death benefits;

  - make false or misleading statements about the seg fund's benefits;

  - make misleading or incomplete comparisons to other investment products; or

  - make unfair criticisms of competing products.

- Seg fund marketing information must include a number of disclaimers, including the following:

  - Any mention of death benefits must also disclose any subsequent reduction in such benefits.

  - A warning about fluctuating market values.

  - All related fees must be disclosed.

  - They cannot espouse the immediate tax benefits, but describe such benefits as being more long-term.

  - When being recommended for RRSPs, they must disclose the age at which such plans must be terminated or converted to RRIFs or annuities.

- When seg funds advertise their past performance, they must adhere to certain guidelines, including the following:

  - They must report performance for standard measurement periods, including one-year, three-year, five-year, and 10-year compound annual returns (if available).

  - They should refer to any provisions that might prevent the holder from redeeming the funds prior to an advertised period performance.

  - They must state any restrictions on withdrawals.

  - Comparisons with market benchmarks or other investments are permitted, as long as the performance is determined using the appropriate reporting requirements.

Chapter 8: Review Questions

( )   1. In general, segregated fund are:

a) not protected from creditors

b) not exempt from bankruptcy protection

c) normally exempt from being included in the property divided among creditors

d) none of the above

( )   2. The assets of a segretgated fund are owned by _____.

a) the fund itself through a separate legal entity

b) the unit holders

c) an insurance company

d) provincial securities regulators

( )   3. Unlike mutual funds, segregated funds:

I. may have death benefits

II. are regulated by provincial securities regulators

III. must file annual financial statements

IV. have maturity guarantees

a) I and IV

b) II and III

c) I, III, and IV

d) II, III, and IV

( )   4. The requirement(s) set out by the Office of the Superintendent of Financial Institutions (OSFI) for segregated funds include:

a) The initial term of the segregated fund must not be longer than 10 years.

b) The amount of the maturity guarantee payable at the end of the term must exceed 100%.

c) There can be no guarantee of any amounts payable on redemption of the contract before death or the maturity date.

d) all of the above

( )   5. The unique needs of segregated funds include:

a) Trustee services, investment management, and foreign content regulation.

b) Trustee services, investment management, asset valuation, custodial services, and monitoring of foreign content.

c) Hedging requirements, monitoring of foreign content, asset valuation, and investment management.

d) Trust services, investment management, asset valuation, and custodial services.

6. What does CompCorp guarantee? ( )

   a) The death benefits and maturity guarantees applicable to a segregated fund contract.

   b) The principle amount should the segregated fund default.

   c) The principle amount should the segregated fund's insurance company go bankrupt.

   d) The principle amount should the investor wish to break the segregated fund contract.

Refer to the following information to answer Questions 7 8:

Assume Bill invested a lump sum of $100,000 on a deferred-sales-charges basis, and the policy was held long enough so there were no redemption fees at the time the policy is surrendered.

7. What are the tax consequences if Bill wishes to redeem his deposit after 10 years when the market value of his deposit was $145,000? ( )

   a) A capital gain of $45,000 is taxable in the year of redemption.

   b) There are no taxes payable.

   c) Bill can defer the capital gains payable for seven years.

   d) none of the above

8. What are the tax consequences if Bill wishes to redeem his $100,000 deposit after 10 years when the market value of his deposit is $78,000? ( )

   a) Bill can carry forward the capital loss for seven years.

   b) A net capital gain of $22,000 is taxable.

   c) There are no taxes payable.

   d) none of the above

9. Insurance agents and sponsors must communicate to clients and the public adhering to _____ guidelines. ( )

   a) benefits and advantages contract

   b) CIA

   c) provincial securities regulators

   d) CLHIA

10. Like mutual funds, segregated funds offer: ( )

    a) professional investment management

    b) portfolio diversification

    c) insurance contracts

    d) both a) and b)

DERIVATIVE SECURITIES

INTRODUCTION

- Derivatives are so-called because they derive their value from the price of another underlying asset such as a stock, stock or bond index, commodity price, etc. They are suitable for hedging or speculative purposes by more sophisticated investors and are used extensively by institutional investors. Investment advisors dealing in derivatives require additional research, specialized knowledge, and particular skills, and are required to take special courses to deal in some of these products. Conversion, retraction, or extendible features that are attached to debt and preferred equity securities are securities that include embedded options, and are also derivative securities.

RIGHTS AND WARRANTS

Rights and **warrants** are similar to call options (discussed later in this chapter) because they both *give the holder the right to purchase shares at specified prices until the expiration date*. Unlike options, they are *issued by the corporation itself*, and result in dilution of the common equity capital base.

Rights are generally *short-term* in nature, while warrants tend to be issued with *three to five years to maturity*.

A right provides a shareholder the opportunity to acquire additional shares at a predetermined (subscription) price which is generally *lower* than the current market price. This creates value for the shareholder and induces them to exercise this option.

! Rights are usually transferable, and certificates are mailed to shareholders on the **record date**. Shares trade **ex rights** *two business days prior to a record date*, and the stock is said to be **cum rights** before the ex rights date. Typically the share price will drop by the theoretical intrinsic value of the right on the ex rights date.

! Rights may be offered because:

1. Current market conditions are not conducive to traditional common share issues.

2. Management wants to give existing shareholders the opportunity to acquire shares, possibly at a discount to present market price.

3. It enables new funds to be raised while providing existing shareholders the right to maintain their proportionate ownership of the company (which is known as the **pre-emptive right** associated with common share ownership).

- No commission is levied on the exercise of rights, and a ready secondary market can develop, which provides holders who do not wish to exercise their rights, the option to sell their rights. If the shares trade on an exchange, the rights are listed on the exchange automatically and trading takes place until they expire.

! Regular delivery requires settlement within *three business days* on the TSE and the CDNX *up to three days* before the expiry date. On the TSE, they settle in *two days* for trades *three days prior to expiry*, the *next day* for trades *one and two days prior* to the expiry date, and must be settled in *cash* on the expiry date. For the CDNX, rights are settled on a cash basis from three days prior to, and including the expiry date. Because of their short lifetime, they are often bought and sold on a "when issued" basis, which implies that sellers agree to deliver the rights when they are received.

! A rights holder may take four courses of action:

1. Exercise some or all of the rights.
2. Sell some or all of the rights.
3. Buy additional rights for trading or exercise purposes.
4. Do nothing and let the rights expire: this would represent suboptimal behaviour since the investor would gain no benefit through this action, and would lose the value of the rights they were provided with.

! Usually *each shareholder receives one right* and a certain *number of rights (N) is required to purchase one share* (purchase of fractional shares may or may not be permitted, depending on the details of the issue).

! The theoretical **intrinsic value (IV)** of a right is calculated using two methods:

1. **During the cum rights period:**

   IV = (market price of the stock − subscription price) ÷ (N+1)

   The addition of 1 to N, reflects the fact that the market price of the share includes the value of one right during this period.

2. **During the ex rights period:**

   IV = (market price of stock − subscription price) ÷ (N)

Example 1:

(a) Determine the intrinsic value of a right for a share that is trading for $40 cum rights. Four rights are required to purchase a share at the subscription price of $35.

Solution:

$IV = (40 - 35) / (4 + 1) = \$1.00$

(b) Determine the intrinsic value of the right in part (a) two days after the ex rights date if the share price above has fallen to $39.20.

Solution:

$IV = (39.20 - 35) / 4 = \$1.05$

The term *warrants* may have two meanings, which are described below. The first definition is by far the most common, and it is the one that the remaining discussion is based upon.

1. Warrants are certificates that contain an option to buy shares from the issuer at a given price for a predetermined period of time. Companies often attach warrants to debt or preferred share issues as *sweeteners* (i.e., to make the issue more attractive to investors). Most are *detachable* either immediately or after a certain holding period, after which time they may be traded separately from the original security to which they were attached.

2. Warrants may also be referred to as certificates that provide ownership of rights, although this is much less common.

Investors may be attracted to warrants because they provide "**leverage**," which is attractive to speculators. In other words, the market price of a warrant is generally much lower than the price of the underlying security, yet its price moves together with the underlying asset price. The result is greater swings in prices for warrants than for the underlying asset, which magnifies gains (or losses) in percentage terms.

A ratio that may be used to measure this leverage potential is:

leverage potential = (market price of the underlying) ÷ (market price of the warrant)

In general, larger ratios imply a greater leverage effect; however, other factors such as the amount of over-valuation must also be considered.

Example 2:

Determine the leverage potential of the following warrants:

(a) share price is $50, warrant price is $8, and exercise price of warrants is $52

(b) share price is $40, warrant price is $15, and exercise price of warrants is $30

Solution:

(a) leverage potential = 50 / 8 = 6.25

(b) leverage potential = 40 / 15 = 2.67

- Some other factors that investors should consider before purchasing warrants include *marketability* and *protection against stock splits and/or stock dividends* (which are usually covered).

Similar to rights, the **intrinsic value** (IV) of a warrant is the amount that the market price of the underlying asset (P_0) exceeds the exercise or subscription price (S) of the warrant. It may never go below zero, since exercise is at the option of the warrant holder. It is also typical to estimate the **time value** of a warrant, which refers to the amount by which the price of the warrant exceeds its intrinsic value. We can express these relationships using the folowing equations:

$$\textbf{IV} = \textbf{Max } (\textbf{P}_0\textbf{ - S, 0})$$

$$\textbf{Time Value} = \textbf{Price of warrant} - \textbf{IV}$$

Example 3:

Determine the intrinsic value and time value for the warrants in Example 2.

Solution:

(a)   IV = Max (50 − 52, 0) = 0; Time Value = 8 − 0 = $8

(b)   IV = Max (40 − 30, 0) = 10; Time Value = 15 − 10 = $5

Some particular types of warrants include:

1. **Piggy back warrants:** additional warrants may be received as part of the exercise of original warrants (and typically have higher exercise prices).

2. **Warrants issued by third parties:** these warrants are issued by third parties on a variety of assets such as the Nikkei 255 index, gold prices, or U.S. T-bonds. One of the most popular of these warrants issued in Canada has been put warrants on the Nikkei 255 index, which is issued by Bankers Trust. These warrants provide the option to "sell" at pre-determined exercise prices. They are settled in cash on the exercise date, based on the difference between the exercise price and the value of the Nikkei.

OPTIONS

Options are contracts between a buyer and a seller, based on an underlying security. Unlike rights and warrants, they are not issued by a company as a form of capital. The **buyer** pays a "**premium**" or fee and *receives the right, but not the obligation*, to exercise certain rights provided in the contract. Each equity option contract is for *100 underlying shares*, therefore if the quoted price is $2, the cost of purchasing the option contract would be $2 \times 100 = 200. The **seller** or "**writer**" of the option contract is "*obligated*" to undertake certain actions specified in the contract, when notified to do so by the buyer (or the clearing corporation).

The **expiration** (or **expiry**) **date** is the date at which the option contract expires. Options expire on the *third Friday* of the stated expiration month.

The "**exercise**" or "**strike**" **price** refers to the price specified in the contract at which the underlying security may be *bought* (in the case of a "**call**" option) or *sold* (in the case of a "**put**" option).

European style options can be exercised *only* at the expiry date, while **American** style options can be exercised *any time up to and including the expiry date*. Most exchange listed equity options are American style, while index options and OTC options are typically European.

Options can be bought or sold through an exchange facility or privately arranged (OTC options).

- The Chicago Board of Options Exchange began trading in options in 1973. Liquidity problems, which had plagued the OTC options markets were overcome by:

    1. standardizing option contracts; and
    2. introducing a clearing corporation that would guarantee the performance of the seller of an options contract (i.e., effectively it becomes the buyer and seller for each option contract).

The **Canadian Derivatives Clearing Corporation (CDCC)** is the sole clearing corporation in Canada, and issues and guarantees all equity, bond, and stock index option positions. Since April of 2000, the Montreal Exchange (ME) has been the only exchange where financial options and futures are traded in Canada, and it is now the sole owner of the CDCC. In the U.S. all listed options are cleared through the Options Clearing Corporation (OCC).

Exercise is accomplished by submitting an exercise notice to the clearing corporation, which "assigns" the exercise notice to a member firm, which then assigns it to one of its accounts.

The **open interest** represents the number of options of a particular series that are presently outstanding. It is often used as a measure of liquidity, along with the **volume** of trading.

An investor may **purchase a call** for any of the following reasons:

1. leverage;
2. to fix a future price (at the combined price of the option premium paid now and the exercise price);
3. buying calls instead of purchasing the underlying security and investing the difference;
4. as an alternative to buying the underlying security; and
5. to close out a position (i.e., for a written call).

Call writing may be done:

1. to generate additional income;
2. to close out a position (i.e., for a call that was previously purchased); and
3. as protection against a price decline in the underlying security.

- **Naked (uncovered) call writers** do not own the underlying security and are subject to a great deal of risk, since they are obligated to buy the underlying security for delivery at market prices, which can increase substantially. As such, they are required to maintain margin accounts. **Covered call writers** already own the stock, and thus are not required to maintain margins, since they merely have to deliver their own shares if required.

Buying a put may be done:

1. to create leverage;
2. as insurance against a drop in the underlying security's price;
3. as an alternative to selling (or short selling) the underlying security; and
4. to close out a "short" put position.

Writing a put may be done:

1. to earn additional income;
2. to close out a "long" put position; and
3. to acquire the underlying security (at desired prices).

- New option contracts are created in the primary market. The contracts must be issued under the option prospectus, which is a short-form prospectus that is a generic publication from the clearing corporation outlining the risks of options trading. There is no fixed number of options outstanding and they do not have certificates.

Option sales *settle the next business day*. Exercise of options settle in three days.

An existing option holder (or writer) enters into a **closing transaction** by selling (or buying) an identical option, thereby closing their previous open position in the option. It is one of the functions of the clearing corporation to match all buy and sell orders.

Call options are said to be "**in-the-money**" when the price of the underlying security (P_0) is greater than the strike price (S) (puts − when $P_0 < S$).

Call options are said to be "**out-of-the-money**" when $P_0 < S$ (puts − when $P_0 > S$).

Call options are said to be "**at-the-money**" when $P_0 = S$ (puts − when $P_0 = S$).

The **intrinsic value** of an option is the amount it is in the money, or zero if it is at or out-of-the money (since exercise is optional, the IV can never be negative). It is obviously determined by the relationship between share price and exercise price.

For calls: $IV = Max (P_0 - S, 0)$

For puts: $IV = Max (S - P_0, 0)$

- The **time value** of an option is the difference between the option premium and the intrinsic value. It is affected by time to maturity, dividends, interest rates, and volatility of the underlying security. For puts and calls, we can say:

Time value = Option price − IV

Example 4:

An investor obtains the following market prices for a call and put option on a common share that is presently trading at $7.00 per share:

call option: exercise price is $8 and the call premium is $1.00

put option: exercise price is $9 and the put premium is $2.50

(a) Determine the intrinsic values and time value premiums for each option, and state whether they are in-, at-, or out-of-the money.

Solution:

Call: IV = Max (7 − 8, 0) = 0; Time value = 1 − 0 = $1.00; out-of-the money

Put: IV = Max (9 − 7, 0) = $2.00; Time value = 2.50 − 2.00 = $0.50; in-the-money

(b) Determine the net profit (ignoring transactions costs) for an investor who purchases one contract of each of these options if they hold the options to expiration date at which time the share price is $9.00.

Solution:

Call: Cost = 100 × $1.00 = $100; Profit = ([$9 − $8] × 100) − $100 = $0

Put: Cost = 100 × $2.50 = $250; Profit = 0 − 250 = −$250 loss

Net profit = $0 − $250 = −$250 (loss)

- Option exchanges introduced combinations of **standardized expiration dates** (known as trading cycles) and **standardized exercise prices.** For example there would be 18 different option "series" trading for a stock trading at $35: puts and calls with strike prices of $30, $35, and $40, with maturities of three, six, and nine months. Additional series are started as time passes and if the price changes (for example, if the share price decreased to $28, a $25 series would begin in addition to those already established).

- Exceptions to these short-term maturities are Long-Term Equity AnticiPation Securities (**LEAPS**), which are **long-term options** that can be exercised any time up to the expiry date. Technically, equity options expire on the Saturday following the third Friday of the month, and clients must make their exercise decisions on the Friday.

- Available option products include:

  1. **Equity options:** these are traded on the ME, along with index options and futures, bond options, and futures, and financial futures. Options on agricultural futures trade on the Winnipeg Commodity Exchange (WCE).

2. **Currency options:** trade on the Philadelphia Stock Exchange.

3. **Bond options:** trade on the ME on Government of Canada bonds covering $25,000 face value at maturity (since 1982).

4. **Stock index options:** index options used to trade on the TSE 35 Index in Canada until they were recently replaced by options on the newly created S&P/TSE 60 Index. In the U.S., index options exist on Standard and Poor's 100 Index plus many other indices. Index options are "cash-settled," based on a multiple (often 100) of the value of the index.

5. **OTC options:** these can be tailor-made, and are used a great deal by larger institutional investors (note that default risk is more of a concern for these options since there is no clearing corporation to guarantee performance).

The following factors affect option prices. For example, we can see the effect on option prices of **increases** in the following factors:

Factor	Call	Put
1. Share price (P_0)	up	down
2. Exercise price	down	up
3. Volatility	up	up
4. Riskless rate	up	down
5. Time to expiration	up	up
6. Dividends paid—(P_0 decreases)	down	up

The first two factors determine the intrinsic value, and their impact on option prices is straightforward. Volatility increases the likelihood of price changes on the underlying assets, which will increase the potential payoffs to options. As interest rates increase, the benefit of delayed ownership afforded by call options increases, since the opportunity cost of purchasing the shares increases. This increases the value of call options. The time to expiration offers additional time to benefit from the option, thereby increasing the time value premium. When dividends are paid, the share price of the underlying asset will decrease, which decreases call values and increases put values.

An investor must receive a risk disclosure statement issued by the clearing corporation before the initial order is executed. Some of the risks involved in options trading are:

1. limited lifespan;

2. substantial risks of naked writing;

3. no guarantee of a liquid secondary market;

4. writers of options cannot control the assignment process; and

5. cash delivery can have unique risks because of the settlement process.

Warrants and options are similar in the following ways:

1. They are both leveraged equity investments.
2. Owners of either type of security do not receive dividends or voting rights.
3. Their prices are determined by similar factors, and option pricing models are often applied to warrants.

Warrants and options differ from one another in the following ways:

1. Options are issued by individuals, not the underlying corporations.
2. New shares are created when a warrant is exercised, which is not true for options.
3. The number of option contracts that may be outstanding is not limited.
4. Option exercise prices never change, while some warrants may provide for changing exercise prices.

FUTURES AND FORWARDS

Futures and **forwards** are used to reduce risk or for speculation purposes. Futures contracts are legal contracts to deliver or take delivery of a specified quantity and quality of a specified asset at a specified future time period at a predetermined price. Unlike options, both sides of the contract must satisfy their side of the contract (i.e., there is no option to be exercised).

• Futures are traded in the trading pit of a commodity or futures exchange by means of public outcry. Delivery time periods can range from one day for an index contract, to a window of four or five weeks for some commodity futures contracts.

• A futures contract is set at today's prices, but is for delivery at some future point in time. Most contracts are closed out in the market ahead of time, so that physical deliveries are rare (roughly 2% of all contracts).

• Futures trade on agricultural products, commodities including some metals, lumber and plywood, heating oil, and financial instruments such as interest rate products and stock indices.[1] Options on futures contracts have also become popular because they entail more limited risk than the underlying futures contract (where exercise is NOT optional).

• The Chicago Board of Trade and the Chicago Mercantile Exchange are the two largest commodity exchanges in North America. Other important exchanges include the Commodity Exchange in New York, the New York Mercantile Exchange, the New York Coffee Exchange, the Sugar and Cocoa Exchange, the New York Cotton Exchange, and the New York Futures Exchange.

---

[1] Recently, the ME began offering futures contracts on the stock price of Nortel Networks. The London Stock Exchange also initiated futures on individual stock prices in 2001, and in December 2000, the U.S. Congress passed a bill permitting such contracts in the U.S. These are expected to surface in the U.S. in 2002.

- In Canada, the only commodity exchange is the **Winnipeg Commodity Exchange (WCE)** where canola futures are by far the most active commodity future traded (1.819 million contracts 1999-2000).

- The ME trades contracts on three-month bankers' acceptances (which call for cash delivery), as well as on Government of Canada bonds. The number of futures contracts cleared through the CDCC was 8.3 million, down from 9.1 million in 1998, but up subtantially from 3.5 million in 1995.

Hedgers are generally participants who deal in the underlying commodity or financial asset, and wish to limit their financial losses by:

1.   selling futures contracts to effectively pre-sell inventories at current market prices; or
2.   buying futures to lock in a future purchase price for the underlying asset.

- The hedging effect can be achieved without delivery taking place, as illustrated in the following example. Suppose a farmer grows canola and wishes to pre-sell his expected harvest at current prices. This can be achieved by selling a futures contract promising November delivery of 10,000 tonnes at $365 per 100 tonnes. In November, if the price of canola is $365 per 100 tonnes, the futures contract will be worth nothing and the farmer will sell the harvest in the open market. If the price has fallen to $335 (which is the risk that was being hedged), he can close out his futures position at a profit of $30 per 100 tonnes, which will offset the lower price he obtains for selling the canola in the market. If the price has risen to $385, the farmer loses $20 per 100 tonnes on the futures contract. This offsets the higher selling price for the canola; however, this is the cost of obtaining "insurance."

Speculators invest through futures to exploit the leverage and flexibility afforded by these contracts. In the example above, the farmer may have sold the futures contracts to a speculator who was speculating that the price of canola would increase. Therefore, we observe that the futures market can serve as a mechanism for transferring risk from those wanting to avoid it, to those willing to accept it.

- Financial futures contracts permit investors to hedge their equity or debt instruments relatively inexpensively, since only a margin deposit is required. In addition, they are ideal for speculation due to the leverage they provide.

Program trading involves the use of computers to track the prices of several assets, and make purchase and sale recommendations based on the stated program objectives. For example, an arbitrage trading program might track the prices of all assets in the S&P/TSE 60 Index, and search for an opportunity to profit from discrepancies between these prices and the prices of futures or options contracts on the index. Typically, exploiting these discrepancies will only be possible for professional traders facing low commission costs.

Futures markets use a **clearing corporation** to reduce default risk and to arrange deliveries as required. They also ensure that futures traders maintain adequate margin deposits.

Forwards are the *OTC equivalent of futures*. Unlike futures, the contracts are not standardized and may be tailor-made. There is no clearing corporation, so default risk is a concern to the parties involved, and forwards can also suffer from illiquidity.

- The largest users of forwards are banks, who issue these contracts to hedgers such as pension funds, manufacturers, and corporations. The banks trade foreign exchange and interest rate products, often in the form of swaps.

Chapter 9: Review Questions

1. Rights trade ex rights _____ business days prior to a record date.　　　　( )

   a) two

   b) three

   c) four

   d) five

2. _____ warrants may be received as part of the exercise of original warrants and typically have higher exercise prices.　　　　( )

   a) Put

   b) Piggy back

   c) Commodity-indexed

   d) Call

3. Most OTC options are _____ style.　　　　( )

   a) European

   b) American

   c) Canadian

   d) British

Refer to the following information to answer Questions 4-6:

An investor obtains the following market prices for a call and put option on a common share that is presently trading at $12.00 per share: (i) call option—exercise price is $15.00 and the call premium is $3.00; and (ii) put option—exercise price is $16.00 and the put premium is $4.50.

4. What is the intrinsic value of each option?　　　　( )

   a) Call: $3; put: 0

   b) Call: $3; put: $4

   c) Call: 0; put: $4

   d) Call: 0; put: 0

( )

5. What is the total profit for an investor who purchases one contract of each of these options if they hold them to expiration date at which time the share price is $16.00?

    a) loss of $650

    b) gain of $100

    c) gain of $650

    d) loss of $100

( )

6. An *increase* in which of the following will cause the price of a call option to decrease?

    I. Share price

    II. Volatility

    III. Exercise price

    IV. Riskless rate

    V. Time to expiration

    VI. Dividends paid

    a) I, IV

    b) I, VI

    c) II, IV

    d) III, VI

( )

7. Refer to the variables in Question 6 above. An increase in which variables will cause an increase in both the price of a call option and the price of a put option?

    a) III, IV

    b) IV, V

    c) II, V

    d) II, VI

Use the following information to answer Questions 8-9:

A company has issued warrants which are presently outstanding. One warrant is required to purchase one common share. The common share price is presently $10, the warrant price is $3, and the exercise price of the warrant is $12.

( )

8. The intrinsic value of one warrant is:

    a) 0

    b) $2

    c) $5

    d) none of the above

9. The time value of one warrant is: ( )

   a) $0

   b) $2

   c) $3

   d) none of the above

10. Which of the following statements are true? ( )

    I. Futures markets use a clearing corporation to reduce default risk and to arrange deliveries as required.

    II. Forward contracts are not standardized and may be tailor-made.

    III. Forward markets use a clearing corporation similar to the future markets.

    IV. Futures markets suffer from illiquidity.

    a) I, II, III

    b) I, III, IV

    c) I, II

    d) I, II, III, IV

Refer to the following information to answer Questions 11-12:

Suppose ABC Company issued rights with a subscription price of $35 with an ex rights date of June 6 where four rights are required to purchase one common share and: (a) June 5: share price is $40; (b) June 6: share price is $38; and (c) June 10: share price is $21.00.

11. What is the intrinsic value of the rights on June 5? ( )

    a) $5.00

    b) $2.50

    c) $1.25

    d) none of the above

12. What is the intrinsic value of the rights on June 6? ( )

    a) $3.00

    b) $1.50

    c) $0.75

    d) $0.60

ANALYZING MARKETS AND PRODUCTS

chapter

10

OVERVIEW

- This chapter deals with the factors that affect equity and bond markets including: the economy and the business cycle, industry cycles, interest rates, and government policies. The objective is to determine the risks and rewards associated with investing in these securities.

Expected profitability and **interest rates** are the two most important factors affecting the value of a security. However, they are affected by the other factors identified above.

Fundamental analysis looks at the economy, the industry, and the company. The most important factor affecting security prices is considered to be the expected future profitability of the issuer. **Technical analysis** looks at stock trading prices, trading volumes, and other market data, in the hopes of identifying recurring patterns. Both methods may use **quantitative analysis** to identify historical patterns of interest rates, economic variables, and industry or stock valuations to measure the factors influencing investment decisions.

- Investors are assumed to be rational, profit seeking individuals who react quickly to, and try to anticipate, new information.

The **Efficient Markets Hypothesis (EMH)** states that asset prices fully reflect available information.

The Random Walk Theory suggests that in efficient markets, prices will follow a "random walk" where prices change randomly (in response to new information which by nature is unpredictable). In other words, there should be no persisting patterns in asset returns.

The Rational Expectations Hypothesis assumes that people are rational and make intelligent economic decisions that are consistent with the evaluation of all available information. It assumes everyone has access to the same information and uses it wisely to best serve their own interest.

- Many studies have been conducted which suggest that markets are in general efficient despite the existence of temporary or small inefficiencies or anomalies. However, it seems unlikely that new information is available to all investors at the same time, that they will react immediately to all information in the same way, and that everyone has the ability to make accurate forecasts and correct decisions. Therefore, it is reasonable to assume that there may exist "opportunities" to earn abnormal returns, and intelligent investors will be ready to exploit them as they arise. With this in mind, a better understanding of how macroeconomic, industry, and company factors influence asset valuation should lead to better investment results.

FUNDAMENTAL MACROECONOMIC ANALYSIS

- Some of the macroeconomic factors that affect investor expectations and thus security prices include:

  1. **External Effects:** include international events such as wars and election results, as well changes in the forces of demand and supply which impact on commodity prices and currency markets.

  2. **Fiscal Policies:** taxes, government spending, and accumulated government deficits impact securities prices through their impact on investment and corporate profitability.

  3. **Monetary Policy:** changes in monetary policy impact interest rates and corporate profitability in several ways. U.S. monetary policy decisions made by the U.S. Federal Reserve Board are a crucial factor affecting Canadian securities prices. This is partially attributable to our reliance on foreign funding to finance our large accumulated debt. The large amount of outstanding government debt has led to substantial growth in bond markets. In addition, monetary policy has a large impact on inflation, which in turn affects the level of T-bill and bond yields. When inflation concerns mount, the Federal Reserve Board must do something to calm bond market uncertainty (i.e., by raising short-term rates to combat inflationary pressures), which can lead to more moderate economic growth or even a growth recession. Since equity markets compete directly with bond markets, this impacts on the value of all securities.

     A "**tilting of the yield curve**" refers to a situation where short-term rates rise while long-term rates fall. This tends to be good news for equity markets, since the short-term rate increase relieves inflationary pressures, while the decline in long-term rates enhances the attractiveness of equities relative to bonds, whose yields are falling. Strong evidence suggests that U.S. and Canadian equity markets rally when the yield curve tilts, and the gains increase as the degree of tilt increases. These tilts have occurred more frequently since the 1980s.

4. **Flow of Funds:** large capital flows from one asset class to another are determined by shifts in Canadian retail and institutional investors' demand for stocks and bonds, and by changes in the demands by foreign investors. Net Canadian equity mutual fund purchases is often cited as an important factor influencing the TSE 300. Since falling interest rates lead to increased stock prices, we would expect equity fund purchases to rise as interest rates fall, which is generally the case.

5. **Inflation:** inflationary pressures cause uncertainty regarding the future, which often leads to higher interest rates, lower profitability, and lower price-earnings (P/E) multiples. Inflation causes higher inventory and labour costs to manufacturers, who may not be able to pass on the total increase in these costs. The growth in the level of the return on equity (ROE) for the TSE 300 (which serves as a proxy for the general level of corporate profits), is highly correlated with changes in GDP and changes in inflation.

INDUSTRY ANALYSIS

- Industry and company profitability may be as much a function of industry structure as it is of the product which the industry sells. This structure, in turn, reflects the strategies pursued by companies within the industry.

- The TSE 300 Composite Index has traditionally been classified into 14 major groups and 40 subgroups of stocks.[1] It is important for investors to try and assess the prospects for growth and degree of risk associated with different industries. Three basic questions to examine are: the comparison of industry growth in sales with that of nominal GDP; the comparison of volume sales with real GDP; and how an industry price index compares with the overall inflation rate.

In order to sustain a competitive advantage that will enable them to survive in both the short- and long-run, companies generally strive to become either:

- a **low-cost producer**
- a producer of a **"differentiated" product**, which has perceived distinct advantages or features from potential competing products.

---

[1] In February 2001, the TSE announced that it would eliminate its 14 industry groupings and phase in a new 10-sector system devised by Standard & Poor's Corp.

Generally all industries exhibit a **life cycle** which includes the following stages:

1. **Emerging** or **Initial Growth:** these industries are generally in the process of introducing new goods or services, and may be experiencing negative cash flows and profitability. As a result, these industries may exhibit low or meaningless P/E ratios, provide low dividend yields, and are very risky in nature.

2. **Rapid Growth:** during this stage, sales and earnings are growing more rapidly than most other industries, and profit margins and cash flows may increase. Typically, growth will be financed to the extent possible from reinvested earnings, and these industries will exhibit low dividend yields. They may exhibit high P/E ratios to reflect the growth opportunities available; however, they may also exhibit above-average risk.

3. **Mature Industries:** these are characterized by a dramatic slowing of growth and a "squeeze" on profit margins as competition escalates. These industries are characaterized by slower, more stable growth rates in sales and earnings, and firms usually have greater financial resources available to them. As a result, dividend yields tend to be higher.

4. **Declining Industries:** growth rates may begin to decline, and profit margins may fall.

Five competitive forces determine the attractiveness of an industry, and its prospects for future growth:

1. ease of entry or exit;
2. degree of competition;
3. availability of substitutes;
4. ability to exert pressure over selling price of products; and
5. ability to exert pressure over the purchase price of inputs.

The **return on equity (ROE)** is a financial ratio of particular importance to shareholders of a company because it measures the profitability of the business, relative to the equity investment in that business. It is calculated as:

Return on Total Equity = (net earnings before extraordinary items) ÷ (total common equity)

This ratio shows how well the capital contributed by common shareholders has been used to generate profits.

Industries are often classified as **cyclical**, **defensive**, or **speculative**. Cyclical industries are those whose earnings are affected to a larger than average amount by downturns in the business cycle. As a rule the ROE of cyclical industries would vary by at least 100% over a complete business cycle, versus one-third for defensive industries, and about 55% for the TSE 300. The TSE 300 has about 80 deeply cyclical companies and about 220 stable companies; however, the cyclical ones are larger, so the resulting percentages of market capitalization of the index are close to 50/50.

- Most TSE 300 cyclical companies are large international exporters of commodities such as lumber, nickel, copper, and oil. **Commodity based cyclicals** include industries such as forestry products, mining, and chemicals. **Industry cyclicals** include transportation, capital goods, and basic industries (steel, building materials), while **consumer cyclicals** include merchandising companies and automobiles.

- Defensive stocks are those whose sales and earnings are less affected by swings in the business cycle, resulting in more stable values of ROE. **Blue chip stocks** are those that can be considered of superior investment quality, and their earnings are more stable during periods of growth or recession. Usually they have a solid record characterized by a dominant market position, strong internal financing, and effective management. While Canadian banks fit the profile of blue chip stocks in many regards, their earnings fluctuate a great deal in response to changes in interest rates. This is true because they are forced to offer higher savings rates when interest rates rise, but they are locked in to fixed rates for mortgage income, which results in a squeeze on profits. Also, as with utility companies, they pay out relatively high dividend amounts, and their prices will decline as a result of increasing interest rates.

- Speculative industries are usually so called because there is a great deal of risk and uncertainty associated with them due to the absence of definitive information.

FUNDAMENTAL COMPANY ANALYSIS

- Fundamental company analysis involves: quantitative analysis, which focuses on financial statement and market data; and qualitative analysis, which assesses less tangible factors such as the quality of management and firm reputation. The objective is to gain insight into the factors that affect company profitability. A good starting point is an examination of the company's financial statements.

- Earnings statement analysis examines trends, and reasons for trends, in variables such as:

  - sales;
  - operating costs and profitability;
  - key financial ratios relating to profitability such as the pre-tax profit margin;
  - the net profit margin;
  - the ROE;
  - cash flow measures;
  - earnings per share (EPS); and
  - the company's dividend record.

- Balance sheet analysis provides a picture of the company's overall financial position and examines:

    ○ the effect of leverage on earnings;

    ○ the company's capital structure, which provides a picture of the company's overall financial soundness; and

    ○ what types of securities have been or might be issued.

- Investors will also be concerned with the degree of liquidity associated with corporate securities.

- Timing of share transactions may be a crucial factor in successful investments. Changing market sentiment can produce large swings in equity prices. These sentiments are determined largely by investor expectations regarding future economic conditions and corporate earnings. The P/E ratio is often used as a timing device by assessing reasonable values for stocks at any time in the business cycle, since they tend to increase during rising stock markets and/or during periods of rising earnings or falling interest rates. P/E levels also reflect overall levels of investor confidence.

- It is essential that investors continually monitor their investments and the companies whose shares they purchase, since conditions change quickly and continuously.

INTERPRETING FINANCIAL STATEMENTS

- Ratio analysis is one of the most commonly used approaches to examine a company's financial performance. A single ratio has limited value; however, they provide "relative" measures of performance/risk characteristics of firms when they are compared with other ratios. Normally this involves:

    1. trend analysis; and
    2. comparison with similar companies or industry averages.

Four areas of firm operations that are often analyzed by reference to ratios are:

    1. **Liquidity:** the firm's ability to generate required cash in a hurry to meet its short-term obligations.

    2. **Risk Analysis:** concerned with the company's ability to deal with its debt, with regards to its ability to repay, and its ability to assume more debt.

    3. **Operating Performance:** concerned with the company's ability to make efficient use of its assets to generate profits.

    4. **Value:** relates the market value and returns associated with the company's shares to its accounting values.

- Internal trend lines are constructed by selecting a base period, and setting the ratio for that period as 100, and relating future ratio values to this figure. For example if the earnings per share (EPS) figures for five successive years are $1.00, $1.20, $1.30, $1.10, and $0.90 and we set the base of 100 equal to the first year's EPS figure, the trend line values will be 100, 120, 130, 110, and 90. The advantages of this approach are that it is simple arithmetically and is easy to interpret changes through the years. Two disadvantages of using trend lines arise if the base year does not have a typical value, or is negative (e.g., if a loss occurred).

- External comparisons must be careful to compare firms with similar firms, and whose ratios have been calculated according to the same basis. For example, it would be incorrect to compare the P/E ratios of two companies if one was calculated based on the year-end price, while the other was determined using the average price over the year. In Canada, Dun and Bradstreet, the Canadian Manufacturers Association, and some banks provide industry ratios for comparison purposes.

- This section presents a large number of ratios, some are difficult to remember and calculate, while others are more straightforward. As you work your way through the material, there are four main things to remember about the ratios:

  1. what they measure (i.e., what type of information they provide);
  2. if a higher ratio is better (or worse) for the company;
  3. the rules of thumb (where applicable); and
  4. how to calculate the ratio.

  The exam will include a variety of questions covering most of these topics with regards to the ratios included on the exam.

- Ratios will be calculated for the following company throughout the remainder of this section.

XYZ COMPANY
Income Statement and Balance Sheet

INCOME STATEMENT

Total Revenue	$1,426,000
Cost of Goods Sold	1,238,700
Depreciation/Amortization	40,100
General, Selling & Admin. Expense	33,100
Earnings before Interest and Taxes	114,100
Interest Expense	5,300
Pre-tax Income	108,800

Income Tax:

Current	10,900
Deferred	9,000
Earnings before Extraordinary Items	88,900
Extraordinary Items	0
Income after Extraordinary Items	88,900
Dividends—Preferred Shares	3,500
Income Available to Common Shares	85,400
Earnings / Common Share	0.68
Common Shares—Year End	125,658
Common Shares—Average	125,536
Preferred Shares—Year End	3,166
Dividends—Common Shares	14,700
Market Price per Share (Close)	6.69

BALANCE SHEET

Assets:

Cash & Equivalents	$150,000
Accounts Receivable	174,000
Inventory	220,200
Total Current Assets	544,200
Fixed Assets—Gross	1,372,700
Less: Accumulated Depreciation	(766,200)
Fixed Assets—Net	606,500
Total Assets	1,150,700

Liabilities & Equity:

Bank Loans & Equivalents		147,800
Accounts Payable		347,200
Current Portion of Long-Term Debt		5,400
Total Current Liabilities		500,400
Long-Term Debt		83,500
Deferred Taxes		41,600
Equity:	Preferred Stock	158,300
	Common Stock	190,600
	Retained Earnings	176,300
	Total Equity	525,200
Total Liabilities & Equity		1,150,700

ANALYZING LIQUIDITY:

Commonly used liquidity indicators include the following:

1. **Working Capital (or net current assets) = current assets − current liabilities**
2. **Current Ratio = (current assets) ÷ (current liabilities)**
3. **Quick (or Acid Test) Ratio = (current assets − inventory) ÷ (current liabilities)**

The **current ratio** measures a firm's ability to repay current obligations from current assets, while the **quick ratio** is a more conservative estimate of liquidity that reflects the fact that inventories are generally not as "liquid" as other current assets. As with most ratios there is no absolute standard for these ratios, but higher values suggest greater firm liquidity. Cash forecasts can provide additional insight into the firm's liquidity situation.

Example 1: For Company XYZ: ─────────────────

Working Capital   = 544,200 − 500,400 = $43,800
Current ratio   = 544,200/500,400 = 1.09
Quick ratio   = (544,200 − 220,200)/500,400 = 0.65

General **rules of thumb (ROT)** are that current and quick ratios should be greater than 2.0 and 1.0 for both utilities and industrials. Thus, Company XYZ does not satisfy the suggested ROT for the current or quick ratios, and may not have adequate liquidity, according to these guidelines.

RISK ANALYSIS:

- Commonly used indicators of a firm's debt situation are:

1. asset coverage;
2. debt percentage of total capital;
3. debt / equity ratio;
4. cash flow / total debt;
5. interest coverage; and
6. preferred dividend coverage.

All of these ratios are discussed below.

1. **Asset Coverage = (total assets − deferred charges − intangible assets − [current liabilities *less* short-term debt such as bank advances and the current portion of long-term debt]) ÷ (total debt outstanding/$1,000), where total debt = short-term debt + current portion of long-term debt + long-term debt**

- This measures the protection provided by the firm's tangible assets, after all prior liabilities have been met. Assets well in excess of company debt are required to generate sufficient earnings to meet interest obligations and repay indebtedness. Additionally, asset coverage shows the book value amount of assets backing the debt securities.

Example 2: For Company XYZ: ——————————

Asset coverage = (1,150,700 − 0 − 0 − [500,400 − 147,800 − 5,400]) ÷ ([147,800 + 5,400 + 83,500] / $1,000) = (803,500) / (236.7) = $3,394.59

As **rules of thumb**, utilities and industrials should maintain at least $1,500 and $2,000 of net tangible assets per $1,000 of debt outstanding. Thus, Company XYZ exceeds the ROT for both utilities and industrials, and provides more than adequate coverage of debt in the form of tangible assets, according to these guidelines.

2. **Debt Percentage of Total Capital = (total debt) ÷ (invested capital), where, invested capital = short-term debt + current portion of long-term debt + long-term debt + preferred stock + common equity**

    Note: some analysts also include deferred taxes as a source of capital, but not the CSC.

- This shows what percentage of total invested capital debtholders are entitled to.

Example 3: For Company XYZ: ——————————

Debt percentage of invested capital = ([147,800 + 5,400 + 83,500] / [147,800 + 5,400 + 83,500 + 158,300 + 190,600 + 176,300]) × 100% = 31.1%

Rules of thumb are that total debt outstanding for utilities and industrials should not exceed 60% and one-third of total capital. Thus, XYZ satisfies the ROT for both utilities and industrials, and does not appear to have too much debt financing according to these guidelines.

3. **Debt/Equity Ratio = (total debt outstanding) ÷ (book value of shareholders' equity)**.

- This ratio pinpoints the relationship of debt to equity and is a direct measure of financial risk.

Example 4: For Company XYZ: ——————————

Debt/equity ratio = (147,800 + 5,400 + 83,500) / 525,200 = 0.45

Rules of thumb suggest that utilities and industrials maintain debt/equity ratios below 1.5 and 0.5. Thus, XYZ satisfies the ROT for both utilities and industrials, and does not appear to have assumed too much debt according to these guidelines.

4. **Cash Flow/Total Debt = (cash flow) ÷ (total debt), where, cash flow = net earnings before extraordinary items (BEI) − equity income + minority interest in earnings of subsidiary companies + deferred income taxes + depreciation + any other deductions not paid out in cash (e.g., depletion, amortization, etc.)**

- Cash flow provides a better indicator of a firm's ability to cover interest payments, pay dividends, and finance expansion because of the substantial size of non-cash items on earnings statements.

Example 5: For Company XYZ:

Cash flow/total debt = ([88,900 − 0 + 0 + 9,000 + 40,100] / [147,800 + 5,400 + 83,500]) × 100% = 55.8%

Rules of thumb suggest that utilities and industrials maintain debt repayment capacity of at least 20% and 30% for each of the last five years. Thus, XYZ satisfies the ROT for both utilities and industrials for this year, and has more than adequate debt coverage, according to these guidelines.

5. **Interest Coverage = (net earnings BEI − equity income + minority interest in earnings of subsidiary companies + all income taxes + total interest charges) ÷ (total interest charges)**

- This ratio is generally considered to be the most important quantitative test, since it measures a firm's ability to meet debt obligations, and a stable trend is important.

Example 6: For Company XYZ:

Interest coverage = (88,900 − 0 + 0 + 19,900 + 5,300) / 5,300 = 21.53

Rules of thumb are that utilities and industrials exhibit coverage ratios of at least 2.0 and 3.0 for each of the last five years. Thus, XYZ satisfies the ROT for both utilities and industrials for this year, and has more than adequate coverage according to these guidelines.

6. **Preferred Dividend Coverage = (net earnings BEI − equity income + minority interest in earnings of subsidiary companies + all income taxes + total interest charges) ÷ (total interest charges + before-tax preferred dividend payments), where, Before-tax dividend payments = actual dividend payments × (100 / [100 − tax rate])**

- Since it is not always possible to determine a company's actual tax rate, it is often useful to determine its apparent tax rate which may be calculated as follows:

   Apparent Tax Rate = (current and deferred income taxes) ÷ (net earnings BEI − equity income + minority interest in earnings of subsidiary companies + current and deferred taxes)

- This is similar to interest coverage, except that before-tax preferred dividend payments are added to interest payments, as the fixed obligation to be covered.

Example 7: For Company XYZ: ————————————————

Apparent tax rate = ([10,900 + 9,000] ÷ [88,900 − 0 + 0 + 10,900 + 9,000]) × 100% = (19,900) / (108,800) × 100% = 18.29%

Before-tax dividend payments = 3,500 × (100 / [100 - 18.29]) = $4,283

Preferred dividend coverage = (88,900 − 0 + 0 + 19,900 + 5,300) / (5,300 + 4,283) = 11.91

Rules of thumb are the same as for interest coverage ratios. Thus XYZ satisfies the ROT for this year for both utilities and industrials, and offers adequate coverage according to these guidelines.

OPERATING PERFORMANCE:

- Some commonly used measures of operating performance are:
    1. gross profit margin;
    2. operating profit margin;
    3. pre-tax profit margin;
    4. net profit margin;
    5. pre-tax return on capital;
    6. net (or after-tax) return on capital;
    7. net (or after-tax) return on common equity; and
    8. inventory turnover ratio.

All of these ratios are discussed below.

1. **Gross Profit Margin = (net sales − cost of goods sold) ÷ (net sales)**

- This ratio indicates the efficiency of management in turning over the company's goods at a profit. There are no recommended rules of thumb, but higher is better.

Example 8: For Company XYZ: ————————————————

Gross profit margin = ([1,426,000 − 1,238,700] / 1,426,000) × 100% = 13.1%

2. **Operating Profit Margin = (net sales − cost of goods sold − selling, general and administrative expenses) ÷ (net sales)**

- This is similar to the gross margin; however, it is more stringent and also takes into account selling, general, and administrative expenses incurred in producing earnings. There are are no recommended rules of thumb, but higher is better.

Example 9: For Company XYZ:

Operating profit margin = ([1,426,000 − 1,238,700 − 33,100] / 1,426,000) × 100% = 10.8%

3. **Pre-Tax Profit Margin = (net income before taxes) ÷ (net sales)**

- This measure accounts for profitability after the affect of interest expenses, but before consideration of taxes. There are are no recommended rules of thumb.

Example 10: For Company XYZ:

Pre-tax profit margin = (108,800 / 1,426,000) × 100% = 7.6%

4. **Net Profit Margin = (net earnings BEI − equity income + minority interest in earnings of subsidiary companies) ÷ (net sales)**

- This measure accounts for expenses and taxes, and effectively sums up in one figure management's ability to run the business. Adjustments for minority interest and equity income are made to enhance comparability across firms, since not all companies have these items. There are no recommended rules of thumb, but higher is better.

Example 11: For Company XYZ:

Net profit margin = ([88,900 − 0 + 0] / 1,426,000) × 100% = 6.2%

5. **Pre-Tax Return on Capital = (net earnings BEI + income taxes + total interest charges) ÷ (invested capital)**

- This ratio is calculated without reference to who supplied the capital, and demonstrates how well management has employed the assets at its disposal. There are are no recommended rules of thumb, but higher is better.

Example 12: For Company XYZ:

Pre-tax return on capital = ([88,900 + 19,900 + 5,300] / [147,800 + 5,400 + 83,500 + 525,200]) × 100% = 15.0%

6. **Net or After-Tax Return on Capital = (net earnings BEI + total after-tax interest charges) ÷ (invested capital), where, total after-tax interest charges = total interest charges × (1 − tax rate)**

- This is the same as (4), except that taxes are also considered. There are no recommended rules of thumb, but higher is better.

! **Example 13: For Company XYZ:** ————————

After-tax interest charges = 5,300 × (1 − 0.1829) = $4,331

After-tax (net) return on capital = ([88,900 + 4,331] / [147,800 + 5,400 + 83,500 + 525,200]) × 100% = 12.2%

! 7. **Net (After-Tax) Return on Common Equity = (net earnings BEI − preferred dividend) ÷ (total common equity)**

- This ratio shows how well the capital contributed by common shareholders has been used to generate profits.

! **Example 14: For Company XYZ:** ————————

Net return on common equity = ([88,900 − 3,500] / [190,600 + 176,300]) × 100% = 23.3%

- Some analysts suggest that taxes are an expense of doing business, and note that the proportion of equity to capitalization changes from period to period and, therefore, prefer measure (6) to measures (5) and (7).

! 8a. **Inventory Turnover Ratio = (cost of goods sold) ÷ (inventory)**

Sometimes net sales is used to replace cost of goods sold, so if this information is unavailable, we also have:

8b. **Inventory Turnover Ratio = (net sales) ÷ (inventory)**

- There are no general rules of thumb. This ratio varies significantly across industries. Higher ratios suggest that a company is selling existing inventory more quickly than their competitors. As a result it faces less risk of being caught with too much inventory in the event of price declines, or maintaining obsolete or damaged inventory. Low inventory turnover can cause a significant increase in financing charges if inventory accumulates, since it represents a large part of a company's working capital. Low turnover could be due to:

  - large portions of unsaleable goods;
  - the firm has too much inventory on hand; or
  - the inventory value is inflated.

! **Example 15: For Company XYZ:** ————————

Using (8a) Inventory turnover = 1,238,700 / 220,200 = 5.62 times

ANALYZING VALUE:

- Some commonly used value ratios are:

  1a. dividend payout ratio (including preferred);

  1b. dividend payout (common);

  2a. earnings per share;

  2b. fully diluted earnings per share;

  3. dividend yield;

  4. price-earnings ratio;

  5a. equity value (book value) per preferred share; and

  5b. equity value (book value) per common share.

These ratios are discussed below. They provide a way of relating market value to dividends and earnings.

1a. **Dividend Payout (Including Preferred) = (total dividends) ÷ (net earnings BEI)** !

1b. **Dividend Payout (Common) = (common dividends) ÷ (net earnings BEI − preferred dividends)** !

- These ratios indicate the percentage of earnings being paid out as dividends, and the amount being reinvested for future growth. Since management generally tries to maintain steady dividend payments, an unstable payout ratio is usually associated with unstable earnings. There are no general rules of thumb.

Example 16: For Company XYZ: !

Dividend payout (including preferred) = ([14,700 + 3,500] / [88,900]) × 100% = 20.5%

Dividend payout (common) = ([14,700] / [88,900 − 3,500]) × 100% = 17.2%

2a. **Earnings per Share (EPS) = (net earnings BEI − preferred dividends) ÷ (number of common shares outstanding)** !

- It is one of the most widely used and understood of all ratios, and provides common shareholders with a measure of earnings available to them after all other obligations have been met, and provides a clue as to the company's ability to maintain or increase dividend payments. There are no general rules of thumb, but higher is better.

2b. **Fully Diluted EPS = (adjusted net earnings BEI) ÷ (adjusted common shares outstanding)** !

- This figure reflects the EPS available to common shareholders if all securities such as convertible preferred stock or debentures, stock options, and warrants were converted into common shares. The adjusted earnings figure would reflect the fact that interest would no longer be payable on convertible debt, and it would not be necessary to subtract the preferred dividends on the convertible preferred shares. The adjusted common shares figure would be increased to reflect the new number of shares outstanding if all securities were converted.

Example 17: For Company XYZ:

Earnings per share = (88,900 − 3,500) / 125,658 = $0.68

There is no mention of convertible securities, warrants, or other dilutive securities for this company; therefore, the fully diluted EPS = basic EPS.

3. **Dividend Yield = (annual dividend per share) ÷ (current market share price)**

- This ratio offers a superficial comparison of the yield offered by different common shares. There are no general rules of thumb.

Example 18: For Company XYZ:

Common dividend per share = common dividends / number of common shares outstanding = 14,700 / 125,658 = $0.117

Dividend yield (common) = (0.117 / 6.69) × 100% = 1.75%

4. **Price-Earnings (P/E) Ratio = (current market share price) ÷ (EPS)**

- This is probably the most useful and widely used ratio, because it is, in fact, all the other ratios combined into one figure. It represents the ultimate evaluation of a company and its shares by the investing public, with due consideration for tangible and intangible factors such as quality of management, future growth opportunities, and risks faced by the company. In fact, a major reason for calculating EPS is to enable a comparison with the share's market price. It enables comparisons across firms, provided they are in the same industry. The calculation above uses the most recent 12 month EPS figure; however, in practice, P/E ratios are often calculated based on projected earnings. There are no general rules of thumb.

Example 19: For Company XYZ:

Price-earnings ratio = 6.69 / 0.68 = 9.8 times

5a. **Equity Value (Book Value) per Preferred Share = (total shareholders' equity) ÷ (number of preferred shares outstanding)**

5b. **Equity Value (Book Value) per Common Share** = (total common equity) ÷ (number of common shares outstanding)

- This ratio measures the amount of assets that shareholders are entitled to if the company was to be liquidated.

Example 20: For Company XYZ:

Equity value per preferred share = (525,200) / (3,166) = $165.89

Equity value per common share = (525,200 − 150,000) / (125,668) − $2.02

The **rules of thumb** for (5a) for utilities and industrials is that they should maintain book value per preferred share of at least two times the value of assets that each preferred share would be entitled to receive in the event of liquidation, in each of the last five years. Therefore, XYZ satsifies this rule for this year, since the par value per preferred share is $50. This can be calculated by dividing the book value of preferred shares (158,300) by the number of preferred shares outstanding (3,166), which implies coverage is 165.89 / 50 = 3.32 times. There are no general rules of thumb for (5b).

ADDITIONAL RATIOS:

- Additional ratios that may be applied to companies include:
  - price to equity per share;
  - working capital to stockholders' equity;
  - working capital turnover; and
  - earnings per common share/dividend per common share.
- Some ratios are used when analyzing companies in specific industries such as:
  - sales per square foot of retail space (for retailers such as supermarkets);
  - cushion ratio (net cash flow as a percentage of gross income), which is used for evaluating real estate investments; and
  - loan loss provisions as a percentage of loans outstanding or expressed as cents per dollar of sales, which are used by banks.

FUNDAMENTAL VALUATION MODELS

The Dividend Discount Model (DDM) assumes that we value common shares according to the present value of expected future cashflows associated with the security. If we assume dividends are the relevant cash flows, we can express the relationship as:

$$P_0 = \frac{Div_1}{(1 + r)^1} + \frac{Div_2}{(1 + r)^2} + \frac{Div_3}{(1 + r)^3} + \cdots + \frac{Div_t}{(1 + r)^t} \cdots,$$

where P_0 is the intrinsic value of share price today, Div_1 is the expected dividend at the end of year one, and the required rate of return by the common shareholders (r), is the appropriate market determined risk-adjusted discount rate. If we make the assumption that dividends will grow at a constant rate (g) indefinitely, the equation above reduces to the following equation which is often referred to as the constant-growth version of the DDM or Gordon's Dividend Growth Model:

$$P_0 = \frac{Div_1}{r - g}$$

Notice that the discount rate depends largely on the general level of interest rates.

Example 21:

Determine the share price of a stock that is expected to pay an annual year-end dividend of $1.00, which is expected to grow indefinitely at an annual rate of 5% per year, if the required return on these shares is 15%.

Solution:

$$P_0 = \frac{Div_1}{r - g} = \frac{\$1.00}{.15 - .05} = \$10.00$$

- The DDM has a great deal of intuitive appeal, because it links equity prices to three important "fundamentals": corporate profitability (through their link with dividends); the general level of interest rates; and risk (the latter two through their impact on the discount rate).

In particular, all else being equal, the model predicts that the intrinsic value of common shares will **increase** as a result of:

1. increases in expected dividends as measured by Div_1, which are closely related to profitability;

2. increases in the growth rate (g) of these dividends; and

3. decreases in the appropriate discount rate (r), which will be an increasing function of the general level of interest rates, as well as the riskiness of the underlying security.

The constant-growth version of the DDM can be rearranged in the following manner, using the present market price in place of intrinsic value, to obtain an estimate of the return required by investors on a particular share:

$$r = \frac{Div_1}{P_0} + g$$

Example 22:

Determine the required rate of return on a stock that is expected to pay an annual year-end dividend of $2.00, which is expected to grow indefinitely at an annual rate of 4% per year, if the shares are trading at $20.

Solution:

$$r = \frac{2.00}{20} + .04 = .140 \text{ or } 14\%$$

An expression for the P/E ratio can be derived from the DDM, by determining the payout ratio (b) associated with a given dividend. In other words, if we define EPS_1 as the expected earnings per share during year one, we can express the DDM as:

$$P_0 = \frac{EPS_1 \times b}{r - g}$$

Dividing both sides of this by EPS_1, we get:

$$\mathbf{P/E} = \frac{\mathbf{b}}{\mathbf{r - g}}$$

This equation implies, all else being equal, that P/E ratios will increase:

1. as a firm increases its payout ratio;
2. as the discount rate falls—which could be caused by falling inflation (which will cause the general level of interest rates to decline), and/or a decline in the riskiness of expected cash flows; and
3. as the growth rate in dividends (or earnings) increases.

• Generally, existing shareholders like to see high P/E ratios as they indicate good growth prospects and/or lower riskiness associated with the firm's cash flows. It is important to remember the phrase "other things being equal" because usually other things are not equal and the preceding relationships do not hold by themselves. It is quite obvious, upon reflection, that if a firm could increase its estimated P/E ratio, and therefore its market price, by simply raising its payout ratio, it would be very tempted to do so. However, such an action would in all likelihood reduce future growth prospects, lowering g, and thereby defeating the increase in the payout. Similarly, trying to increase g by taking on particularly risky investment projects would cause investors to demand a higher required rate of return, thereby raising r. Again, this would work to offset the positive effects of the increase in g. Variables 2 and 3 are typically the most important factors in the preceding determination of the P/E ratio because a small change in either can have a large effect on its value.

! Example 23:

Determine an appropriate P/E ratio for a stock, if the company maintains a payout ratio of 53.5% under the following conditions:

(a)   r = 15%, and g = 7%

(b)   r = 16%, and g = 7%

(c)   r = 15%, and g = 8%

Solution:

(a) $\text{P/E} = \dfrac{0.535}{0.15 - .07} = 6.69$

(b) $\text{P/E} = \dfrac{0.535}{0.16 - .07} = 5.94$

(c) $\text{P/E} = \dfrac{0.535}{0.15 - .08} = 7.64$

- Often people say that a share represents a "buy" opportunity due to a low P/E ratio. The implication is that the share is undervalued relative to its earnings. However, market efficiency implies that this need not be (and in fact should not be) the case, as each security should be priced to reflect all relevant information about the firm.

STOCK INDICES AND AVERAGES

! An **index** is a number that measures a number of stock prices so that a percentage change in this index may be calculated over time. They are used for performance comparisons and to gauge overall movements in the stock market. An **average** is used for the same purposes as an index, but it is unlike an index because it is determined by summing a number of prices and dividing this sum by the number of items composing the average; therefore it is composed of equally weighted items.

! The present TSE 300 Composite Index System was introduced in 1977; however, historical data is available as far back as 1956. The value of the **TSE 300 Composite Index** is determined by the total market capitalization (the number of common shares outstanding times the market price per share) of a portfolio of 300 of the largest Canadian stocks. In other words, it is *a market- or value-weighted index*. Thus, a stock's weight changes in response to changes in share price and/or the number of shares outstanding. The stocks that are included in the TSE 300 are reviewed every year, and new stocks are added to replace those that no longer satisfy the criteria for inclusion.

- The 300 stocks included in the TSE 300 are classified by industry to form 14 major group indices, and 40 sub-groups are also tracked. As mentioned previously, this system is scheduled to be replaced by a 10-industry classification system devised by Standard & Poor's Corporation (S&P) in the near future. The base value of 1,000 was set for all indices for the base year of 1975.

- The TSE 100 and TSE 200 were introduced in 1993 and are designed primarily for institutional investors as an instrument for index or passive management. The base value for both of these indices was set at 250 as of August 31, 1993. The TSE 100 includes the 100 largest and most liquid TSE stocks, and includes Consumer, Industrial, Interest Sensitive, and Resource sectors. The TSE 200 includes the remaining 200 stocks in the TSE 300, and is used as a proxy for returns on small-cap stocks.

- Total Return indices were introduced in 1980 and measure the return on the indices if all dividends had been reinvested. As such, they measure the actual total returns that would have been achieved by holding those stocks on a continuous basis. Their base value is set at 1,000 as of December 31, 1976.

The **S&P/TSE 60**, which is also a market-weighted index, was introduced on December 31, 1998. It is managed by S&P and the index base value was set equal to 100 as of January 29, 1982 (which differs from the base year of 1975 for the TSE 300 Index). This base period was chosen due to concerns regarding data reliability prior to this date. This is the index upon which the value of i60 units is based. It is also the basis for equity index option and futures products that trade on the ME.

The **S&P/TSE SmallCap** and **MidCap** stock indices were introduced in April 1999. The MidCap index contains the 60 TSE 300 stocks that are ranked below those in the S&P/TSE 60 Index in terms of market capitalization; while the SmallCap Index contains the remaining TSE 300 stocks.

- A relative strength graph plots the performance of stocks or indices relative to other benchmarks and is useful for comparative purposes.

The Canadian Venture Exchange (CDNX) maintains four indices:

1. the **CDNX Composite Index**, which is the main index, and three sector indices below;
2. mining;
3. oil and gas; and
4. technology.

The indices are equally weighted, and each is composed of the top 80% of index-eligible securities by market capitalization. The indices were set to a value of 2,000 at the start of CDNX trading on November 29, 1999.

The **Dow Jones Industrial Average (DJIA)** is the most widely quoted measure of NYSE stock performance, despite the fact that it includes only 30 of over 2,300 stocks that trade on the NYSE. It is a *price-weighted average* and is therefore affected more by changes in higher priced stocks. It is calculated by adding the prices of the 30 stocks

> together and dividing by a divisor, which has been revised downward through the years to reflect the impact of stock splits. The DJIA is comprised of the highest quality blue chip stocks that trade in the U.S. These stocks have relatively low risk and have tended to underperform broader based indices such as the S&P 500 Index (discussed below) in the long term as a result. Other Dow Jones indices include the Transportation average (20 companies), a Utility average (15 companies), and a Composite average (65 companies), which are all price-weighted.

> The **S&P 500 Index** is a broader based market-weighted index that measures U.S. stock performance. It is widely used to measure the investment performance of institutional investments.

- The NYSE maintains market-valued indices which include all listed equities for a given group: composite; industrials; transportation; finance and real estate; and utilities. The AMEX index is a market value weighted index, based on the market capitalization of all 800 or so stocks that trade on the American Stock Exchange. The NASDAQ Composite Index includes over 3,700 OTC stocks (market cap around 13% of NYSE stocks) and is market-valued. The Value Line Composite Index measures the average percentage change in about 1,700 stocks that are mainly second tier issues. The Wilshire 5000 Equity Index is a market-valued index that measures as many stocks as possible for which quotations are available, and is the broadest based U.S. index.

- Important international indices include:

    1. The Nikkei Stock Average (225) in Japan, which is price-weighted and has been available since 1950.
    2. The FT-SE 100 Index in the United Kingdom, which is market-weighted.
    3. The DAX in Germany, which consists of 30 blue chip stocks, and is value-weighted (assuming reinvested equity income).
    4. The CAC 40 Share Price Index in France.
    5. The Swiss Market Index in Switzerland.

TECHNICAL ANALYSIS

Technical analysis is based on three main assumptions:

1. All market actions are automatically accounted for in price activity; therefore fundamental analysis is a fruitless exercise.
2. Prices move in a series of trends and patterns that tend to persist through time.
3. The past repeats itself in the future.

- Some commonly used tools in technical analysis are discussed below. They include the following:

1. Chart Analysis;

2. Quantitative Analysis;

3. Sentiment Indicators; and

4. Cycle Analysis.

1. **Chart Analysis:** this technique uses graphs to examine where security prices have been in order to determine in which direction they may be heading. They use these charts to try to identify support and resistence levels, as well as to identify normal trading patterns. **Resistence levels** are price levels that stock prices have difficulty exceeding, because investors begin to sell the underlying securities as the prices approach these values (i.e., supply increases and demand falls at these points). **Support levels** are price levels that stock prices have difficulty falling below because investors begin to buy the underlying securities as the prices approach these values (i.e., demand increases and supply falls at these points). Some of the commonly used tools and patterns are described below.

- The most commonly used graph is a **bar chart**. Bar charts plot the range of prices over a particular interval, such as a day, a week, etc. They also usually include trading volume at the bottom of the chart.

- **Reversal patterns** are those that often precede a substantial price swing. For example, a **Bottom Head and Shoulders** formation refers to a stock price pattern that depicts an accumulation range. Once the price breaks out of this accumulation range, by breaking through the "neckline" from below, it begins a *bull* surge (i.e., prices are expected to increase). The **Top Head and Shoulders** formation implies the opposite. Once the price breaks through the neckline from above, prices are expected to decline significantly.

- **Continuation patterns** represent "sideways" patterns that are thought to represent pauses in a prevailing price trend. They are often referred to as "consolidations," with the triangle pattern representing one of the most important patterns.

2. **Quantitative Analysis:** this approach focuses on identifying trends, or providing early signals that a given trend is losing momentum. Two general categories include:

   ○ **Moving Averages (MAs):** these are calculated by adding the closing prices for a stock (or index) over a given period of time (usually 40 weeks or 200 days to attempt to align with the market primary trend). If the overall trend has been down, the MA line will be above the current individual prices, and if the price "breaks through" the moving average line from below, it generates a "buy" signal. If the overall trend has been up, the MA line will be below the current individual prices, and if the price "breaks through" the moving average line from above it generates a "sell" signal.

   ○ **Oscillators:** oscillator indicators generally fluctuate in values between 0 and 100, or from 21 to 11. They may be used to provide:

     – a signal of when a market is "overbought" or "oversold," which would be indicated when the values are near the extreme values;

- a warning regarding a weakening trend, which may occur when the oscillator diverges from the underlying price; or

- important trading signals when the oscillator crosses the zero line.

One of the most important oscillators is the **moving average convergence-divergence (MACD)** indicator. It finds the difference between two moving averages (such as the 20-day MA and the 30-day MA), and generates a smoothing line based on the difference.

3. **Sentiment Indicators:** these indicators focus on measuring investor expectations. **Contrarians** invest based on the premise that the majority of market beliefs will be wrong, on average. Therefore, they take the opposite position from prevailing confidence indicators. For example, if a survey indicated that 90% of market particpants were bearish (i.e., believed markets would decline in the near future), a contrarian would buy on such information, based on the belief the market is currently "oversold."

4. **Cycle Analysis:** this approach focuses on identifying the overall direction of market movements. They tend to focus on four different cycle lengths:

   ○ long-term (greater than two years);

   ○ seasonal (one-year);

   ○ primary/intermediate (nine to 26 weeks); and

   ○ trading (four weeks).

One of the most popular theories is the **Elliot Wave Theory**. This theory suggests that the market moves in a series of large waves and cycles, which are superimposed by smaller waves, and so on. In particular, it suggests that the market moves up in a series of five waves and down in a series of three waves, all of which have smaller waves superimposed upon them.

- **Equity Market Analysis** may use the some of the following indicators of the soundness of equity markets in general, which are discussed below:

  1. Volume Changes;
  2. Breadth of Market:
     ○ Advance-Decline Line;
     ○ New Highs and New Lows; and
  3. Sentiment.

1. **Volume Changes:** when volume is increasing during a bull (bear) market, it indicates a lot of buying (selling) pressure, which confirms support for the the trend. If volumes are lower, the trend is not well-supported and may begin to reverse.

2. **Breadth of Market:** measures the number of different issues being traded, an increase in which suggests *bullish* conditions. Two important breadth measures are:

- **The Advance-Decline Line:** the cumulative advance-decline line adds the difference between advances and declines every day to its starting value, an increase in which suggests *bullish* conditions.

- **New Highs and New Lows:** when new highs are increasing (and new lows are decreasing), it is a *bullish* signal, while the opposite provides a bearish signal.

3. **Sentiment:** one important equity market sentiment indicator is provided by CONSENSUS INC., which is based on sentiment data for all futures markets, including S&P 500 Index futures. When the CONSENSUS Index of Bullish Market Opinion finds more than 75% of those surveyed are bullish, the market may be considered overbought and due for a correction, while when the value dips below 25%, the market is considered oversold.

- Many of the demand and supply factors that technical analysts monitor change in response to fundamental factors that affect earnings. Therefore, technical analysis is related to fundamental analysis in some sense, and it may help in timing purchases or sales, since it may indicate turning points. Its main disadvantage is the subjectivity involved in interpreting the charts and signals.

Chapter 10: Review Questions

1. All of the following would likely exert a positive influence on the general level of stock prices except for: ( )

    a) A minority government is replaced by a majority government.

    b) Short-term interest rates rise while long-term interest rates fall.

    c) Unemployment approaches the full employment unemployment rate.

    d) The government announces a significant cut in corporate tax rates.

2. The rationale for the use of technical analysis is inconsistent with: ( )

    a) the Random Walk Theory

    b) the Efficient Markets Hypothesis

    c) neither (a) nor (b)

    d) both (a) and (b)

3. Technical analysis involves: ( )

    a) looking at stock trading prices, trading volumes, and other market data

    b) looking at P/E ratios and dividend yields

    c) looking at the economy, the industry, and the company

    d) none of the above

( )   4. What is the intrinsic value of a common share that has an expected payout ratio of 37.5%, and has expected earnings per share of $4.00, if earnings and dividends are both expected to grow indefinitely at an annual rate of 5% per year, and the required return on the shares is 11%?

        a) $25.00

        b) $30.00

        c) $66.67

        d) insufficient information

( )   5. What is the implied P/E ratio for a stock that has an expected EPS of $5.00 and an expected year-end dividend of $2.00, if the appropriate discount rate is 12%, and the expected annual growth rate in dividends is 4%?

        a) 3.0 times

        b) 5.0 times

        c) 10.0 times

        d) 25.0 times

( )   6. Which of the following increases the attractiveness of an industry, with regards to the prospects for enhanced profitability of the companies within the industry?

        a) entry into the industry entails limited technological requirements

        b) there are many competitors

        c) there are very few complementary products available

        d) there are very few substitute products available

( )   7. Which of the following are cyclical industries?

        I. Forest products

        II. Automobiles

        III. Utilities

        IV. Food merchandisers

        a) I and II

        b) III and IV

        c) I and III

        d) II and IV

( )   8. Rising inflation causes P/E ratios to _____ due to the upward pressure it exerts on _____ .

        a) increase; interest rates

        b) decrease; interest rates

        c) increase; corporate profits

        d) decrease; corporate profits

9. Which of the following situations represents a bearish signal?   (   )

    a) an increase in the advance-decline line

    b) new lows are decreasing

    c) bottom head and shoulders formation

    d) none of the above

10. An investor whose primary investing objective is income would be interest-   (   )
    ed in common shares of a company in an industry in the
    life cycle stage.

    a) emerging

    b) initial growth

    c) rapid growth

    d) mature

11. Earnings statement analysis would examine each of the following except: (   )

    a) operating costs

    b) sales

    c) the effect of leverage

    d) cash flow

12. Which of the following statements about the DJIA and the TSE 300 are   (   )
    true?

    a) The DJIA is more greatly affected by stocks with a higher market cap than
        is the TSE 300.

    b) The TSE 300 is more greatly affected by stocks with a higher market cap
        than is the DJIA.

    c) Both are equally affected by stocks with a higher market cap.

    d) none of the above is true

13. What is the implied rate of return on common shares that are trading at   (   )
    $50, if they are expected to pay a year-end dividend of $4.00, that is expect-
    ed to increase at an annual rate of 4% per year?

    a) 8%

    b) 12%

    c) 14%

    d) none of the above

( )   14. Two companies A and B, are of similar size and operate in the same industry, yet the P/E ratio of A is 20, while the P/E ratio of B is 12. This may be due to the fact that:

      a) the market believes that A has greater growth potential than B

      b) the market believes that A is riskier than B

      c) both (a) and (b)

      d) neither (a) nor (b)

( )   15. The _____ is the most widely used benchmark by investment professionals in the United States.

      a) DJIA

      b) S&P 500

      c) Value Line Composite Index

      d) Nasdaq Composite Index

( )   16. The basic factor affecting shifts in demand for stocks and bonds by institutional investors is:

      a) the level of interest rates

      b) net purchases by non-residents

      c) the level of P/E ratios

      d) external effects

( )   17. "Tilting of the yield curve" is a common phrase which refers to:

      a) substituting long-term bonds for short-term bonds in a portfolio

      b) substituting short-term bonds for long-term bonds in a portfolio

      c) short-term rates rising while long-term rates fall

      d) long-term rates rising while short-term rates fall

Refer to the following Income Statement and Balance Sheet for ABC Company to answer Questions 18-21.

ABC COMPANY
Income Statement and Balance Sheet

INCOME STATEMENT

Total Revenue	$150,000
Cost of Goods Sold	105,700
Depreciation/Amortization	6,000
General, Selling & Admin. Expense	14,000
EBIT	25,00
Interest Expense	10,000
Pre-tax Income	15,000

Income Tax:

Current	5,000
Deferred	2,000
Less: Minority Interest in subsidiaries	2,000
Add: Equity Income	1,000
Earnings before Extraordinary Items	7,000
Extraordinary Items	4,000
Income after Extraordinary Items	3,000
Dividends—Preferred Shares	1,500
Common Shares—Year End	20,000
Dividends—Common Shares	2,000
Market Price per Share (Close)	10.00

BALANCE SHEET

Assets:

Cash & Equivalents	$15,000
Accounts Receivable	20,000
Inventory	30,000
Total Current Assets	65,000
Fixed Assets—Net	100,000
Goodwill	5,000
Total Assets	170,000

Liabilities & Equity:

Bank Loans & Equivalents	10,000
Accounts Payable	15,000
Current Portion of Long-Term Debt	5,000
Total Current Liabilities	30,000
Long-Term Debt	35,000
Deferred Taxes	5,000
Equity: Preferred Stock	15,000
Common Stock	20,000
Retained Earnings	65,000
Total Equity	100,000
Total Liabilities & Equity	170,000

18. What is ABC's debt-to-equity ratio?   (   )

    a) 2.00:1

    b) 0.50:1

    c) 0.55:1

    d) insufficient information

( )   19. What is ABC's book value per common share?

      a) $1.00

      b) $4.25

      c) $5.00

      d) insufficient information

( )   20. What is ABC's P/E multiple?

      a) 20.0 times

      b) 28.6 times

      c) 36.4 times

      d) 66.7 times

( )   21. What is ABC's preferred dividend coverage ratio?

      a) 1.95 times

      b) 2.50 times

      c) 8.95 times

      d) insufficient information

( )   22. What are the suggested rules of thumb for the interest coverage ratio?

      a) above 2.0 for both industrials and utilities

      b) above 2.0 for industrials and 3.0 for utilities

      c) above 3.0 for industrials and 2.0 for utilities

      d) there are no rules of thumb for this ratio

Refer to the following information to answer Questions 23-25:

Firms X and Y are in the same industry, and are roughly the same size. Based on the following ratios for the previous year:

Ratios	Firm X	Firm Y
Current	2.0	1.8
Net Return on Invested Capital	7.0%	6.0%
Net Return on Common Equity	12.5%	14.0%
Cash Flow/Total Debt	0.32	0.25
Quick	1.2	1.1
Inventory Turnover	20 times	25 times
Debt Percentage of Total Capital	30%	40%
Interest Coverage	3.5 times	2.6 times
Preferred Dividend Coverage	3.5 times	2.4 times
Debt/Equity	0.5	1.1

23. Which company appears to be more profitable according to the ratios presented?   (   )

    a) Firm X, because it has a higher Net Return on Invested Capital.

    b) Firm Y, because it has a higher Net Return on Common Equity.

    c) Firm Y, because it has a higher Inventory Turnover ratio.

    d) Cannot say without further analysis.

24. Which of the following statements is true?   (   )

    I. Firm X satisfies the suggested rule of thumb for cash flow to total debt for utilities, but not for industrials.

    II. Firm X satisfies the suggested rule of thumb for cash flow to total debt for utilities and industrials.

    III. Firm Y satisfies the suggested rule of thumb for cash flow to total debt for utilities, but not for industrials.

    IV. Neither Firm X nor Firm Y satisfy the suggested rule of thumb for cash flow to total debt for utilities or for industrials.

    a) I and III

    b) II and III

    c) II only

    d) IV only

25. Which of the following statements is true?   (   )

    I. Firm X satisfies the suggested rules of thumb for utilities for debt as a percentage of total capital and preferred dividend coverage, but not for industrials.

    II. Firm X satisfies the suggested rules of thumb for debt as a percentage of total capital and preferred dividend coverage for both utilities and industrials.

    III. Firm Y satisfies the suggested rules of thumb for debt as a percentage of total capital and preferred dividend coverage ratios for utilities, but not for industrials.

    IV. Neither Firm X nor Firm Y satisfy the suggested rules of thumb for debt as a percentage of total capital and preferred dividend coverage ratios for utilities or for industrials.

    a) I and III

    b) II and III

    c) II only

    d) IV only

FINANCIAL PLANNING AND TAXATION

THE PROCESS OF FINANCIAL PLANNING

- Financial planning requires the consideration of many factors including the client's: age, wealth, career stage, marital status, tax situation, estate considerations, risk tolerance, investment objectives, legal situation, and other matters. This enables the investor and financial planner to obtain a comprehensive picture of the investor's present situation, so that it will be easier to identify future investing objectives. The financial planner's role is to coordinate information and advice from relevant experts in various fields.

Four objectives of a financial plan are that it:

1. is do-able;
2. accommodates small changes in lifestyle and income level;
3. is not too intimidating; and
4. provides necessities, but has some room built-in to allow some luxuries.

The financial planning process involves the following six steps:

1. Collect and Assess All Relevant Data
2. Identify Objectives and Constraints
3. Identify Financial Constraints
4. Develop a Written Plan
5. Implementation of Recommendations
6. Review, Revision, and Recommendations

! 1. COLLECT AND ASSESS ALL RELEVANT DATA:

This includes tax information, bank statements, pay slips, and documents such as wills and insurance policies. Personal data such as age, marital status, number of dependents, health, and employment help define an acceptable level of risk for the investor. Information must be gathered regarding the net worth, income, and tax status of clients. It is important that complete client records are maintained and kept up to date.

! 2. IDENTIFY GOALS AND OBJECTIVES:

It is important that the client objectively assess personal strengths and weaknesses, including their career status and future earnings potential. Personal circumstances such as risk preferences, marital status and job security can greatly affect the financial plan. **The New Client Application Form** includes clearly stated investment objectives that must be used to guide investment actions. These objectives can generally be described as in Chapter 1: income, growth, preservation of capital, tax minimization, or liquidity.

The Life Cycle Theory is a helpful approach, which suggests that the typical risk-return preferences or needs change for individuals at different points in their life:

1. Early Earning Years (to age 35): the investor is building a career, family, and net worth; therefore, priorities include savings plans and liquidity for emergencies, while the primary investing objective is growth.
2. Mid Earning Years (to age 55): expenses begin to decline, while income and savings generally increase; therefore objectives tend to focus on growth and tax minimization.
3. Peak Earning Years (to retirement): preservation of capital becomes very important, and risk reduction measures should be undertaken.
4. Retirement Years: during this period, preservation of capital and income will be the primary objectives.

While this appproach is useful as general guideline, many individuals do not fit the typical profile.

- It is important to consider the investor's individual situation, and one useful tool in this regard is the **financial planning pyramid**. It indicates the strength of the base for investor objectives. Levels build one on top of the other:
  1. security: insurance, will;
  2. independence: debt elimination, house, RRSP, emergency fund;
  3. conservative: fixed income securities and certain mutuals funds;
  4. moderate: stocks, mutual funds;
  5. aggressive: tax shelters, commodity derivatives; and
  6. very aggressive: art, IPOs, OTC securities, real estate, precious metals.

3. IDENTIFY FINANCIAL CONSTRAINTS:

These include many factors including income, risk tolerance, and time horizon.

4. DEVELOP A WRITTEN PLAN:

The written statement should include clearly defined goals, and a schedule for achieving them. It should be straightforward, and easy to put into practice.

5. IMPLEMENTATION OF RECOMMENDATIONS:

The investor must carefully put the plan into practice after reviewing the details of the plan. The advisor should make sure that the investor is aware of the risks and rewards of all of the recommended investments.

6. REVIEW, REVISION, AND RECOMMENDATIONS:

This is probably the most important step and should be undertaken at regular intervals (at least annually) or if a change in circumstances warrants reconsideration of the plan (e.g., change in employment conditions or marital status).

TAXES AND TAXATION ISSUES

Proper tax planning should be incorporated in all financial plans; however, it should not be the overriding objective, as discussed in Chapter 1. It is best to establish the tax plan early and continually reassess it. Legitimate and effective tax avoidance measures include:

1. full utilization of allowable deductions;
2. conversion of non-deductible expenses into deductible expenditures;
3. postponing receipt of income;
4. splitting income with other family members; and
5. selecting investments that provide better after-tax yields.

• The *Income Tax Act* (ITA) governs federal income taxes, while the provinces have separate laws. The federal government collects taxes for all provinces except Quebec (both individuals and corporations), and Ontario and Alberta (corporations). Canada imposes taxes on all income (domestic and foreign) earned by its residents (individual or corporate), as well as on foreign companies with management and control in Canada.

• Individuals and corporations must calculate income and pay taxes annually. Individuals must use the calendar year, but corporations can choose any fiscal year-end, as long as it is used consistently

The following four steps are followed to determine income tax:

1. Determine income from employment, business, or investments.
2. Make allowable deductions to determine taxable income.
3. Determine gross or basic taxes payable based on taxable income.
4. Claim various tax credits to determine the net tax payable.

Income is treated differently, depending on its source:

1. employment income: is taxed on a gross receipt basis, and individuals cannot deduct related costs in earning this income;
2. income from business: requires activity by the firm, in earning net income as calculated using GAAP;
3. income from property: is earned passively; however, reasonable expenses such as property taxes, repairs and maintenance, and possibly financing costs for acquisition purposes may be deductible; and
4. capital gains or losses: which arise when capital assets are sold at price above (or below) their original acquisition cost.

- Basic federal income tax rates as of 2001, are:

    1. 16% for taxable income up to $30,754;
    2. $4,921 + 22% on the next $30,574 up to $61,509;
    3. $11,687 + 26% on the next $38,490 up to $100,000; and
    4. $21,694 + 29% on all income above $100,000.

    The provinces also charge taxes based on the amount of taxable income. For example in 2001, a Nova Scotia tax payer with $29,000 in taxable income would be in the 16% federal tax bracket and be subject to an 9.77% provincial tax rate, resulting in a combined marginal tax rate of 25.77%.

Employers must withhold income tax on employee salaries, and pay it to the government on behalf of its employees. Most individuals pay income tax on an annual basis, unless they earn more than 25% of their income from sources that do not withhold tax. These individuals must make payments quarterly based on the lessor of: taxes for the previous year; an average over the previous two years; or, an estimate for the current year. Corporations pay income taxes monthly.

TAXABLE AND TAX DEDUCTIBLE ITEMS

Dividends (whether they are cash, stock or reinvested dividends) received from Canadian corporations are taxable in the following manner for all provinces except Quebec:

1. The amount of the dividend is "grossed-up" by 25% to obtain the taxable amount of dividend which is used in determining net income.

2. The taxpayer is able to claim the **dividend tax credit** (which reduces taxes payable) in the amount of 13.33% of the taxable amount of dividend.

3. The provincial tax is calculated after the tax credit is claimed.[1]

Example 1:

Consider a Nova Scotia investor who receives $80 in dividends, the grossed up amount of $100 would be added to taxable income. This would produce a federal tax figure of $16, if the investor is in the 26% bracket. This amount is then reduced by $13.33 (13.33% of $100) to arrive at the federal taxes payable figure of $12.67. Assume the Nova Scotia provincial tax would be 53% of $12.67 or $6.72, and total taxes payable would be $19.39, so the net dividend amount would be $80.61. The marginal tax rates on dividends are lower than on interest, but are now higher than those applying to capital gains. Any shift from interest-bearing securities to dividend-paying ones should enhance after-tax returns.

Example 2:

Quebec calculates taxes payable on dividends differently. In particular, the federal tax payable is reduced further by a standard federal tax abatement (currently 16.5%). For the example above this amount would be $0.165 \times \$12.67 = \$2.09$, leaving federal taxes payable at $12.67 − $2.09 = $10.58. The provincial tax rate (assume 26%) and provincial tax credit (rate is currently 8.87%) are both applied to the grossed up amount of $100, which implies provincial tax of $0.26 \times \$100 = \$26$ less the credit of $0.0887 \times \$100 = \$8.87$, which leaves provincial taxes payable of $17.13 and total taxes payable of $10.58 + $17.13 = $27.71.

- Foreign dividends are usually taxed by the source country, and there is an allowable credit which is the lower of the foreign tax paid and the Canadian taxes payable on foreign income.

- If a private corporation pays a dividend out of its capital dividend account, the dividend is not taxable and also has no effect on the adjusted cost base of the underlying shares.

- Interest earned through an investment contract is taxable based on an annual accrual basis, rather than on a cash basis.

The following items related to investment income are tax deductible:

1. Carrying charges: including interest on borrowed funds, investment counseling fees, fees paid for administration or safe custody of investments, safety deposit box charges, and accounting fees paid for recording investment income.

---

[1] Note that the example in the CSC textbook on page 11-16 assumes that provincial taxes are levied as a percentage of the federal taxes payable, which is no longer the case after January 1, 2001. The example below follows the format presented in the CSC textbook for consistency purposes.

2. Interest on borrowed funds: is deductible only if the investor had a legal obligation to pay the interest, the purpose of the borrowing was to earn income, and the income earned from the investment is not tax exempt (note: it does not need to be an arms-length transaction). In addition, the interest charge: (a) cannot exceed the amount of interest earned on debt securities unless they are convertible; (b) is disallowed as a deduction if it exceeds the grossed-up amount of preferred dividends; and (c) is for the most part deductible if it is for the purchase of common shares.

CAPITAL GAINS AND LOSSES

A **capital gain** occurs when capital assets are sold for more than their cost of acquisition. As of October 2000, only 50% of the capital gain is taxable, provided the transaction involved a taxpayer whose ordinary business does not involve the trading of securities, or that Canada Customs and Revenue Agency did not determine the trading to be "speculative" in nature. The general rule is that:

Capital gain = (selling proceeds [i.e., selling price − commission costs])

− (the adjusted cost base [which includes commission costs])

The **adjusted cost** base is complicated when shares were purchased at different purchase prices, and is based on the **average cost method**.

Example 3:

(a) If 100 shares were purchased for $5 (including commission) and an additional 300 shares were purchased for $8 (including commission), then the average adjusted cost per share would be ($500 + $2,400) / 400 = $7.25 per share.

(b) If 300 shares were later sold for $10 each, with $80 commision costs, the resulting capital gain would be:

Capital Gain = ([$10 × 300] − $80) − ($7.25 × 300) = $2,920 − $2,175 = $745

No capital gain or loss arises when *convertible features* are exercised. However, the adjusted cost base of the shares acquired through conversion are based on the cost of the original securities. For example, if 200 preferred shares are purchased for a total cost of $4,000 and each share is convertible into 10 common shares, the adjusted cost base of one common share (after conversion), will be $4,000 / (10 × 200) shares = $2 per common share.

The adjusted cost base for "*units*" is determined based on the proportional cost of the relevant securities at the time of purchase. If a unit consisting of one common and one preferred share is purchased for $20, when prevailing market prices are $18 for preferred and $4 for common, the adjusted cost base is: (1) preferred = $18 × (20/22) = $16.36; and (2) common = $4 × (20/22) = $3.64.

Warrants and rights may be acquired: through direct purchase; by owning the shares associated with a rights offering; or, by purchasing units with rights or warrants attached. When they are purchased they are treated the same as convertibles. However, if they are the result of owning underlying shares, the adjusted cost base of the original shares is adjusted. When warrants or rights are not exercised, a capital gain or loss may result, unless they were acquired at zero cost.

Taxes on the sale of *debt securities* such as bonds, are applied as above. However, the accrued interest portion of a bond purchase price is not included as part of the adjusted cost base, and is treated as taxable income in the hands of the bond seller.

Capital losses may be used to offset capital gains income. They cannot be claimed by the security holder unless ownership is transferred in writing to another person. The exception to this rule occurs when the security becomes worthless due to bankruptcy of the underlying company.

Superficial losses occur when the same security is sold, but then repurchased within 30 days and it is still held 30 days after the sale. They are *not* tax deductible; however, the amount of the superficial loss is added to the original cost base of the repurchased shares, which lowers the ultimate capital gain. They do not apply if the losses arise because the investor is leaving Canada, dies, or due to the expiry of an option.

Investors may consider **tax loss selling** to produce tax losses which will offset capital gains, if the funds can be more attractively employed elsewhere. The following factors should be considered:

1. Timing must be such as to avoid a superficial loss.
2. The settlement date must be within the current tax period or else the loss is attributed to the following tax year.

TAX DEFERRAL PLANS

Tax deferral plans are designed to reduce taxes during periods of high income (and high-tax brackets), by deferring payment until a period such as retirement, when income levels (and tax brackets) are lower. Total contributions to retirement savings plans that provide tax advantages are limited to *18% of earned income* to a maximum dollar amount of *$13,500* from 1996 to 2003.

The amount contributed to **registered pension plans (RPPs)** and **deferred profit sharing plans (DPSPs)** is called the **pension adjustment (PA)**. When an increase in benefits materializes due to the introduction of a new pension plan, the adjustment to define contributions to the new plan versus the old plan is called the **Past Service Pension Adjustment (PSPA)**. Both the PA and PSPA reduce the allowable contributions to an RRSP by a taxpayer. Carry-forward provisions enable the taxpayer to make up contributions below their maximum amount in subsequent years.

! Registered pension plans (RPPs) are established by the employer for the employees' benefit. Both employer and employee make contributions, which are tax deductible.

! RPPs may be set up in one of two forms:

1. **Money purchase plans** (or **defined contribution plans**): the contributions are defined and benefits vary with the value of the fund (employer/employee contributions are limited by the limits mentioned above).

2. **Defined benefit plans:** benefits are predefined and contributions vary (the current DBP limits are 2% of pre-retirement earnings per year of service with a limit of $1,722.22 (until 2004). In addition employee current contributions are restricted to the lesser of:

   ○ 9% of current compensation and
   ○ $600 plus 70% of the employee's PA for the year.

! **Registered Retirement Savings Plans (RRSPs)** allow annual tax-deductible contributions up to predefined limits. The income earned on the plan is not taxed as long as it remains in plans that are registered with Canada Customs and Revenue Agency and meet Canadian content requirements.

! There are two types of RRSPs:

1. **Single vendor RRSPs:** the holder invests in one or more pooled or mutual funds which are managed by fund managers.

2. **Self-directed RRSPs:** the investor contributes permissable securities into a plan that is administered for a fee; however, the investor directs the investment transactions himself. The foreign content limit was 25% in 2000, which increased to 30% in 2001.

! RRSPs are trust accounts set up for the investor's benefit upon retirement and access to funds cannot be gained immediately, without paying a withholding tax. In addition, RRSPs are not eligible to provide security for loans.

! RRSP contributions must be made within 60 days of year end and are limited to 18% of the previous year's earnings or $13,500, less the previous year's PA and PSPA plus the unused RRSP deduction room. A penalty tax of 1% per month is levied on "over-contributions" of $2,000 or more. Investors may contribute securities they already own to the plan (referred to as a "**contribution in kind**"), and they must pay taxes on any capital gains; however, they are unable to claim any capital losses that result.

! Investors may contribute to a **spousal RRSP** provided the contribution does not put them over their own maximum contribution limit. It does not affect the contribution limits of the spouse. For example, if a wife contributes $7,000 of her $13,500 limit to her own plan, she may also contribute $6,500 to her husband's plan, without affecting his contribution limits. The proceeds from deregistering a spousal plan is taxable income for the spouse (not the contributor), except for contributions made in the year of deregistration and the two calendar years before the plan is deregistered.

- The following pension income transfers to an RRSP are tax-free and do not affect contribution limits:

  1. direct transfers from RPPs and other RRSPs and
  2. allowances of $2,000 for long service upon retirement for each year of service after 1988.

RRSPs may be de-registered at any time, but must occur by the time the planholder is 69. Available options for **deregistering the plan** include:

  1. withdraw the full lump sum amount, which is fully taxable;
  2. purchase a life annuity with a guaranteed term or a fixed term annuity which provides benefits to age 90;
  3. purchase a **Registered Retirement Income Fund (RRIF)**, which provides annual income to age 90 or life;
  4. change it to allow transfer of funds to another RRSP or RPP; or
  5. combinations of the above options.

Upon death, remaining benefits on an annuity or RRIF can be transferred to a spouse or child, or else the value is included in the deceased's income in the year of death and is fully taxable.

Major **advantages** of RRSPs include:

  1. They reduce taxable income during high taxation years.
  2. They shelter income from taxation by transferring them into an RRSP.
  3. They allow for tax-exempt accumulation of retirement funds.
  4. They allow deferral of some taxes.
  5. They provide income-splitting opportunities, which may result in lower total tax payments.

RRIF holders must make taxable withdrawals of a certain portion of assets from the fund annually. The minimum withdrawals are designed to provide benefits for a desired term; however, the payout may be accelerated if the owner elects. Individuals may own more than one RRIF and they may be self-directed if desired.

- Payments from **immediate annuities** start right away, while **deferred annuities** start at a later date specified in the contract. Unlike immediate annuities that must be paid in full, deferred annuities can be paid for in monthly installments. While the contributions to a deferred annuity are not tax deductible, they defer the taxes paid on investment income. If the annuities are not purchased using RRSP proceeds, only the interest portion of the payments is taxable; however, the full amount is taxable if received from an RRSP (since the principal has never been taxed). Finally, some deferred annuities are RRSP-eligible investments. They are sold by life insurance companies.

- **Stock savings plans (SSPs)** provide tax deductions or credits for qualifying investments (shares of local companies), and are offered by some provinces. There are maximum dollar limits and the funds must stay in the plan for a minimum period of time.

BASICS OF TAX PLANNING:

Attribution rules apply to the transfer of income to family members under many circumstances and they serve to pass the tax consequences back to the transferor. Exceptions to attribution may occur when:

1. the property or assets are transferred at fair market values or through a loan that is established at fair market rates, and where interest is paid within 30 days of year end;

2. the transfer was a gift, and it can be shown that tax avoidance was not the main purpose of the transaction; or

3. business income is generally not subject to attribution.

• Certain income splitting opportunities exist, which may result in reduced taxes:

1. Have the higher-income spouse pay the bills, while the lower-income spouse invests more; therefore, the investment income will accrue to the lower-tax-bracket spouse.

2. The higher-income spouse can loan funds for investment opportunities to the lower-income spouse at fair market rates, which results in taxation of only the net investment income over interest paid at the lower tax rates.

3. Direct discharge of a spouse's debts is not subject to attribution.

4. It may pay to have the taxpayer claim dividends as income if the dividend income would reduce the marital tax credit; therefore, a spousal dividend swap may be advantageous.

5. Capital losses may be transferred by selling the asset to a third party, and then having the spouse purchase it within 30 days. This would not represent a capital loss (but rather a superficial one); however, if the spouse then sells it they can obtain a capital loss.

6. Payment of debts by way of a gift.

7. Splitting CPP income: must split both plans and be agreed to by both parties.

8. Asset swaps at fair market value are allowed, so higher tax bracket may trade income generating assets for non-income generating assets at fair market values.

9. Salaries for legitimate services rendered to spouses from proprietorships are deductible.

10. Gifts are not subject to attribution.

REGISTERED EDUCATION SAVINGS PLANS (RESPS):

RESP contributions are not tax-deductible; however, income earned on these plans is not taxable. The beneficiary of the plan will be taxed upon withdrawal of funds, provided they are enrolled in qualifying educational programs.

The maximum annual contribution per beneficiary is $4,000, with a lifetime maximum of $42,000. Contributions can be made for 21 years, but the plan must be collapsed within 25 years of its initiation.

The plans may be individual or self-directed plans, and more than one beneficiary may be named to a plan. In this way, if any children do not attend a qualifying post-secondary institution, any beneficiaries that do qualify will have access to the proceeds of the plan.

Since 1998, the contributor is permitted to withdraw the invested capital and income from the plan if none of the beneficiaries attends a qualifying institution by age 21, provided the plan is at least 10-years old. Under the same situation, the contributor may also transfer up to $50,000 to an RRSP, provided they have sufficient contribution room. Once the contributor begins to withdraw funds from the plan, it must be terminated by February 28 of the next year.

Canada Education Savings Grants (CESGs) provide an additional attraction for RESPs. As of 1998, the federal government will match 20% of the first $2,000 contributed each year to an RESP (up to $400 per year). These grants do not count towards the contributor's annual or lifetime maximum contributions, and unused grant room can be carried forward up to a maximum of $7,200 per child. If the student does not pursue post-secondary education, the grant must be repaid.

Chapter 11: Review Questions

1. An investor buys 300 XYZ preferred shares at a total cost of $7,500. Each preferred share is convertible into two and a half XYZ common shares. If the investor converts into common shares at a later date, what is the adjusted cost base per share?   ( )

   a) $25

   b) $62.50

   c) $10

   d) $15

2. The following are examples of a capital loss except: ( )

   a) a stock that was originally purchased for $20 is sold for $15, but is repurchased 21 days later

   b) a stock that was originally purchased for $20 is sold for $15, and is not repurchased

   c) common shares that were acquired through the purchase of a warrant for $40, that had an associated exercise price of $20, were sold for $50

   d) all of the above represent capital losses

( )   3. An investor purchases 200 XYZ common shares at $20 and pays $60 in commission, then buys another 300 shares at $25, and pays $100 in commissions. What is the adjusted cost base per share?

      a) $22.50

      b) $23.00

      c) $23.32

      d) none of the above

( )   4. An investor is in the 40% marginal tax bracket (combined federal and provincial tax rate), and receives $200 in dividends from a Canadian corporation. How much tax must they pay on the dividend?

      a) $33.33

      b) $66.67

      c) $80.00

      d) none of the above

( )   5. The following represent desirable objectives for a financial plan except:

      a) it covers necessities

      b) it is designed primarily to minimize taxes

      c) it accommodates small lifestyle changes

      d) it is not intimidating

( )   6. RRSPs differ from RRIFs because:

      a) RRSPs shelter income earned within the plan.

      b) RRSPs may hold stocks, bonds, mutual funds, and T-bills.

      c) RRSPs do not require minimum annual withdrawals.

      d) RRSPs may be self-directed.

( )   7. Which of the following statements is false?

      a) Corporations pay taxes in quarterly instalments.

      b) Individuals that earn more than 20% of their income from sources that do not deduct taxes must pay taxes quarterly.

      c) neither (a) nor (b) is false.

      d) both (a) and (b) are false.

( )   8. According to the life cycle approach to financial planning, investors in the _____ stage, should focus primarily on _____ .

      a) early earning years; growth

      b) peak earning years; tax minimization

      c) mid-earning years; income

      d) retirement years; liquidity

THE PORTFOLIO APPROACH

chapter

12

INTRODUCTION

The final step of the investment management process (after **security selection** and **market timing** decisions) involves **portfolio management**. Portfolio management considers securities based on their contribution to the risks and expected returns of the entire portfolio.

RISK AND RETURN

In an ideal world, investors could obtain high returns, without assuming any risk. Unfortunately, high expected returns usually go hand in hand with high risk. Thus, financial decisions usually entail the classic **risk-return trade-off**: reducing risk tends to reduce expected returns, while increasing expected returns tends to increase risk.

It is common to make the assumption that investors are **risk averse**. This means that investors will require additional expected return in return for assuming additional risk. Given the risk-return trade-off faced by investors, they will attempt to either:

- minimize risk for a given level of required return, or
- maximize expected return for a given level of risk.

In other words, if an investor is presented with two equally risky investments, they will choose the one that offers the higher return. Similarly, if presented with two investments with equal expected returns, they will choose the one with the lower risk.

- While all investors are assumed to be risk averse, some are more so than others. More risk averse investors should pursue investment strategies that are consistent with their low tolerance for risk. They may be attracted to securities such as Guaranteed Investment Certificates (GICs) and Canada Savings Bonds (CSBs), which have low risks, but also relatively low expected rates of return. Less risk averse investors will be comfortable pursuing riskier investment strategies, and may invest more heavily in common shares and other riskier securities.

RETURNS:

The **total return (TR)** for any security consists of the sum of two components:

1. cash flow yield
2. price change

Formally, the TR for a given holding period is expressed as a decimal (or percentage) number (Return%) relating all the cash flows received by an investor during a designated time period to the purchase price of the asset:

$$\text{Return\%} = \frac{\text{Cash Flow} + (\text{Ending Value} - \text{Beginning Value})}{\text{Beginning Value}} \times 100$$

Example 1: ──────────────────────────────

Determine the return for each of the following investments:

(a) A common stock is bought for $20 and sold one year later for $21, and did not pay any dividends during the year.

(b) A common stock is bought for $10 and sold one year later for $8, and paid a $1 dividend just before it was sold.

(c) An 8% $1,000 face value bond was bought for $950 and sold after one year for $980.

Solution:

(a) Return% = (0 + 21 - 20) / 20 = 1 / 20 = 0.0500 = 5.00%

(b) Return% = (1 + 8 − 10) / 10 = −1 / 10 = −0.1000 = −10.00%

(c) Return% = (80 + 980 − 950) / 950 = 110 / 950 = 0.1158 = 11.58%, where $80 is the annual amount of coupons received on an 8% $1,000 face value bond.

Historical returns provide investors with insight into the nature of the risk-return characteristics of different securities. Generally, various asset categories are ranked in the following manner with regards to expected return and risk (as measured by standard deviation, which will be discussed later in this section). Starting from the lowest-risk, lowest expected return and increasing to the highest-risk, highest expected return, we have:

1. Treasury Bills
2. Bonds
3. Debentures
4. Preferred Shares
5. Common Shares
6. Derivatives

The **real rate** of return for an investment represents how much their values have increased in real terms, after adjusting for inflation. It may be approximated by subtracting the **inflation rate** from the actual rate of return, referred to as the **nominal rate**. This relationship is depicted in the following equation:

Real Return = Nominal Rate − Inflation Rate

Example 2: ————————————————————

Assume that the rate of inflation over the past year has been 3%.

(a) Determine the real rate of return for an investment that provided a 7% nominal return.

(b) Determine the nominal return for an investment that provided a 2% real return.

Solution:

(a) Real Return = 7 − 3 = 4%

(b) Nominal Return = 2 + 3 = 5%

RISK:

Risk may be defined as the chance that the actual outcome from an investment will differ from the expected outcome. The more variable the possible outcomes that can occur (i.e., the broader the range of possible outcomes), the greater the risk. An investor who purchases a stock for $20 that they expect to sell after one year for $30 faces a great deal of uncertainty (or risk) associated with their expected return. On the other hand, an investor who purchases a one-year federal government T-bill faces very little uncertainty, since the face value of the T-bill will be paid to them after one year, barring default by the federal government.

Some of the more common types of risks include the following:

1. **Inflation Rate Risk:** a factor affecting all securities is purchasing power risk, or the chance that the purchasing power of invested dollars will decline. With uncertain inflation, the real (inflation-adjusted) return involves risk even if the nominal return is safe (e.g., a T-bill).

2. **Business Risk:** the risk of doing business in a particular industry or environment, as measured by variability in a company's earnings, is called business risk.

3. **Political Risk:** with more investors investing internationally, both directly and indirectly, the political, and therefore economic stability and viability of a country's economy need to be considered.

4. **Liquidity Risk:** liquidity risk is the risk associated with the particular secondary market in which a security trades. An investment that can be bought or sold quickly and without significant price concession is considered liquid. The more uncertainty about the time element and the price concession, the greater the liquidity risk. A T-bill has little or no liquidity risk, whereas a small OTC stock may have substantial liquidity risk.

5. **Interest Rate Risk:** this refers to the variability in a security's return resulting from changes in the level of interest rates. Such changes generally affect securities inversely; that is, other things being equal, security prices move inversely to interest rates. Some securities, such as bonds, are more sensitive to interest rates than others.

6. **Foreign Exchange Risk:** those who invest globally face the prospect of uncertainty in the returns after they convert the foreign gains back to their own currency. Foreign exchange risk may be defined as the variability in returns on securities caused by currency fluctuations.

7. **Default Risk:** this is the risk associated with a company not being able to pay its debt obligations as they come due. It is a large concern for investors in corporate or foreign securities, and less of a concern for federal government debt issues.

An investor can construct a diversified portfolio and eliminate part of the total risk, the diversifiable or non-market part. What is left is the non-diversifiable portion or the market risk. Variability in a security's total returns that is directly associated with overall movements in the general market or economy is called **systematic (market) risk**. The investor cannot escape this part of the risk because no matter how well he or she diversifies, the risk of the overall market cannot be avoided. If the stock market declines sharply, most stocks will be adversely affected; if it rises strongly, most stocks will appreciate in value.

The variability in a security's total returns not related to overall market variability is called the **non-systematic (non-market) risk**. This risk is unique to a particular security and is associated with such factors as business and financial risk as well as liquidity risk. Although all securities tend to have some non-systematic risk, it is generally connected with common stocks.

Investors must be able to quantify and measure risk. Three commonly used measures of risk are variance, standard deviation, and beta. The first two measure the total risk associated with the expected return, while the last is a measure of systematic or market risk.

o The **variance** or its square root, **standard deviation**, are typically used to measure total variability in outcomes. Variance and standard deviation measure the spread or dispersion in the distribution of possible security returns. The larger this dispersion, the larger the variance or standard deviation.

- ○ Market risk is usually measured by a variable called "**beta**." Beta measures the risk of an individual stock relative to the market portfolio of all stocks. The higher the beta, the riskier the security.

ASSET ALLOCATION:

- The asset allocation decision is a critical one, which involves deciding how much of an investment portfolio should be invested in each of the three major asset classes (cash, fixed income, and equities). As discussed in Chapter 1, cash and near-cash assets provide safety; fixed income assets provide income and a reasonable level of safety; while equities provide the greatest growth potential.

- The investor's objectives, along with their risk tolerance, dictate appropriate asset mixes. For example, a mix of 5% cash, 15% fixed income, and 80% equities might be considered appropriate for a young, knowledgeable investor with a long time horizon, and high risk tolerance. At the opposite end of the spectrum, a mix of 20% cash, 60% fixed income, and 20% equities, might be more appropriate for a retired investor, with a short to medium time horizon with low risk tolerance, and a need for current income from her investments.

Investment returns are influenced by the following factors:

1. asset mix (asset allocation);
2. market timing decisions;
3. security selection; and
4. chance.

It is estimated that asset allocation accounts for 80% to 90% of investment returns.

- The **expected return (or actual return) on a portfolio** can be calculated as the *weighted average of the expected (or actual) returns* of the individual assets within the portfolio.

Example 3:

The expected return on a portfolio that has $10,000 invested in security A (which has an expected return (ER_A) of 8%), $10,000 in security B (with $ER_B = 10\%$), and $20,000 in security C (with $ER_C = 12\%$), is determined as follows:

Solution:

Weight in A (W_A) = 10,000 / 40,000 = 0.25; W_B = 10,000 / 40,000 = 0.25; W_C = 20,000 / 40,000 = 0.50

Expected portfolio return = W_A (ER_A) + W_B (ER_B) + W_C (ER_C) = 0.25 (8%) + 0.25 (10%) + 0.50 (12%) = 2 + 2.5 + 6 = 10.5%

! Research shows that most non-systematic risk can be eliminated by holding as few as 32 securities in a portfolio. Holding a great deal more securities than this provides limited diversification benefits and may entail additional tracking, accounting costs, etc.

- Investment managers often use a number of hedging strategies to limit losses on investments, such as the use of put options on indiviual equities, and/or the use of equity and bond index futures or options.

COMBINING SECURITIES.

! The number one principle of portfolio management is to diversify and hold a port-folio of securities; therefore, the risk of individual securities is relevant only to the extent that they add risk to the total portfolio. As discussed, diversification reduces many of the unique risks associated with a particular security, such as the interest rate risk and default risk associated with a particular debt security, or the business risk associated with a common stock investment.

- Portfolio risk is a unique characteristic and not simply the sum of individual secu-rity risks. A security may have a large risk if it is held by itself but much less risk when held in a portfolio of securities. Since the investor is concerned primarily with the risk of their total wealth position, as represented by their overall invest-ment portfolio, individual securities are risky only to the extent that they add risk to the total portfolio.

! The co-movements between securities' returns is often referred to as the correlation between their returns. The correlation measures how security returns move in rela-tion to one another. It is a relative measure of association that is bounded by $+ 1.0$ and $- 1.0$, with:

  - $+1.0$ indicating perfect positive correlation;
  - -1.0 indicating perfect negative (inverse) correlation; and
  - 0.0 indicating zero correlation (uncorrelated).

- If two stocks A and B display perfect positive correlation, the returns have a per-fect direct linear relationship. Knowing what the return on one security will do allows an investor to forecast perfectly what the other will do. When stock A's return goes up, stock B's does also. When stock A's return goes down, stock B's does also. With perfect negative correlation, the securities' returns have a perfect inverse linear relationship to each other. Therefore, knowing the return on one security provides full knowledge about the return on the second security. When one security's return is high, the other is low. With zero correlation, there is no relationship between the returns on the two securities. Knowledge of the return on one security is of no value in predicting the return of the second security. In the real world, these extreme correlations are rare. Rather, securities typically have some positive correlation with each other since all security prices tend to move with changes in the overall market and/or economy.

Obviously, there are little benefits to be had from diversification if the securities have high positive correlations. For example, an investor would not eliminate much risk by diversifying across the stocks of the "Big Five" banks, since their fortunes (and future returns) are linked to the same variables. However, investing in five stocks in five different industries would likely provide an investor with the opportunity to eliminate a substantial amount of unique risk. The lower the correlations between the security returns, the greater the benefits from diversification. In fact, studies have shown that most non-systematic risk can be eliminated by holding as few as 32 securities in a portfolio.

Beta measures the volatility of an individual security relative to that of the entire market. Technically, it is a measure of the correlation between individual security returns and those on a chosen market portfolio.

The higher the beta, the riskier the security. If the security's returns move more (less) than the market's returns as the latter changes, the security's returns have more (less) *volatility* (fluctuations in price) than those of the market. The market portfolio has a beta of 1.0, while a security with a beta of 1.5 indicates that, on average, its returns are 1.5 times as volatile as market returns, both up and down. In other words, its returns rise or fall on average 15% when the market return rises or falls 10%. A security with a beta greater than 1.0 is said to be an aggressive, or volatile, security. If the beta is less than 1.0, it indicates that, on average, the stock's returns have less volatility than the market as a whole. For example, a security with a beta of 0.6 indicates that stock returns move up or down, on average, only 60% as much as the market as a whole.

Betas for individual securities and portfolios tend to change through time.

The **Capital Asset Pricing Model (CAPM)** is a model that recognizes the risk-return trade-off, and argues that investors require a higher expected return to compensate them for assuming additional risk. In essence, CAPM states that the expected rate of return on an asset or portfolio (R_p) is a linear function of two components: the **risk-free rate of return (R_f**, which is usually measured by the short-term federal government T-bill yield), and a **risk premium**. Thus,

$$R_p = R_f + \text{Risk premium}$$

The central relationship of the CAPM is given by the **security market line**, which is provided below:

$$R_p = R_f + \beta(R_M - R_f)$$

where

R_M = the expected rate of return on the market portfolio

β = the beta for the security

$R_M - R_f$ = market risk premium

- The security market line provides an explicit measure of the risk premium, which is based on expected market returns and the company's level of market risk, as measured by beta. It indicates that securities with betas greater than the market beta of 1.0 should have larger risk premiums than that of the average stock, and therefore, when added to R_f, larger required rates of return. This is exactly what investors should expect, since beta is a measure of risk, and greater risk should be accompanied by greater expected return. Conversely, securities with betas less than that of the market are less risky and should have required rates of return lower than that for the market as a whole.

! Example 4: ————————————————————

The expected return on the market is 12%, and T-bills presently offer a 5% return.

(a)   What is the market risk premium?

(b)   What is the expected return on a stock with a beta of 1.2?

(c)   What is the beta of a portfolio with an expected return of 10%, if it is priced correctly according to CAPM?

Solution:

(a) $R_M - R_f = 12 - 5 = 7\%$

(b) $R_P = 5 + 1.2(12 - 5) = 5 + 8.4 = 13.4\%$

(c) $10 = 5 + \beta(7)$,

      so $7\beta = 10 - 5$,

      and $\beta = 5/7 = 0.714$

THE PORTFOLIO APPROACH

! A critical feature of portfolio formation is that portfolio returns will be an *average of the returns* on all securities within the portfolio, but the risk will be *lower than the weighted average of risks*, as long as the securities are not perfectly correlated. This implies that risk can actually be eliminated by forming portfolios.

! Portfolio management is a continuous *process* consisting of four steps:

1. Designing the investment policy.
2. Developing and implementing the asset mix.
3. Monitoring the economy, the markets, and the client.
4. Adjusting the portfolio and measuring performance.

DESIGNING AN INVESTMENT POLICY

- The **investment policy** dictates the guidelines and objectives that were agreed upon by the portfolio manager and the investor. It is a legal agreement that dictates the role of the manager. Inputs tend to be complex, but they include investment objectives and constraints, as well as a summary description of the investing style of the manager.

Investment objectives must take into account the following factors:

- risk;
- return;
- time horizon;
- liquidity;
- taxation;
- market timing; and
- other objectives, such as purchasing a business or vacation property, or having the intention of retiring by a given age.

Constraints include:

- legal;
- moral/ethical;
- emotion: including investment knowledge and tolerance for risk;
- basic minimum income to be provided by the portfolio (without liquidating securities);
- realism: the client must understand that some objectives are not realistic (e.g., achieving high returns with low risk and high liquidity); and
- other (e.g., illness, pending divorce, etc.).

The information above must be related to the three primary investment objectives of income, capital gains, and preservation of capital, and to the secondary objectives of liquidity and tax minimization.

- The importance of preservation of capital can be inferred from objectives and constraints related to: risk, market timing, inflation, return, and emotion.
- The importance of income relates to: taxation, return, risk, inflation, and basic minimum income.
- The importance of capital gains relates to: taxation, risk, return, market timing, and emotional considerations.

These objectives can be related to asset allocation decisions, and it is essential to communicate to clients the basis for any conclusions that are reached.

- The following table (which was also included in Chapter 1) shows in general, how well suited bonds, preferred stocks, and common stocks are to satisfying each of these objectives:

	Safety	Income	Growth
Bonds:			
Short-term	best	very steady	very limited
Long-term	next best	very steady	variable
Preferred Stock	good	steady	variable
Common Stocks	often the least	variable	often the most

- Managing investor objectives is critical. This is true because it is not possible to simultaneously maximize safety, income, and growth potential:

    ◦ In order to maximize safety, some growth potential and income must be sacrificed.

    ◦ In order to maximize growth potential, some safety and income must be sacrificed.

    ◦ In order to maximize income, some safety and growth potential must be sacrificed.

- Managing the trade-offs involved in satisfying the various investing objectives requires that balanced portfolios are weighted in asset classes to varying degrees to reflect the importance of each objective. In addition, diversification is important, and one security should generally never exceed 10% of the value of an investment portfolio.

- Conservative investors will prefer investment grade investments; while more aggressive investors may be inclined to have some portion of their wealth tied up in speculative investments, which may hold greater growth potential.

Manager style will determine how well the investor's objectives and constraints "fit" with the manager's style.

Three commonly referred to styles employed by equity managers are:

1. **Growth managers:** invest in growth stock portfolios that tend to be very volatile. The securities are subject to risk from market cycles, and individual securities are sensitive to earnings meeting or exceeding analysts expectations. Their portfolios tend to include securities with low dividend yields, high price-earnings (P/E) ratios, high price/cash flow ratios, and high price/book ratios. Investors should be less risk averse and possess relatively long-term investment horizons.

2. **Value managers:** look for "bargain" based on intensive "bottom-up" stock research. The portfolios tend to be less volatile than growth portfolios, with lower standard deviations and betas, which reflects the fact that prices are already low. Value stocks tend to possess low P/E ratios, low price/cash flow ratios, low price/book ratios, and high dividend yields. Investors should be reasonably risk tolerant, with long-term investment horizons.

3. **Sector rotators:** focus on particular sectors (e.g., industries) in accordance with a top-down analysis (discussed in Chapter 10). This approach may result in higher volatility and greater risk (due to lower diversification).

Fixed income managers may use several styles, some of which are described below:

1. **Interest Rate Anticipators:** these managers lengthen the term of their bond holdings when they expect interest rates to fall, and shorten the term when they expect rates to increase. They do so in order to attempt to maximize capital gains on the portfolio. This strategy is active and entails more risk than a typical buy-and-hold bond strategy, since future interest rates are difficult to predict accurately.

2. **Term to Maturity:** this approach limits the manager to invest in bonds with specified terms to maturity (e.g., less than 10 years to maturity). This limits the risk of the fund. Short-term managers will hold T-bills and bonds with maturities less than three years, mid-term managers will hold three- to 10-year bonds, while long-term managers will hold those with more than 10 years to maturity.

3. **Credit Quality:** these managers focus on the credit quality of bonds, relative to their yields. In general, corporate bonds provide higher yields than government bonds, and lower rated corporate bonds provide higher yields than higher rated ones. Bonds rated BBB or above are considered investment grade bonds, while those rated below BBB are referred to as high-yield securities, or junk bonds.

4. **Spread Traders:** bond managers may engage in spread trading (i.e., trading based on beliefs that yield spreads between different categories of bonds will narrow or widen in the future).

THE INVESTMENT POLICY STATEMENT

- The **investment policy statement** is a formal written document that dictates the guidelines and objectives that were agreed upon by the portfolio manager and the investor. It is a legal agreement that dictates the role of the manager. Inputs tend to be complex, but they include investment objectives and constraints, as well as a summary description of the investing style of the manager.

DEVELOPING AND IMPLEMENTING AN ASSET MIX

- It is important to determine which asset categories (cash, fixed income, and equity securities) will be targeted for investment. Additional asset classes such as international investments and derivatives may warrant inclusion for more sophisticated investors. The portfolio composition should be determined based on the client's individual characteristics and risk tolerance.

THE ASSET MIX:

- **Cash** includes currency, money market securities, CSBs, GICs, and other debt instruments such as bonds with maturities of one year or less. It usually makes up at least 5% of a diversified portfolio; however, this amount may increase for more risk-averse investors. In addition, the levels will vary as a result of changing market conditions, or portfolio rebalancings.

- **Fixed income** assets include medium- to long-term bonds, strip bonds, mortgages, and other debt securities, as well as non-convertible preferred shares. Diversification within this asset class may occur across: credit quality, duration or maturity of instruments, and types of fixed income securities. The amount of the total portfolio allocated to fixed income can vary from 15% to 95%, based on several factors including:

  - desire for current income;
  - basic minimum income required;
  - desire for preservation of capital; and
  - other considerations such as tax and time horizon.

- **Equity assets** include common shares, but also derivatives such as warrants, rights, options, LEAPs, i60s, convertibles, etc. The amount of the total portfolio allocated to equities can account for anywhere from 15% to 95%.

SETTING THE ASSET MIX:

The **equity cycle** refers to the cyclical movements in stock market prices. The phases include: **expansionary, peak, contraction**, and **trough**. It is important to note that there may be temporary set backs or corrections within the overall phases. Equity cycles are very similar to the economic (or business) cycles discussed in Chapter 2; however, they tend to lead the latter (which is why stock prices are considered to be leading economic indicators).

- The rationale behind **asset class timing** (or asset allocation) is that improved returns can result when investors recognize when to shift from stocks to T-bills and/or bonds. This is logical, since more than 80% of portfolio returns may be attributed to asset mix.

General strategies in relation to the equity cycle include:

1. Lengthen terms of bond holdings and avoid stocks during *contraction phase*.
2. Sell long-term bonds which rally ahead of stocks in response to falling interest rates, during the *trough phase*.
3. Maintain or increase stock position during *expansionary phase*, since stocks tend to do well during sustained economic growth periods.
4. Stop buying stock and invest in short-term instruments as *peak phase* approaches, since interest rates are likely to increase.

The difficulty of implementing these strategies is that variations occur within the cycles and it is difficult to anticipate the arrival and duration of these phases.

The Dividend Discount Model (DDM), which was discussed in Chapter 10, is given below:

$$P_0 = \frac{Div_1}{r - g}$$

where

P_0 = the intrinsic value of the share price today

Div_1 = the expected dividend at the end of year one

r = the required rate of return by the common shareholders, and

g = the constant annual growth rate in dividends to infinity

The DDM can be used to interpret changes in equity prices in relation to the equity cycle. In particular:

1. *r* is rising and *g* is falling during the *contraction phase* (one to two years), which causes prices to fall;

2. *r* is falling faster than *g* is falling during the stock market *trough*, which causes an interest rate driven rally in stock prices (five to 13 months);

3. *r* briefly rises faster than *g* rises during the *expansionary phase*, which causes a brief decline in stock prices (six to nine months); or

4. *g* rises faster than *r* from the *expansionary to peak phase*, which causes stock prices to rise (one to three years).

- **Industry rotation** can also lead to improved results, if one can successfully predict economic cycles and their impact on the security prices of various industries. This approach can be implemented using several strategies such as shifting in and out of cyclical and defensive industries, or moving in and out of interest-rate-sensitive industries in response to interest rate forecasts.

- The appropriate asset mix for an investor should reflect their objectives, constraints, investment knowledge, and risk tolerance. The following represent some asset mixes that might be considered appropriate for three different investors; although in practice specific circumstances must be known in order to develop appropriate mixes:

  ○ A young, knowledgeable investor with a long time horizon, and high risk tolerance: 5% cash, 20% fixed income, and 75% equities.

  ○ A retired investor, with no other source of income, a medium time horizon, and low risk tolerance: 10% cash, 60% fixed income, and 30% equities.

  ○ A middle-aged white collar worker, with two children, who has reasonable investment knowledge, and is concerned with providing for her children's education, and her own retirement: 10% cash, 30% fixed income, and 60% equities.

- Managers can take actions to control the risk and limit losses on individual securities or on the entire portfolio by monitoring maturities of debt instruments, credit quality of security issuers, and/or by using put options on broad indices. For example, within the Cash asset class, government issues have lower risk than corporate issues. Within the Fixed Income asset class, short-term debt instruments (less than three years) have the lowest risk, medium-term instruments (three to 10 years) have moderate risk, while long-term (over 10 years) instruments possess the most risk. For Equities, conservative (large cap, blue chip) stocks have the lowest risk, growth stocks have medium risk, while venture and speculative securities have the highest risk.

- The asset allocation decision can account for 80% to 90% of a portfolio's total return, and is therefore much more critical to an investor than security selection and market timing decisions. For example, the total return of one fund may exceed that of another due to the asset mix, even though it underperformed the other in each asset class. Historical evidence regarding the performance of different asset classes highlights this fact.

ASSET ALLOCATION TECHNIQUES

The desired long-term asset mix of a portfolio is referred to as its **strategic asset allocation**. Maintaining this desired mix involves continual monitoring and rebalancing of the portfolio because the asset mix changes continuously as a result of dividend and interest payments, and as market prices change. For example, consider a portfolio that has a desired (or base) asset mix of 50% bonds and 50% equities. At the beginning of the period, the portfolio had $10,000 invested in bonds, and $10,000 invested in stocks. After six months, as a result of interest and dividend payments, as well as changes in bond and stock prices, the value of the bonds is $10,000, and the value of the stocks is $8,000. In order to maintain the desired mix, the portfolio manager must sell $1,000 worth of bonds and purchase $1,000 in stocks.

Several **asset allocation techniques** may be employed:

1. **Constant-weighting asset allocation:** involves rebalancing the portfolio to maintain a strategic long-term position, which essentially involves buying bonds (or stocks) when they are relatively less expensive and selling them when they are relatively more expensive.

2. **Tactical asset allocation:** a moderately active approach which allows managers short-term deviations from longer-term asset mixes to take advantage of market timing skills.

3. **Dynamic asset allocation:** an active approach that adjusts the asset mix as market conditions change by selling equities when markets fall and buying when they rise.

4. **Insured asset allocation:** allows managers discretion in managing asset amounts only if they exceed a base portfolio value whose value must be guaranteed.

5. **Integrated asset allocation:** this strategy may incorporate any or all of the above approaches.

- Some portfolios are managed in a passive manner, based on the belief that markets are relatively efficient. These portfolios strive to match the performance of a market benchmark, and attempt to reduce portfolio management costs.

Passive portfolio management may involve the use of:

- buy and hold strategies;
- indexing; or
- index particpation units, such as i60s.

MONITORING THE ECONOMY, THE MARKETS, AND THE CLIENT

- Managing a portfolio is an ongoing process that requires systematic monitoring of:

  1. changes in the investor's circumstances and
  2. market conditions.

  The objective is to incorporate anticipated changes into portfolio adjustments in a systematic manner.

- Portfolio managers must continually monitor information that has the potential to affect portfolio performance. The planner must monitor client circumstances, including changes in their objectives, preferences, and financial position. In addition, market and economic conditions must be followed. This involves analyzing a number of factors, and categorizing their overall impact on the portfolio (or asset class) as positive, neutral, or negative. These factors are used as inputs, when obtaining estimates of expected returns for the various asset classes.

- For equities, factors may include many of the fundamental, technical, economic, and value indicators that were discussed in previous chapters.

- Fixed income factors generally try to predict future interest rate levels, and focus on factors such as monetary policy, fiscal policy, economic indicators, inflation, and foreign exchange factors.

- Returns on cash are generally easy to determine due to their short-term nature and merely involve taking the interest rate forecasts used for analyzing fixed income securities.

- All of the return expectations can be aggregated to estimate the expected total return on the portfolio.

- A general checklist that considers some of the following factors may assist the manager:
    1. Is the portfolio well aligned with investor objectives and risk tolerances?
    2. Is the asset mix appropriate for the current market outlook?
    3. Is the portfolio overdiversified and too difficult to manage?
    4. Is it too concentrated?
    5. Are liquid reserves sufficient?
    6. Is it tax friendly?
    7. What about other assets of the investor?
    8. Are future funds likely to be available for investment in the portfolio?
    9. Are any withdrawals likely?
    10. Does it include any weak securities that should be sold?
    11. Is the degree of leverage appropriate?
    12. Is sufficient income being generated?
    13. What are current opinions of research analysts?
    14. Has the client been informed of the current market outlook?

- The following points should be considered regarding the cash component:
    1. Should the term be changed?
    2. Should the quality be adjusted?
    3. Should some CSBs be sold?

- The following points should be considered regarding the fixed income component:
    1. Is the average maturity appropriate?
    2. Is any yield spread switching appropriate?
    3. Are coupon levels appropriate?
    4. Are there any deadlines approaching for conversion, retraction, or calls?
    5. Is the weighting of dividend versus interest income appropriate?
    6. Have any credit ratings changed?
    7. Are interest and dividend payments adequately covered by issuers?

- The following points should be considered regarding the equity component:
    1. Is the risk level appropriate?
    2. Are industry weightings reasonable?
    3. What are the reasons for omitting or duplicating industry representations in the portfolio?
    4. Are any odd lots held?
    5. Have any rights been declared?
    6. Have records been updated?
    7. Are there any "buy" opportunities available (both domestic and foreign)?

8. Are dividends secure?

9. Are any warrants or options due to expire?

10. Are there any hedging or speculative uses for options?

11. Should any individual companies be reviewed in depth?

EVALUATING PORTFOLIO PERFORMANCE

Portfolio performance is usually evaluated by comparing its total rate of return to the average return of *comparable portfolios* during the same time period. Such comparisons may enable portfolio performance to be ranked relative to their peers.

- Total return may be determined by dividing the portfolio's total earnings (income plus capital gains or losses) by the average amount invested in the portfolio. A formula for determining the Pre-Tax Total Return is:

Total (Pre-Tax) Return = Increase in Market Value / Average Amount Invested

$$= \frac{[\text{Closing Value} - (\text{Opening Value} + \text{Net Contributions or} - \text{Net Deductions})]}{[\text{Opening Value} + (\text{Net Contributions or} - \text{Net Deductions}) / 2]^1}$$

Example 5:

Suppose a growth portfolio had: a beginning of period market value of $500,000; investor deposits during the period of $30,000 and withdrawals of $20,000; and an end of period market value of $530,000.

Solution:

Its total return is:

Return = [530,000 − (500,000 + 30,000 − 20,000)] ÷ [500,000 + (30,000 − 20,000) /2]
= 20,000 / 505,000 = 3.96%.

- This approach is subject to distortions if large withdrawals or deposits are made toward the end of the measurement period.

- Differences in portfolio characteristics also make accurate performance comparisons difficult. For example, asset mixes and risk characteristics may differ significantly from one fund to another, even within the same fund category.

- After-tax rates of return "net" out the income taxes payable by the portfolio in determining the return, while the real rate of return is approximated by subtracting the inflation rate for the period from the total return.

---

[1] There is an error in the formula presented on page 12-56 of the CSC textbook. The brackets in the numerator should appear before "Opening Value," as it appears here. The numbers provided in the example on pages 12-55 and 12-56 of the CSC textbook are calculated correctly using this version of the equation.

Chapter 12: Review Questions

( )   1. A client has approached you with the following information:

Security	Expected Return	Market Value
ABC Co.	7%	$20,000
DEF Co.	12%	$25,000
GHI Co.	15%	$45,000

If the client holds the given market values of the above securities in their portfolio, what is the return the investor can expect?

a) 11.33%

b) 12.39%

c) 12.41%

d) 11.83%

( )   2. Refer to the information in Question 1. If the portfolio is strictly growth oriented with the only expectation being capital gains, what will the portfolio be worth in one year if the expected growth translates into capital appreciation?

a) $99,000

b) $100,200

c) $101,151

d) none of the above

( )   3. You purchase a stock for $18 and hold it for two years. The annual dividend for this stock is $1.50. If you sell the stock at the end of the two years for $21, what is the percentage return on this stock?

a) 25%

b) 33.3%

c) 16.6%

d) 28.6%

( )   4. An investment plan is devised with a primary investment objective for growth, with a secondary objective of tax minimization. The asset mix for this plan should include:

a) mostly value stocks

b) mostly growth stocks

c) mostly speculative stocks

d) cannot say without more information

5. A fixed income manager who actively rebalances her portfolio weights in government versus corporate bonds in response to beliefs regarding changes in the relative yields on these securities would be referred to as a: ( )

   a) maturity switcher

   b) interest rate anticipator

   c) spread trader

   d) credit quality manager

6. The following represent constraints that should be considered when designing an investment policy except: ( )

   a) emotion

   b) ethical considerations

   c) investment knowledge

   d) market timing

7. A "value" manager would invest in stocks with relatively _____ P/E ratios and _____ dividend yields.   ( )

   a) high; high

   b) high; low

   c) low; low

   d) low; high

8. A _____ asset allocation strategy, results in buying stocks when they fall in price, and selling them when they rise in price.   ( )

   a) constant-weighting

   b) strategic

   c) tactical

   d) dynamic

9. Determine the total return on a portfolio with a beginning of period value of $50,000 that reached an ending value of $51,000, and received no interest or dividend income, if the net period contributions were $2,000.   ( )

   a) +1.96%

   b) −1.96%

   c) 0.0%

   d) none of the above

10. Each of the following risks can be reduced through diversification except: ( )

   a) interest rate risk

   b) default risk

   c) business risk

   d) systematic risk

( ) 11. Diversification will provide the greatest benefits when two securities display:

   a) perfect positive correlation

   b) perfect negative correlation

   c) zero correlation

   d) similar characteristics

( ) 12. Standard deviation measures total risk, while _____ is a measure of market risk.

   a) variance

   b) beta

   c) correlation

   d) none of the above

( ) 13. A stock with a beta of 0.6, will have an expected return that is:

   a) higher than the risk-free rate and the expected return on the market

   b) higher than the risk-free rate and lower than the expected return on the market

   c) lower than the risk-free rate

   d) cannot say without additional information

( ) 14. Which of the following would be the best asset mix for an aggressive young investor, with good investment knowledge, and a high tolerance for risk?

   a) 20% cash; 30% fixed income; 50% equities

   b) 10% cash; 35% fixed income; 55% equities

   c) 10% cash; 20% fixed income; 70% equities

   d) 5% cash; 40% fixed income; 55% equities

( ) 15. Which of the following is not a general strategy in relation to the equity cycle?

   a) Maintain or increase stock position during expansionary phase.

   b) Lengthen terms of bond holdings and avoid stocks during contraction phase.

   c) Buy long-term bonds that rally ahead of stocks in response to falling interest rates during the trough phase.

   d) all of the above are general strategies

( ) 16. The following investments would be considered as part of the fixed income component in an investor's portfolio except:

   a) two-year bonds

   b) preferred shares

   c) mortgages

   d) Canada Savings Bonds

17. What is the beta of a stock that has an expected return of 15%, if the market expected return is 10%, and the T-bill rate is 6%, according to CAPM?   ( )

    a) 1.11

    b) 2.25

    c) 2.50

    d) none of the above

18. Equity prices often rise due to the growth rate in earnings (and dividends) rising faster than interest rates during the later part of the _____ phase of the equity cycle.   ( )

    a) expansionary

    b) peak

    c) contraction

    d) trough

BUILDING THE RELATIONSHIP WITH THE CLIENT

- In addition to being technically competent, it is important for advisors to deal with clients effectively with respect to information gathering, ongoing communication, and education. In addition, advisors must ensure that they comply with industry regulations and adhere to ethical standards in all dealings with clients.

INFORMATION GATHERING, COMMUNICATION, AND EDUCATION

Information gathering is critical for financial advisors. They should be aware of essential details of each of their clients, including an understanding of the client's:

- current financial and personal status;
- investment goals and preferences; and
- risk tolerance.

Advisors also need to be aware of their clients' unique personal needs and goals, including:

- Their decision-making process.
- Their preferred method(s) of communicating with the advisor.
- Their psychological profile.
- The needs, goals, and desires of their family.

- Advisors need to be good listeners since many clients will not communicate their motivation for many decisions directly. Advisors also need to be aware that discussing personal financial matters is an emotional topic for most individuals.

- It is important to maintain regular contact with clients. This reassures clients that the advisor is acting in their best interests, and also enables the advisor to maintain current knowledge of the client's financial and personal situation.

- In order to develop a good working relationship with a client, it is advantageous for the client to be able to understand why certain decisions have been made. This suggests that it will pay to try and educate the client with respect to several matters.

In order to establish an investor's risk tolerance, it will be helpful to educate them regarding the various types of investment risks they face in addition to market risks, such as:

1. the risk of not investing, or investing too conservatively;
2. the risk of not diversifying;
3. purchasing power risk;
4. default risk; and
5. currency risk.

ETHICS AND THE FINANCIAL ADVISOR

- **Ethics** may be defined as a set of moral values that guide behavior and establish standards for judging whether actions are right or wrong.

All sellers of securities and mutual funds must adhere to the **Code of Ethics** for the securities industry. This code is based upon the following *principles*:

- Trust
- Integrity
- Justice
- Fairness
- Honesty
- Responsibility
- Reliability

The code imposes the following **primary ethical values** on registrants:

1. They must use proper care and exercise independent professional judgement.
2. They must conduct themselves with trustworthiness and integrity, and be honest and fair in all dealings with the public, clients, employers, and colleagues.

3. They must conduct business in a professional manner that will reflect positively on the industry, and encourage others to do so. They should also try to maintain and improve their own professional knowledge, and encourage others to do so as well.

4. They must comply with the regulations of the appropriate security act(s), as well as the requirements of any Self-Regulatory Organizations (SROs) of which they are members.

5. They must hold client information in strict confidence.

- There is an important distinction between ethical behaviour and complying with rules. While conformance with rules is one component of ethical behaviour, it is not always enough. Ethical behaviour implies making moral judgements and acting accordingly in situations that may not be covered by any specific rules.

STANDARDS OF CONDUCT

The **Standards of Conduct** for the securities industry expand on the Code of Ethics, establishing behaviour requirements that are based to a large extent on provincial securities acts and SRO rules. Some of the more important standards are discussed below, while the complete description of these standards is included in the appendix to Chapter 13 of the CSC text.

Know Your Client and Suitability: Advisors must make a concerted effort to *know the client*, including details of their financial and personal situation. This ensures the advisor cannot be faulted for providing the best advice possible, given their knowledge of the client's situation. The client's account should document the information provided, and the information should be updated in order to ensure the suitability of all investment recommendations.

Trustworthiness, Honesty, and Fairness: Clients need to be able to trust their financial advisors. This trust must cover two dimensions: *competency* and *integrity*. A competent advisor with little integrity cannot be trusted to make the best financial decisions for a client; neither can an advisor with integrity who is incompetent. One important aspect of maintaining integrity is the disclosure of all current and potential conflicts of interest. In order to promote competency among advisors, they must satisfy proficiency requirements, as well as participating in continuing education programs.

- **Fiduciary Duty and Professionalism:** The ongoing nature of the advisor-client relationship dictates a **fiduciary relationship** between advisors and their clients. Fiduciary relationships involve two or more parties where there may be an imbalance of knowledge or control, which invokes moral issues. In particular, financial advisors act as agents on the behalf of investors (the principals). Trust is of utmost importance in this principal-agent relationship because the principal's well-being is vulnerable to decisions made by the agent, who is expected to have greater expertise and/or authority. In order to ensure professionalism, the standards require that general business activity as well as attempts to solicit business, are conducted in a professional and responsible manner that promote respect and confidence from the public.

CASE STUDIES

- The following two case studies are similar in nature to those at the end of Chapter 13 in the CSC text. They apply the concepts developed in Chapters 12 and 13 of the CSC text, as well as some of the tax planning considerations discussed in Chapter 11.

CASE #1: BRIGID

- **Situation:** Brigid is single, 27 years old, and has been working at the same job for the past five years. She has no plans to leave her job and her current salary is $36,000 per year. It is reasonable to assume this amount will increase approximately 5% per year over the next 30 to 35 years. She has never invested in RRSPs, but has contributed to the CPP and her company pension plan for the past five years. She has recently finished paying off her student loan, and her only remaining debt is a car loan in the amount of $10,000. She rents a modest one bedroom apartment which costs her $550 per month and feels that she can live comfortably on $1,500 a month. Discuss what her primary investment objectives should focus on, and discuss what type of investment mix she should consider.

- **Personal Evaluation:** Brigid has steady employment, with good earnings potential and an employee registered retirement plan. She has good control over her debt situation and likely has room to borrow additional funds if necessary (for investment, housing, or consumption purposes). If we assume she is adequately insured and that she has no immediate plans to purchase a house, it is reasonable to assume that she is in a position to start investing for retirement. Given the fact that she has quickly paid off her student loan and has not borrowed a great deal of additional funds, it may be reasonable to assume she has a fairly conservative attitude toward managing her finances. In addition, the fact that she has not invested in RRSPs at all suggests that she may not be an extremely knowledgeable investor. Alternatively, it may signal that she is extremely conservative and wishes to pay off her debt first, even at the expense of foregoing the tax deduction benefits associated with RRSP contributions.

- **Investment Objectives:** Her primary investment objective should be *growth*, since she should generate more than sufficient income in the coming years to satisfy her cash flow requirements, and since retirement is some years away. Her secondary objectives would be *tax minimization* and *safety* since she is likely to be in the moderate-to-high tax bracket in the coming years, and since she appears to have a fairly conservative attitude toward managing her finances.

- **Investment Strategy:** Brigid's first move should be to take full advantage of her available RRSP contribution limit, which should be substantial due to the carry-over amounts available from previous years. This will minimize her tax obligations and the funds placed in RRSPs should be primarily invested in growth equities to satisfy her primary investment objective of growth. In order to maintain sufficient portfolio diversification, and in light of her apparent conservative disposition, she may want to maintain 5%-10% in money market funds and an additional 10%-20% in fixed income securities. Once she has exhausted her RRSP contribution limits, she may want to invest additional funds into more aggressive equity funds with long-term growth potential, since capital gains will only be realized when the shares are sold, and given the preferential tax treatment associated with any dividends received in the interim.

CASE #2: BRENNAN AND ANGELA

- **Situation:** Brennan and Angela have been married for 25 years and their children, Jason and Siobhan, are grown up and on their own. Angela and Brennan are both 53 years old and both of them have been teaching high school at the same school for the past thirty years. They both earn $62,000 per year and they plan to retire in five years. Each of them has invested $3,000 per year in RRSPs for the past 20 years, allocating approximately 20% to money market funds and the remaining 80 % to growth equity funds. They have both also contributed to the CPP and teachers' pension plan for the past 30 years. They recently finished paying off the mortgage on their home, which they plan to live in upon retirement and their only remaining debt is a car loan in the amount of $20,000. They feel they can live comfortably on $2,800 a month after retirement.

- **Questions:**

    1. Does there appear to be any opportunities for this couple to reduce taxes by using "income splitting" strategies? Briefly explain.

    2. Identify and briefly discuss what their primary investment objectives should focus on and identify any secondary objectives you feel are relevant.

    3. Prescribe and justify an appropriate investment mix for this couple.

    4. Recommend two options available to them if they decide to deregister their RRSPs immediately upon retirement.

- **Suggested Answers:**

    1. No, they both earn the same amount now and likely will until retirement; therefore, they are likely in the same tax bracket. In addition, they both have contributed about the same amount to registered plans, hence their income (and tax brackets) will remain virtually identical upon retirement.

    2. They are both in the "peak earnings" stage of their life cycle and preservation of capital should be their primary objective, since they plan on retiring in the near future. Since they are in a high tax bracket, tax minimization should be a secondary objective.

3. They should begin "adjusting" their asset mix toward safer securities. Many mixes are possible. For example, an appropriate target might be 20% cash (money market instruments), 40% fixed income securities, and 40% equities (primarily "blue chip" equities).

4. They could use the proceeds to purchase a life annuity with a guaranteed term or a fixed term annuity that provides benefits to age 90. Alternatively, or coincidentally, they could purchase a Registered Retirement Income Fund (RRIF), which provides annual income to age 90 or life. These strategies avoid paying tax on the full amount, which would occur if the full amounts were withdrawn upon deregistration of the plan.

Chapter 13: Review Questions

( )   1. Which of the following is not an investment risk that should be conveyed by a financial advisor to his/her client?

a) the risk of investing too conservatively

b) the risk of not investing

c) the risk of diversifying

d) currency risk

( )   2. Which of the following is a primary ethical value in the Code of Ethics established by the securities industry?

a) Registrants must not solicit business through channels other than those stipulated in the securities act(s).

b) Registrants must use proper care and exercise independent professional judgement.

c) Registrants must act quickly to ensure that all client accounts are settled by the required date.

d) Registrants must never assure their clients that a particular security price or return will be guaranteed in the future.

( )   3. What are the two components of a trust relationship between advisor and client?

a) knowledge and skill

b) competence and integrity

c) honesty and judgement

d) knowledge and disclosure

4. Which of the following statements best describes a fiduciary relationship? (   )

   a) They are agent-principal relationships where the principal is vulnerable and the agent has greater expertise or authority.

   b) They are agent-principal relationships where the agent is vulnerable and the principal has greater expertise or authority.

   c) They are agent-principal relationships where the principal needs the moral and ethical guidance of the agent.

   d) They are agency-principal relationships where the agent needs the moral and ethical guidance of the principal

5. Which of the following would not be classified as a fiduciary relationship? (   )

   a) The relationship between mother and child.

   b) The relationship between doctor and patient.

   c) The relationship between lawyer and client.

   d) They can all be classified as fiduciary relationships.

6. Which of the following is not included in the Canadian Securities Industry Standards of Conduct? (   )

   a) continuous education

   b) disclosure

   c) insider trading

   d) know your client

7. Financial advisors are required to know the essential details about each client which include: (   )

   I. The client's current financial status.

   II. The client's current personal status.

   III. The client's risk tolerance.

   IV. The client's investment goals and preferences.

   a) I, II, III, and IV

   b) I, II, and IV

   c) I, II, and III

   d) II, III, and IV

END–OF–CHAPTER REVIEW QUESTIONS

ANSWERS

Answers to End-of-Chapter Review Questions

Please note that the page references below refer to the chapter and page number(s) in the CSC textbook where you will find the information.

Question	Answer	Level of Difficulty
CHAPTER 1		
1.	B pg. 1-6, 1-7	M
2.	A pg. 1 3	M
3.	B pg. 1-33 to 1-36	D
4.	C pg. 1-1, 1-2	M
5.	B pg. 1-18	D
6.	D pg. 1-53	E
7.	C pg. 1-50	M
8.	B pg. 1-52 It is the Deputy Minister of Finance	D
CHAPTER 2		
1.	D pg. 2-4, 2-5	M
2.	D pg. 2-18, 2-19	E
3.	A pg. 2-36	M
4.	C pg. 2-32	M
5.	D I and IV pg. 2-23, 2-24	M
6.	B II and V pg. 2-24	M
7.	B pg. 2-14, 2-15	M
8.	A pg. 2-24	M
9.	C pg. 2-39	M
10.	B pg. 2-34 to 2-36	D
11.	C pg. 2-34 to 2-36	D
12.	B pg. 2-11	M
CHAPTER 3		
1.	D pg. 3-27	E
2.	B pg. 3-33	M
3.	C pg. 3-15, 3-16	M
4.	D pg. 3-17	M
5.	B pg. 3-18 to 3-20	M
6.	B pg. 3-10, 3-11	M
7.	C pg. 3-25	M

Question	Answer	Level of Difficulty
8.	C pg. 3-39	M
9.	C pg. 3-34	M
10.	D pg. 3-3	D
11.	C pg. 3-15, 3-16	D
12.	D pg. 3-26, 3-27	E
13.	D pg. 3-5	M
14.	A pg. 3-2	M
15.	B pg. 3-24	E

CHAPTER 4

Question	Answer	Level of Difficulty
1.	B pg. 4-10, 4-11	M
2.	C pg. 4-2	E
3.	D pg. 4-6	M
4.	C pg. 4-14	D
5.	A pg. 4-20, 4-21	M
6.	D Depreciation (year 1) = $50,000 \times 0.10 = $5,000$; Depreciation (year 2) = $45,000 \times 0.10 = $4,500$	D
7.	B pg. 4-15	M
8.	D pg. 4-27	M
9.	C pg. 4-13, 4-14, 4-33	M
10.	B pg. 4-30	E
11.	D pg. 4-14, 4-18	E
12.	B pg. 4-11, 4-12	E
13.	A pg. 4-28, 4-29	M
14.	C pg. 4-3	M
15.	D pg. 4-10, 4-11	M

CHAPTER 5

Question	Answer	Level of Difficulty
1.	C pg. 5-36	E
2.	C $[10 + (100 - 113.4)/10] / [(100 + 113.4)/2] = 8.12\%$	D
3.	A $(100\text{-}96)/96 \times (365/90) \times 100\% = 16.9\%$	M
4.	B pg. 5-41, 5-42	M
5.	D pg. 5- 37 to 5-40	M

Question	Answer		Level of Difficulty
6.	B	Price = $50 \times ([1 - 1/\{1.042\}^{28}] /.042) + 1,000 \times (1/[1.042]^{28}) = 814.27 + 316.01 = \$1,130.28$	D
7.	C	pg. 5-17, 5-39	M
8.	C	Accrued interest $= \$1,000 \times 0.10 \times 39/365 = \$10.68$	D
9.	C	pg. 5-35	M
10.	A	pg. 5-37	M
11.	D	pg. 5-37, 5-38	D
12.	B	pg. 5-38, 5-39	D
13.	A	pg. 5-7 to 5-9	M
14.	C	pg. 5-14	M
15.	A	pg. 5-12	E
16.	C	pg. 5-6	M
17.	C	pg. 5-45	M
18.	B	pg. 5-3	M
19.	A	pg. 5-37	E
20.	D	pg. 5-24	M
21.	C	pg. 5-17 to 5-19	M
22.	C	pg. 5-50	M
23.	B	pg. 5-41, 5-42	M
24.	B	pg. 5-5	M
25.	C	Purchase Price = $1,035 + (31/365 \times \$75) = \$1,041.37$	D

CHAPTER 6

1.	B	pg. 6-35	E
2.	D	pg. 6-36, 6-37	M
3.	C	Cost = $\$1.50 \times 500 = \$750$; Max. loan = $0.20 \times \$750 = \$150$; required deposit = $750 - 150 = \$600$	M
4.	D	No loan is permissible, therefore deposit $150 which when added to the initial deposit of $600 covers the $750 purchase price	M
5.	A	Require 130% of market value = $\$8 \times 1,000 \times 1.30 = \$10,400$; Required deposit = $10,400 - 8,000$ (proceeds) = $\$2,400$	M

Question	Answer		Level of Difficulty
6.	D	Require 130% of $7,000 = $9,100; Required deposit = 9,100 − 10,400 = −1,300 (surplus funds that can be withdrawn)	D
7.	A	Profit = ($8 − $5) × 1,000 = $3,000	M
8.	D	pg. 6-48	M
9.	B	pg. 6-47	E
10.	B	Premium % = (35 − [3 × 11]) / (3 × 11) = 6.1%	M
11.	C	Common yield = 0.22 / $11 = 2.0%	M
12.	D	Preferred yield = 2 / 35 = 5.7%; Payback = 6.1 / (5.7 − 2.0) = 1.65 years	D
13.	B	pg. 6-15	E
14.	C	pg. 6-24	D
15.	B	Dividend amount = .08 × 50 = $4; Market yield = 4 / 65 = 6.2%	M
16.	A	pg. 6-19 to 6-23	M
17.	A	pg. 6-18, 6-19	M
18.	B	pg. 6-26	M
19.	C	pg. 6-28, 6-29	M
20.	C	pg. 6-39	M
21.	C	pg. 6-36 to 6-38 (18,000 × .30 = 5,400)	M
22.	D	Max Loan = .70 × 2,000 × $1 = $18,200 Previous Loan = .7 × 2,000 × $9 = $12,600 Excess $ 5,600	M
23.	C	pg. 6-47	D
24.	D	pg. 6-42	D
25.	B	pg. 6-42 to 6-44	M

CHAPTER 7

1.	D	pg. 7-31, 7-32	M
2.	B	pg. 7-36, 7-37, 7-41	M
3.	D	Offering price = 40 / (1 − .06) = $42.55	M
4.	B	Both III and IV are false. pg. 7-59 to 7-61	D
5.	D	pg. 7-65, 7-67	M
6.	C	pg. 7-2, 7-3	M
7.	B	II and IV are both true. pg. 7-70	M

Question	Answer	Level of Difficulty
8.	A pg. 7-6, 7-7	E
9.	C pg. 7-10	M
10.	A pg. 7-11	E
11.	D pg. 7-68, 7-69	D
12.	D pg. 7-74, 7-75	M
13.	C pg. 7-05	M
14.	B pg. 7-53	M
15.	A pg. 7-44, 7-45	M
16.	B pg. 7- 40	E
17.	C pg. 7-13	D
18.	B pg. 7-57, 7-58	M
19.	A pg. 7-62, 7-63	M
20.	A pg. 7-63, 7-70, 7-73, 7-74	D

CHAPTER 8

1.	C pg. 8-3, 8-4	E
2.	C pg. 8-10	M
3.	A pg. 8-10	M
4.	C pg. 8-13	D
5.	B pg. 8-19, 8-20	M
6.	A pg. 8-32	M
7.	A pg. 8-41 $145,000 − $100,000 = $45,000 taxable capital gain	M
8.	C pg. 8-41 Since the capital gain on the guarantee of $22,000 cancels out the capital loss, no taxes are payable	D
9.	D pg. 8-51	M
10.	D pg. 8-1	E

CHAPTER 9

1.	A pg. 9-2	E
2.	B pg. 9-7	M
3.	A pg. 9-10	M
4.	C Call: IV = Max (12 − 15, 0) = 0 Put: IV = Max (16 − 12, 0) = 4	M

Question	Answer	Level of Difficulty
5.	A $[(\$1 \times 100) - (\$3 \times 100)] +$ $[0 - (\$4.50 \times 100)]$ Total loss $= (-200 - 450) = -650$	D
6.	D III and VI are true. pg. 9-21, 9-22	M
7.	C II and V pg. 9-21, 9-22	D
8.	A IV = Max $(10 - 12, 0) = 0$	M
9.	C Time value $= 3 - 0 = 3$	M
10.	C pg. 9-24 to 9-29	M
11.	D IV $= (40 - 35)/(4 + 1) = \$1.00$	M
12.	C IV $= (38 - 35)/4 = \$0.75$	M

CHAPTER 10

1.	C pg. 10-4 to 10-11	M
2.	D pg. 10-2, 10-3	M
3.	A pg. 10-2	E
4.	A $Div_1 = 0.375 \times 4.00 = \$1.50$; Intrinsic value $= 1.50 / (11 - .05) = \$25.00$	D
5.	B Payout $= 2 / 5 = 0.40$; P/E $= 0.40 / (.12 - .04) = 5$	D
6.	D pg. 10-15, 10-16	M
7.	A I and II pg. 10-17	M
8.	B pg. 10-53, 10-54	M
9.	D pg. 10-66, 10-67, 10-71, 10-72	M
10.	D pg. 10-14, 10-15	M
11.	C pg. 10-21	M
12.	B pg. 10-55 to 10-61	M
13.	B $r = (4.00 / 50) + .04 = 0.12$ or 12%	M
14.	A pg. 10-52, 10-53	M
15.	B pg. 10-61, 10-62	M
16.	A pg. 10-9	M
17.	C pg. 10-8, 10-9	M
18.	B $(10,000 + 5,000 + 35,000)$ $/ (100,000) = 0.50$	M
19.	B $(85,000) / (20,000) = \$4.25$	M
20.	C EPS $= (7,000 - 1,500) / 20,000 = \$0.275$, so P/E $= (10) / (0.275) = 36.4$	D

Question	Answer		Level of Difficulty
21.	A	Apparent tax rate = (7,000) /(7,000 − 1,000 + 2,000 + 7,000) = 0.467 Before-tax pref. dividends = 1,500 × (1/[1 − .467]) = 2,814 Coverage = (7,000 - 1,000 + 2,000 + 7,000 + 10,000) / (10,000 + 2,814) = 25,000 / 12,814 = 1.95 times	D
22.	C	pg. 10-35	M
23.	D	pg. 10-38 to 10-42	M
24.	B	II and III pg. 10-33	M
25.	B	II and III pg. 10-31, 10-36	D

CHAPTER 11

1.	C	ACB = ([$7,500 / 300] / 2.5) = $10 per common share	D
2.	A	This is a superficial loss pg. 11-23, 11-24	M
3.	C	ACB = (([200 × 20] + 60) + ([300 × 25] + 100)) / 500 = (4,060 + 7,600) / 500 = $23.32 per share	D
4.	B	Taxes payable = (200 × 1.25 (0.40) − (250 × .1333) = 100 − 33.33 = $66.67	D
5.	B	pg. 11-2	E
6.	C	pg. 11-26 to 11-30	M
7.	D	pg. 11-15	M
8.	A	pg. 11-7, 11-8	E

CHAPTER 12

1.	B	(.07 × [20,000/90,000]) + (.12 × [25,000/90,000]) + (.15 × [45,000/90,000]) = 12.39%	M
2.	C	(90,000 × 1.1239) = $101,151	D
3.	B	([1.5 × 2] + [21-18]) / 18 = 33.3%	D
4.	D	All are possible-would need to know more about risk preferences	M
5.	C	pg. 12-30	M
6.	D	pg. 12-21 to 12-23	E
7.	D	pg. 12-28, 12-29	M
8.	A	pg. 12-45 to 12-47	M

Question	Answer	Level of Difficulty
9.	B Total return = (51,000 − [50,000 + 2,000]) / (50,000 + [2,000 / 2]) = -1,000 / 51,000 = -1.96%.	D
10.	D pg. 12-7, 12-8	E
11.	B pg. 12-11 to 12-14	M
12.	B pg. 12-8, 12-9	E
13.	B pg.12-17	M
14.	C pg. 12-9, 12-40	M
15.	C pg. 12-36	D
16.	D pg. 12-34	M
17.	B Beta (10 − 6) + 6 = 15, so Beta = 9 / 4 = 2.25	D
18.	A pg. 12-38, 12-39	M

CHAPTER 13

1.	C pg. 13-2, 13-3	M
2.	B pg. 13-3, 13-4, 13-44	M
3.	B pg. 13-5, 13-6	M
4.	A pg. 13-7	M
5.	D pg. 13-7	E
6.	C pg. 13-45	D
7.	A pg. 13-1	M

E X A M 1

CSC PRACTICE EXAMINATION

CHAPTERS 1-6

( )   1. Primary markets involve _____ , while secondary markets involve
              _____ .

           a) the sale of securities; the sale of derivatives.

           b) the sale of new securities to investors; trading of previously issued secu-
              rities among investors.

           c) the sale of securities of large corporations on stock exchanges; the sale
              of securities of smaller firms between individual investors.

           d) trading of securities on stock exchanges; trading of securities between
              investors using a dealer as an agent.

( )   2. Bearer bonds differ from registered bonds in that:

           a) bearer bonds have the name of the owner on the face of the bond,
              while registered bonds are considered to be owned by the actual hold-
              er.

           b) bearer bonds have no maturity date.

           c) bearer bonds are considered to be owned by the actual holder of the
              bond, while registered bonds have the name of the owner on the face
              of the bonds.

           d) bearer bonds have no coupon payments.

( )   3. The Canadian Investor Protection Fund (CIPF) covers the personal loss-
              es of an investor's position up to a maximum of:

           a) $100,000

           b) $1,000,000

           c) $60,000

           d) $500,000

( )   4. The Minority Interest item on a balance sheet arises from the use of the
              _____ of accounting.

           a) consolidation method

           b) cost method

           c) LIFO method

           d) equity method

( )   5. _____ is an example of a leading business cycle indicator.

           a) Business investment spending

           b) Housing starts

           c) Labour costs

           d) Inflation levels

6. The _____ sits on the Board of Directors for the Bank of Canada   ( )
   (B of C), but has no voting rights.

   a) Governor of the B of C

   b) Senior Deputy Governor of the B of C

   c) Minister of Finance

   d) Deputy Minister of Finance

7. During periods of rising prices, the _____ method of inventory valuation   ( )
   will lead to the highest profits.

   a) LIFO

   b) FIFO

   c) average cost

   d) equity method

8. GDP will exceed GNP if: ( )

   a) The value of all goods and services produced by the country's nationals
      exceeds the value of all goods produced within a country in a year.

   b) The value of all goods and services produced by the country's nationals is
      less than the value of all goods produced within a country in a year.

   c) GDP will never exceed GNP.

   d) none of the above

9. During a period of declining interest rates, which of the following bonds   ( )
   would an investor prefer to hold, assuming they are from the same issuer?

   a) 5-year, 10% coupon non-callable bonds

   b) 10-year, 10% coupon non-callable bonds

   c) 10-year, 10% coupon callable bonds

   d) 10-year, non-callable strip bonds

10. The settlement date for Government of Canada treasury bills is the   ( )
    _____ the transaction.

    a) the second clearing day after

    b) the third clearing day after

    c) the same day as

    d) the next clearing day after

( )   11. The maximum loan amount by investment dealers to clients for the purchase of shares with a market price of $1.50 per share is:

   a) no loans are permissible

   b) 20%

   c) 40%

   d) 50%

( )   12. If a prospectus contains a misrepresentation, security purchasers have the right of:

   a) rescission

   b) withdrawal

   c) limited liability

   d) due diligence

( )   13. When a security offering requires an offering memorandum rather than a full prospectus, it is generally known as a _____ offering.

   a) initial public

   b) private

   c) final

   d) seasoned

( )   14. Auction markets are characterized as:

   a) a market where buyers and sellers of securities converge to trade with one another.

   b) a network of dealers who trade with each other over the phone or computer network.

   c) always having more buyers than sellers.

   d) a market without a market place.

( )   15. You decide to purchase 10 board lots of the common shares of company A on margin. The share is not eligible for special margin, and is presently trading for $2. How much cash must you deposit with your broker? .

   a) $2,000

   b) $1,000

   c) $800

   d) $1,400

16. Refer to the information given in Question 15. If the price of A dropped immediately to $1.80, how much will you be required to deposit into your margin account?   (   )

    a) $720

    b) $1,280

    c) $280

    d) There is no need to deposit more into the account, but rather you are eligible to withdraw $280.

17. A friend of yours decides to short sell 1,000 shares of a security that is not eligible for special margin, and is trading at $5. What amount must she deposit into a margin account?   (   )

    a) $1,500

    b) $5,000

    c) $2,500

    d) $6,500

18. Refer to the information given in Question 17. What profit (loss) does your friend realize if she closes her short position when the price of the underlying share is $4?   (   )

    a) profit of $1,000

    b) loss of $1,000

    c) profit of $2,500

    d) loss of $2,500

19. _____ is a colloquialism used to describe the unofficial unlisted market for newly issued but as of yet, unlisted securities.   (   )

    a) Auction market

    b) Street certificate

    c) Black market

    d) Grey market

20. During inflationary periods, inventory value as calculated using the LIFO method will be lower than the inventory value calculated using

    _____ .   (   )

    a) FIFO

    b) average cost

    c) none of the above

    d) both (a) and (b)

( )   21. Unemployment that rises when the economy softens and drops when the economy strengthens again is known as:

     a) structural unemployment

     b) cyclical unemployment

     c) natural unemployment

     d) accelerating unemployment

( )   22. The primary difference between depreciation and amortization is that:

     a) Depreciation is the accounting term for amortization.

     b) Depreciation is a non-cash expense while amortization is a cash expense.

     c) Depreciation is applied against fixed assets while amortization is applied against deferred charges and intangible assets.

     d) There is no difference between the two, you can use either term and it will mean the same thing.

( )   23. The Liquidity Preference Theory states that:

     a) Investors prefer longer-term bonds to shorter-term bonds because they exhibit less interest rate risk.

     b) Investors must be compensated for investing in shorter-term bonds.

     c) Investors prefer shorter-term bonds to longer-term bonds because they exhibit less interest rate risk.

     d) Investors prefer to invest in stocks instead of bonds.

( )   24. _____ orders are executed only if a specific price or better can be obtained.

     a) Limit

     b) Market

     c) Stop-Buy

     d) Stop-Loss

( )   25. _____ orders are used to limit losses on short positions.

     a) Limit

     b) Stop-Buy

     c) Good Till Cancelled

     d) Stop-Loss

( )   26. Schedule II banks may be:

     a) owned wholly by residents.

     b) owned wholly by non-residents.

     c) owned *only* partially by either residents or non-residents.

     d) both (a) and (b).

27. Which of the following is NOT a major use of investment capital?   (   )

    a) direct investment in land

    b) direct investment in equipment

    c) indirect investment in financial assets

    d) none of the above

28. The following are all major capital account components except for: (   )

    a) direct investment

    b) international reserves transactions

    c) transfers

    d) portfolio investment

Refer to the following information to answer Questions 29-32:   (   )

A firm presently has $100 million (face value) in non-callable bonds outstanding. They pay annual coupons at a rate of 7% and the bonds will mature 6 years from today.

29. What is the present market price of the bonds if the yield to maturity on "identical" bonds is 8%?   (   )

    a) $88.91m

    b) $95.38m

    c) $102.42m

    d) $96.89m

30. Under which of the following cases would the price of the bond be lower?   (   )

    a) if the bond was callable

    b) if the bond was extendible

    c) if the bond was convertible

    d) if the bond was retractable

31. What would be an investor's one-year pre-tax percentage return on these bonds if they were purchased at a 5% premium over face value and resold after one year, when the yield on the bonds was 7%?   (   )

    a) 1.9%

    b) -1.3%

    c) 7.9%

    d) not enough information to answer this question

( )   32. What is the accrued interest on these bonds 120 days after the last coupon date?

   a) $2.301m

   b) $2.129m

   c) $1.899m

   d) not enough information to answer this question

Refer to the following information to answer Questions 33-35:

A convertible preferred share is presently selling for $40 and is convertible into two common shares which are presently selling for $18.50 each. The annual dividends are $2.00 for the preferred shares, and $0.45 for the common shares.

( )   33. What is the conversion premium percentage?

   a) 8.11%

   b) 8.25%

   c) 7.85%

   d) 7.90%

( )   34. What is the dividend yield on the preferred shares? .

   a) 2.4%

   b) 1.1%

   c) 5.0%

   d) 10.8%

( )   35. What is the payback for these convertibles?

   a) 3.16 years

   b) 1.62 years

   c) 3.33 years

   d) not enough information to answer this question

( )   36. What is the main difference between Collateral Trust Bonds and Equipment Trust Certificates?

   a) Equipment Trust Certificates are secured by pledge of financial assets, while Collateral Trust Bonds are secured by rolling stock.

   b) Collateral Trust Bonds are long-term while Equipment Trust Certificates are for less than one year.

   c) Collateral Trust Bonds are short-term while Equipment Trust Certificates are long-term.

   d) Equipment Trust Certificates are secured by rolling stock, while Collateral Trust Bonds are secured by a pledge of financial assets.

37. The following protective provisions place restrictions on additional bor-   (   )
    rowings by a corporation except the _____ .

    a) after-acquired clause

    b) closed-end mortgage

    c) open-end mortgage with restrictive provisions

    d) the sinking fund clause

Refer to the following information to answer Questions 38-39:   (   )

You decide to purchase common shares of two companies on margin. The first share
(X) is eligible for special margin and is presently trading for $12, while the second
share (Y) is trading at $1.80.

38. What is your total margin requirement if you purchase 1,000 shares of X   (   )
    and 1,000 shares of Y? .

    a) $4,500

    b) $4,680

    c) $2,340

    d) $5,900

39. If the price of X increases immediately to $12.75 and the price of Y falls   (   )
    rapidly to $1.40, how much (if any) will you be required to deposit in
    your margin account?

    a) $0

    b) $195

    c) $1800

    d) able to withdraw $205

40. What is the difference between direct obligation and guaranteed obliga-   (   )
    tion debt securities?

    a) Direct obligation bonds are issued in the name of a crown corporation,
       while guaranteed obligation bonds are issued by the government.

    b) Direct obligation bonds are issued by the federal government, while
       guaranteed bonds are issued by provincial governments.

    c) Direct obligation bonds are issued by the provincial government, while
       guaranteed bonds are issued by the federal government.

    d) Direct obligation bonds are issued by the government, while guaran-
       teed bonds are issued in the name of a crown corporation but backed
       by the provincial government.

( )   41. The following are all advantages to issuing preferred shares except for:

   a) does not affect debt-equity ratio adversely

   b) greater financing flexibility

   c) dividends are paid from after-tax earnings

   d) none of the above

( )   42. What is the yield on a 190-day Government of Canada treasury bill that is priced at 99.45?

   a) 66.97%

   b) 1.06%

   c) 2.19%

   d) not enough information to answer this question

( )   43. What is the yield to maturity on a 10% bond that pays out coupons semi-annually and has 10 years to maturity if the bond is selling at par?

   a) 10.0%

   b) 13.4%

   c) 8.31%

   d) not enough information to answer this question

( )   44. The following is an example of a Eurobond:

   a) A Canadian corporation issues bonds denominated in German Deutsche Marks in the German market.

   b) The U.S. government issues bonds denominated in Swiss Francs in the Swiss market.

   c) A French corporation issues bonds in Italian Lira in the Italian market.

   d) An Australian company issues bonds denominated in Canadian Dollars in the Belgium market.

( )   45. The following are all advantages to listing common shares except for:

   a) prestige and goodwill.

   b) larger equity base can support more debt.

   c) market value of a company is easily established for estate, merger, or takeover purposes.

   d) none of the above

46. Which of the following statements is true of non-competitive bids?   ( )

   a) Non-competitive bids must be in multiples of $5,000, with a minimum of $250,000 per bid, no maximum amount per bid.

   b) Non-competitive bids must be in multiples of $50,000, with a minimum of $250,000 per bid, no maximum amount per bid.

   c) Non-competitive bids must be in multiples of $50,000, with a minimum of $100,000 per bid, and a maximum of $500,000 per bid.

   d) Non-competitive bids must be in multiples of $5,000, with a minimum of $25,000 per bid, and a maximum of $3 million per bidder.

47. The difference between an AON buy order and an any part buy order is: ( )

   a) An any part order is usually at a specific price and remains on the dealer's books until the order is executed or cancelled, while an AON order is one that is good for a specified number of days and then is automatically cancelled if it hasn't been filled.

   b) An AON order is usually at a specific price and remains on the dealer's books until the order is executed or cancelled, while an any part order is one that is good for a specified number of days and then is automatically cancelled if it hasn't been filled.

   c) An any part order is an order than the client will accept all stock in odd, broken, or board lots up to the full amount of the order, while an AON order is one in which the total number of shares as specified in the order must be purchased before the client will accept the fill.

   d) An AON order is an order than the client will accept all stock in odd, broken, or board lots up to the full amount of the order, while an any part order is one in which the total number of shares as specified in the order must be purchased before the client will accept the fill.

48. When is it appropriate to use the consolidated accounting method?   ( )

   a) When a parent company owns less than 20% of a subsidiary.

   b) When the parent company owns between 20% and 50% of a subsidiary.

   c) When the parent owns more than 50% of the voting shares of a subsidiary.

   d) none of the above

( )   49. What are the major functions of the Bank of Canada?

         I. Act as the government's fiscal agent.

         II. Regulate credit and currency in the best interests of the country.

         III. Conduct monetary policy.

         IV. Control and protect the external value of the national monetary unit.

         V. Act for the government in the issuance and removal of bank notes.

     a) I, II, III

     b) II, IV

     c) I, III, V

     d) all of the above

( )   50. The primary investment objectives include:

     a) marketability and tax minimization.

     b) liquidity, growth, and tax minimization.

     c) safety, income, and growth of capital.

     d) both (a) and (c).

( )   51. What difficulties and hazards are associated with short selling a stock?

         I. There can be difficulties borrowing the required quantity of the security sold short to cover the short sale.

         II. The short seller is not liable for any dividends paid during the period the account is short.

         III. There are difficulties in obtaining up-to-date information on total short sales on a security.

         IV. The short seller is responsible for maintaining adequate margin in the short account.

     a) I, II, III, IV

     b) I, II, IV

     c) II, III

     d) I, III, IV

( )   52. Three advantages of incorporation include:

     a) ease of ownership transfer, professional management, and double taxation

     b) loss of flexibility, the possibility of double taxation, and additional administrative costs

     c) limited liability of shareholders, continuity of existence, and ease of ownership transfer

     d) management flexibility, complications involving withdrawal of capital, and possible tax benefits

53. The four key tests employed to analyze preferred share quality include: ( )

    a) interest coverage, preferred dividend coverage, independent credit analysis, and equity per preferred share

    b) debt analysis, preferred dividend coverage, independent credit analysis, and market to book value analysis

    c) preferred dividend coverage, independent credit analysis, book value per preferred share, and record of continuous dividend policy

    d) record of continuous dividend policy, preferred dividend coverage, liquidity analysis, and independent credit analysis

54. Foreign bonds are issued _____, while eurobonds are issued _____ .   ( )

    a) in the currency and country of the issuer; in international markets in any number of different currencies

    b) when the domestic bond market is weak; in international markets in any number of different currencies

    c) in a foreign market in the currency denomination of that country; in international markets in any number of different currencies

    d) in international markets in any number of different currencies; in a foreign market in the currency denomination of that country

55. A dealer market _____ , while an auction market is _____ .   ( )

    a) is designed for the primary markets; where securities in the secondary markets are traded

    b) is where all transactions converge to one location; a network of dealers who trade by phone or computer network

    c) is where institutions trade; designed for individual investors

    d) consists of a network of dealers who trade with each other over the phone or over a computer network; where all transactions converge to one location

Refer to the following information to answer Questions 56-57:

Monika feels that higher fuel prices will be bad for transportation companies. She identifies Air North Inc. as a likely candidate for share depreciation. She decides to short sell 500 shares of Air North Inc. (eligible for reduced margin) which are currently trading for $22.

56. How much money will Monika have to put in her margin account?   ( )

    a) $3,300

    b) $5,500

    c) $7,700

    d) none of the above

( )   57. Would Monika receive a margin call and, if so, how much would she
           need to deposit into her account if the shorted ABC shares immediately
           increased to $25?

       a) She would not receive a margin call therefore no additional funds
          would need to be deposited.

       b) She would receive a margin call and be required to deposit an addition-
          al $1,950.

       c) She would receive a margin call and be required to deposit an addition-
          al $2,250.

       d) none of the above

( )   58. What factors below influence interest rates?

       a) Political stability, unemployment rate, demand and supply of capital,
          inflation, and economy's performance.

       b) Unemployment rate, current account, inflation differentials, default
          risk, central bank creditability, and the exchange rate.

       c) Inflation, demand and supply of capital, default risk, central bank cred-
          itability, central bank operations, and the exchange rate.

       d) Inflation, the exchange rate, political stability, default risk, interest rate
          differentials, and unemployment rate.

( )   59. If a nation is running a fiscal deficit, it is:

       a) worse off as the result of its trade with foreign countries

       b) encountering a balance of payments disequilibrium

       c) spending more on goods and services than it is raising in tax revenues

       d) importing more goods and services than it is exporting

( )   60. The three theories of the term structure of interest rates are:

       a) rational expectations theory, market segmentations hypothesis, and liq-
          uidity preference theory

       b) random walk hypothesis, rational expectations theory, and the market
          segmentations theory

       c) capital market theory, random walk hypothesis, and liquidity preference
          theory

       d) market segmentations theory, liquidity preference theory, and expecta-
          tions theory

( )   61. What are the five phases of the business cycle in the correct order?

       a) recession, peak, contraction, recovery, expansion

       b) peak, recession, recovery, trough, expansion

       c) expansion, trough, recession, recovery, expansion, peak

       d) expansion, peak, recession, trough, recovery

62. Higher interest rates do not affect the economy in which of the following ways?   ( )

    a) They raise the cost of borrowing for investment purposes.

    b) They discourage consumers from spending capital on items such as durable goods.

    c) They reduce available household income because of the higher proportion of income that is needed to service debt.

    d) none of the above.

63. Which depreciation method produces a lower depreciation charge for the first year in which an asset is purchased?   ( )

    a) straight line

    b) declining balance

    c) sum of the year's digit

    d) double declining

Refer to the following bond quote to answer Questions 64-65:

XYZ Company   6.00%   1 July 04/09   100.50   101.20   5.94

64. Which of the following statements regarding this bond is false?   ( )

    a) It is a retractable bond.

    b) It is an extendible bond.

    c) It pays coupons on July 1 and January 1 every year.

    d) none of the above

65. If you were to sell this bond on the date this quote was available, and the date was February 9, how much would you receive from the buyer of the bond?   ( )

    a) $1,005

    b) $1,012

    c) $1,011.58

    d) $1,018.58

66. The underwriting expenses associated with a debt issue are usually _____ those associated with common equity issues.   ( )

    a) similar to

    b) lower than

    c) greater than

    d) unrelated to

( )   67. Governments issue debt for the following reasons, except:

a) to fund deficits

b) to develop income-producing services

c) to increase working capital

d) to fund infrastructure projects

        68. _____ is an example of a coincident business cycle indicator.

( )   a) Business investment spending

b) Housing starts

c) Retail sales

d) Inflation levels

( )   69. The bank rate is set at which of the following levels?

a) The yield on three-month T-bills plus 0.25%.

b) The upper limit of the Bank's operating band for the overnight rate.

c) The lower limit of the Bank's operating band for the overnight rate.

d) none of the above

( )   70. The _____ suggests that the yield curve represents the supply and demand for bonds of various terms, which are primarily influenced by the bigger players in each sector.

a) Liquidity Preference Theory

b) Expectations Theory

c) Market Segmentation Theory

d) Rational Expectations Hypothesis

( )   71. What is the yield to maturity on a 6% bond that pays out coupons semi-annually and has 20 years to maturity if the bond is selling at 120% of par?

a) 6%

b) 6.36%

c) 4.55%

d) none of the above

( )   72. Which of the following individuals would be considered corporate insiders?

a) an individual owning 5.5% of the company's voting shares

b) a director of a parent company

c) both (a) and (b)

d) none of the above

73. Which of the following activities by investment advisors is not prohibited?   (   )

    a) telephoning residences

    b) calling at residences

    c) bucketing

    d) maintaining confidential numbered accounts

74. A _____ preferred share would suit a conservative investment   (   )
    portfolio.

    a) Convertible

    b) Retractable

    c) Variable dividend

    d) Foreign-pay

75. Which of the following statements about fixed income properties is   (   )
    incorrect?

    a) Prices are inversely related to interest rates.

    b) Prices exhibit greater interest rate risk the longer the term to maturity.

    c) The smaller the coupon rate, the less the interest rate risk.

    d) none of the above

76. The third step in the underwriting process involves: (   )

    a) the issuing of securities to the Financing Group

    b) the selling of securities to the Marketing Group

    c) the disposition of securities for sale

    d) the waiting period

77. A fixed asset is purchased for $80,000. The depreciation expense in year   (   )
    three, if it is depreciated on a declining balance method at a rate of 10%,
    will be:

    a) $6,480

    b) $7,280

    c) $8,000

    d) $9,720

78. Refer to the above question. If that fixed asset has a useful life of seven   (   )
    years and an expected salvage value of $10,000, what is the depreciation
    charge in year three if the straight line method is used?

    a) $8,000

    b) $11,430

    c) $10,000

    d) $12,857

(   )   79. The primary difference between treasury issues and secondary issues is that:

a) treasury issues involve the issuance of securities already held by the public while secondary issues include any type of follow up issues

b) secondary issues involve the issuance of securities already held by the public while treasury issues are follow up issues

c) treasury issues occur when a growing firm decides to go public while secondary issues are follow up issues

d) there is no difference between the two

(   )   80. A company has 800,000 shares outstanding before it undergoes a 1 for 4 consolidation. After the consolidation, the number of shares outstanding will be:

a) unchanged

b) 3.2 million

c) 0.2 million

d) 1.6 million

(   )   81. If the real rate of interest is 6% and the rate of inflation is 2%, what is the nominal rate of interest?

a) 6%

b) 4%

c) 8%

d) not enough information available

(   )   82. A company declares a dividend that is payable on March 19 to holders of record on February 1. In order to be entitled to receive this dividend, you must buy the shares prior to:

a) March 19

b) February 1

c) January 31

d) January 30

(   )   83. During the process of issuing shares a _____ is prepared, which is an information circular for in-house use only.

a) preliminary prospectus

b) red herring

c) greensheet

d) primary prospectus

84. Which of the following statements about issuers under the POP system is incorrect?   ( )

    a) Issuers have been filing annual and interim statements for 24 months prior to the issue.

    b) Issuers are not in default of any requirements under the relevant securities legislation.

    c) Issuers have a large public float.

    d) none of the above

85. A _____ preferred share would suit an aggressive and sophisticated investment portfolio.   ( )

    a) Convertible

    b) Retractable

    c) Variable dividend

    d) Participating

86. If the yield to maturity is less than the coupon rate, a bond must be: ( )

    a) selling at a discount

    b) selling at a premium

    c) selling at face value

    d) a zero coupon bond

87. The settlement date for four-year Government of Canada bonds is _____ the transaction.   ( )

    a) the second clearing day after

    b) the third clearing day after

    c) the same day as

    d) the next clearing day after

88. All else being equal, a _____ bond will always sell for more than an otherwise similar _____ bond.   ( )

    a) retractable; callable

    b) callable; retractable

    c) callable; extendible

    d) floating rate; fixed rate

( )   89. _____ would appear at the top of the liabilities side of a company's balance sheet, followed by _____ , then _____ , and then by _____.

a) dividends payable; income taxes payable; accounts payable; bank advances

b) income taxes payable; dividends payable; bank advances; accounts payable

c) bank advances; income taxes payable; accounts payable; dividends payable

d) bank advances; accounts payable; dividends payable; income taxes payable

( )   90. The following are examples of intangible assets except:

a) goodwill

b) deferred charges

c) trademarks

d) none of the above

( )   91. The second paragraph in the auditor's report is known as the _____ paragraph.

a) tertiary

b) scope

c) opinion

d) all of the above

( )   92. The following statements regarding GICs are true except:

a) They are not insured by CDIC.

b) They can be used as collateral for loans.

c) They can be automatically renewed at maturity.

d) Many GICs offer compound interest.

( )   93. A client may request arbitration from a SRO, under which of the following situations?

a) The claim amount is $150,000 and the events in dispute originated in Ontario in January 1998.

b) The claim amount is $150,000 and the events in dispute originated in Quebec in January 1998.

c) The claim amount is $100,000 and the events in dispute originated in Ontario in January 1998.

d) The claim amount is $100,000 and the events in dispute originated in Quebec in January 1998.

94. What would be the market price of 6% preferred shares with a par value of $20 that have a required rate of return of 8%?   ( )

    a) $15

    b) $20

    c) $26.67

    d) none of the above

95. The following suggest that a preferred share of an industrial company is low quality except: ( )

    a) It has a preferred dividend coverage ratio of 2.5.

    b) It has an equity per preferred share ratio that is 1.5 times the par value of the shares.

    c) It is rated P-1 by CBRS.

    d) none of the above

96. The Miscellaneous Assets category on the balance sheet would include all of the following except: ( )

    a) cash surrender value of life insurance

    b) amounts due from directors

    c) copyrights

    d) advances to subsidiaries

97. Contributions to employee pension plans will be deducted in: ( )

    a) the operating section of the earnings statement

    b) the non-operating section of the earnings statement

    c) the owners' section of the earnings statement

    d) they are not deducted on the earnings statement, but rather show up as a liability on the balance sheet

98. Company A owns 25% of Company B. If Company B earns $100 million and pays dividends of $12.5 million to Company A, what entry will Company A make on their earnings statement?   ( )

    a) $100 million in income from subsidiaries

    b) $25 million in equity income

    c) $12.5 million in dividend income

    d) none of the above

( ) 99. _____ are more common than _____ for preferred share issues.

a) Purchase funds; sinking fund provisions

b) Sinking fund provisions; purchase funds

c) Callable features; cumulative features

d) both (b) and (c) are true

( ) 100. Client orders have priority over orders that are labeled as:

a) Pro orders

b) N-C orders

c) either (a) or (b)

d) neither (a) nor (b)

EXAM 2

CSC PRACTICE EXAMINATION

CHAPTERS 7-13

( )   1. The chief difference between a warrant and a right is that:

a) A warrant is generally long term and is issued to enable new funds to be raised immediately, while a right is generally short term and is usually attached to another issue as a sweetener.

b) A warrant is generally long term and is usually attached to another issue as a sweetener, while a right is generally short term and is issued to enable new funds to be raised immediately.

c) A warrant is generally short term and is usually attached to another issue as a sweetener, while a right is generally long term and is issued to enable new funds to be raised immediately.

d) A warrant is generally short term and is issued to enable new funds to be raised immediately, while a right is generally long term and is usually attached to another issue as a sweetener.

( )   2. Which of the following would be likely to exert a positive influence on the general level of stock prices?

I. A majority government is replaced by a minority government.

II. Short-term interest rates rise while long-term interest rates fall.

III. Unemployment approaches the full employment unemployment rate.

IV. There is a significant increase in long-term bond prices.

V. The government announces a significant cut in corporate tax rates.

VI. The consumer price index declines unexpectedly.

VII. The federal government deficit is higher than anticipated.

a) I, II, VI, VII

b) II, IV, V, VI

c) II, IV, VI, VII

d) II, III, VI

( )   3. Refer to the above list of events from Question 2. Which events would exert a negative influence on the general level of stock prices?

a) III, IV, V

b) I, III, VII

c) I, II, VII

d) II, III, VII

Use the following information to answer Questions 4-5:

A company has issued warrants which are presently outstanding. One warrant is required to purchase one common share. The common share price is presently $20, the warrant price is $3 and the exercise price of the warrant is $22.

4. The intrinsic value and time value of one warrant is: (   )

    a) $3 and 0, respectively

    b) $2 and $19, respectively

    c) $2 and $3, respectively

    d) 0 and $3, respectively

5. The leverage potential of the warrant is: (   )

    a) 7.33

    b) 0.07

    c) 1.1

    d) 6.67

6. _____ investment funds invest primarily in short-term instru-   (   )
ments such as T-Bills and commercial paper.

    a) Money market

    b) Mortgage

    c) Bond

    d) Balanced

7. The net asset value (NAV) of a fund that has a 5% sales charge and an   (   )
offering price of $60 per unit is:

    a) $63

    b) $65.20

    c) $57

    d) $56.85

8. One difference between Labour Sponsored Venture Capital Corpora-   (   )
tions (LSVCCs) and mutual funds is that LSVCCS:

    a) may exceed 10% ownership in companies

    b) are primarily long-term investments

    c) are not RRSP eligible

    d) are not RRIF eligible

9. All else being equal, warrants will have higher market prices when: (   )

    a) the prospects are poor for the underlying security

    b) the volatility of the underlying asset increases

    c) the time to expiry decreases

    d) dividends are high for the underlying asset

( )   10. _____ options are primarily European style.

       a) Equity

       b) Currency

       c) Stock Index

       d) Bond

( )   11. Technical analysis would focus on examining:

       a) company financial statements

       b) industry growth opportunities

       c) moving stock price averages

       d) dividend yields

( )   12. Equity prices often rise due to interest rates falling faster than the growth rate in earnings (and dividends) during the _____ phase of the equity cycle.

       a) expansionary

       b) peak

       c) contraction

       d) trough

( )   13. The following indices are value-weighted, except the _____.

       a) TSE 300 Composite Index

       b) S&P 500 Index

       c) S&P/TSE 60 Index

       d) Dow Jones Industrial Average

( )   14. A _____ asset allocation strategy adheres to a long-term asset mix by monitoring and rebalancing as necessary.

       a) strategic

       b) tactical

       c) dynamic

       d) insured

( )   15. The primary difference between a futures contract and a forward contract is that:

       a) forward contacts are not standardized

       b) futures contracts are not standardized

       c) futures contracts are the OTC equivalent of forward contracts

       d) there is no difference between the two

16. The volatility in returns associated with changes in market conditions is   (   )
known as what type of risk?

    a) Unsystematic risk

    b) Cyclical risk

    c) Systematic risk

    d) Natural risk

17. Client portfolios which are managed on a continuing basis by the mem-   (   )
ber for a management fee are known as:

    a) market accounts.

    b) cash accounts.

    c) managed accounts.

    d) Johnny accounts.

18. If a wife who earned $70,000 last year, has contributed $8,000 to her own   (   )
RRSP, how much can she contribute to her husband's plan?

    a) $4,600

    b) $5,000

    c) $5,500

    d) It depends on how much the husband has already contributed.

Refer to the following information to answer Questions 19-21:

A company presently has 500,000 shares outstanding which are trading at $50 per
share. The shares are presently trading cum rights and five rights are required to
purchase one share at the subscription price of $45.

19. What is the intrinsic value of one right before the ex rights date?   (   )

    a) $1.00

    b) $5.00

    c) $0.83

    d) 0

20. What is the theoretical intrinsic value of one right two days after the ex   (   )
rights date if the shares are trading for $49.50?

    a) $0.50

    b) $0.83

    c) $0.90

    d) $4.50

( )

21. How much money will the firm raise if the rights offering is fully subscribed?

a) $4,500,000

b) $4,950,000

c) $5,000,000

d) $2,500,000

Refer to the following Income Statement and Balance Sheet for XYZ Company to answer Questions 22-24:

XYZ COMPANY
Income Statement and Balance Sheet

INCOME STATEMENT

Total Revenue	$1,426,000
Cost of Goods Sold	1,238,700
Depreciation/Amortization	40,100
General, Selling & Admin. Expense	33,100
Earnings before interest and taxes	114,100
Interest Expense	5,300
Pre-tax Income	108,800
Income Tax:	
Current	10,900
Deferred	9,000
Earnings before Extraordinary Items	88,900
Extraordinary Items	0
Income after Extraordinary Items	88,900
Dividends—Preferred Shares	3,500
Income Available to Common Shares	85,400
Earnings / Common Share	0.68
Common Shares—Year-End	125,658
Common Shares—Average	125,536
Dividends—Common Shares	14,700
Market Price per Share (Close)	6.69

BALANCE SHEET

Assets:

Cash & Equivalents	$150,000
Accounts Receivable	174,000
Inventory	220,200
Total Current Assets	544,200
Fixed Assets—Gross	1,372,700
Less: Accumulated Depreciation	766,200
Fixed Assets—Net	606,500
Total Assets	1,150,700

Liabilities & Equities:

Bank Loans & Equivalents	147,800
Accounts Payable	347,200
Current Portion of Long-Term Debt	5,400
Total Current Liabilities	500,400
Long-Term Debt	83,500
Deferred Taxes	41,600
Equity: Preferred Stock	158,300
Common Stock	190,600
Retained Earnings	176,300
Total Equity	525,200
Total Liabilities & Equity	1,150,700

22. What is the value of XYZ's quick ratio?   (   )

    a) 1.09

    b) 0.65

    c) 0.94

    d) 1.03

23. What is XYZ's cash flow to debt ratio?   (   )

    a) 53.0%

    b) 58.3%

    c) 62.9%

    d) not enough information available

( )　24. What is XYZ's book value per common share at year-end?

   a) $2.92

   b) $2.78

   c) $2.66

   d) not enough information available

( )　25. The primary difference between discretionary accounts and managed accounts is that:

   a) Managed accounts are client portfolios which are managed by a member, usually for a fee while discretionary accounts are opened for clients as a convenience to clients who are unable or unwilling to attend to their own accounts.

   b) Discretionary accounts are client portfolios which are managed by a member, usually for a fee while managed accounts are opened for clients as a convenience to clients who are unable or unwilling to attend to their own accounts.

   c) Managed accounts are managed by the client while a discretionary account is managed by a person appointed by the client.

   d) Discretionary accounts are managed by the client while a managed account is managed by a person appointed by the client.

( )　26. The primary difference between diversifiable and non-diversifiable risk is that:

   a) Market risk refers to volatility in returns associated with changes in market conditions while non-market risk is company specific.

   b) Non-market risk refers to volatility in returns associated with changes in market conditions while market risk is company specific.

   c) Diversifiable risk refers to volatility in returns associated with changes in market conditions while non-diversifiable risk is company specific.

   d) Diversifiable risk is market specific while non-diversifiable is firm specific.

( )　27. Only _____ of a capital gain is taxable since October of 2000.

   a) 1/4

   b) 1/2

   c) 2/3

   d) 3/4

28. During the year 2000, the foreign content of RRSPs could not exceed: ( )
    a) 20%
    b) 25%
    c) 30%
    d) 35%

29. What is the intrinsic value of a common share that is expected to pay an ( )
    annual year-end dividend of $1.25, which is expected to grow indefinitely
    at an annual rate of 5.5% per year, if the required return on the shares is
    12%?
    a) $20.29
    b) $19.23
    c) $10.41
    d) $21.54

30. What is the implied P/E ratio for a stock that has an expected EPS of ( )
    $2.25 and an expected year-end dividend of $0.75, if the appropriate dis-
    count rate is 15%, and the expected annual growth rate in dividends is
    3%?
    a) 2.78 times
    b) 6.25 times
    c) .22 times
    d) 11.1 times

31. Which of the following is NOT a competitive force that affects the attrac- ( )
    tiveness of an industry and its prospects for growth?
    a) ease of entry or exit
    b) degree of competition
    c) availability of complements
    d) ability to exert pressure over selling price of products

32. What does "beta" measure? ( )
    a) business risk
    b) non-market risk
    c) unsystematic risk
    d) sensitivity of returns on a security to changes in market returns

Refer to the following information to answer Questions 33-35:

Firms X and Y are in the same industry, and are roughly the same size. Based on the following ratios for the previous year:

Ratios	Firm X	Firm Y
Current	2.0	1.8
Net Return on Invested Capital	7.0%	6.0%
Net Return on Common Equity	12.5%	14.0%
Cash Flow/Total Debt	0.32	0.25
Quick	1.2	1.1
Inventory Turnover	20 times	25 times
Debt Percentage of Total Capital	30%	40%
Interest Coverage	3.5 times	2.6 times
Preferred Dividend Coverage	3.5 times	2.4 times
Debt/Equity	0.5	1.1

( )   33. Which company appears to be more profitable according to the ratios above?

a) Firm X, because it has a higher Net Return on Invested Capital.

b) Firm Y, because it has a higher Net Return on Common Equity.

c) Firm Y, because it has a higher Inventory Turnover ratio.

d) Cannot say without further analysis.

34. Which of the following statements is true?

( )   I. Firm X satisfies the suggested rules of thumb for liquidity ratios for utilities, but not for industrials.

II. Firm X satisfies the suggested rules of thumb for liquidity ratios for utilities and industrials.

III. Firm Y satisfies the suggested rules of thumb for liquidity ratios for utilities, but not for industrials.

IV. Neither Firm X nor Firm Y satisfy the suggested rules of thumb for liquidity ratios for utilities or for industrials.

a) I and III

b) II and III

c) II only

d) IV only

35. Which of the following statements is true? .   (   )

  I. Firm X satisfies the suggested rules of thumb for utilities for debt-to-equity and interest coverage, but not for industrials.

  II. Firm X satisfies the suggested rules of thumb for debt-to-equity and interest coverage for both utilities and industrials.

  III. Firm Y satisfies the suggested rules of thumb for debt-to-equity and interest coverage ratios for utilities, but not for industrials.

  IV. Neither Firm X nor Firm Y satisfy the suggested rules of thumb for debt-to-equity and interest coverage ratios for utilities or for industrials.

  a) I and III

  b) II and III

  c) II only

  d) IV only

36. An investor purchases 400 ABC common shares at $22.40 on January 31, 2000, then buys another 300 ABC common shares at $24.60 on June 30, 2001. What is the adjusted cost base per share?   (   )

  a) $23.34

  b) $23.50

  c) $23.20

  d) $23.46

37. An investor purchases 100 shares for $8 on March 1, 2000, then sells the shares for $6.50 on March 21, 2000. If the investor repurchases the shares on April 10, 2000 for $6.50 and holds them until May, what is the loss incurred?   (   )

  a) capital loss of $150

  b) superficial loss of $150

  c) capital loss of $1.50

  d) there is no loss

38. Which of the following is NOT a part of the portfolio management process?   (   )

  a) Designing an investment policy.

  b) Developing and implementing an asset mix.

  c) Soliciting funds when necessary.

  d) Adjusting the portfolio and measuring performance.

( )   39. What is a "Spread Trader"?

a) An investment manager who looks to profit from differences in bid-ask prices.

b) An investment manager who looks to profit by anticipating the direction of interest rates and structuring their portfolios accordingly.

c) An investment manager who looks to profit from the differences in rates between federal, provincial, and/or corporate bonds.

d) An investor who looks to find the investment manager with the lowest rates, and chooses their manager based upon who has the lowest rate.

( )   40. What is the difference between a defensive and a speculative industry?

a) Speculative industries have a great deal of risk and uncertainty, while defensive industries are relatively stable.

b) Speculative industries are those whose earnings are affected by a larger than average amount of downturns in the business cycle, while defensive industries are relatively stable.

c) Defensive industries have a great deal of risk and uncertainty, while speculative industries are relatively stable.

d) There is no real difference between the two.

( )   41. What is the five-week moving average of a stock that has the following end of week closing prices: week one-$22, week two-$21, week three-$22, week four-$20, week five-$22?

a) $22.50

b) $21.40

c) $21.20

d) $21.00

( )   42. Refer to above question. If the closing price at the end of week six were $20, what is the five-week moving average now?

a) $21.00

b) $21.16

c) $22.30

d) $20.75

( )   43. The portfolio management technique that adjusts the mix between risk-free assets and risky assets as the markets rise and fall is known as:

a) Insured Asset Allocation

b) Tactical Asset Allocation

c) Constant-Weighting Asset Allocation

d) Dynamic Asset Allocation

44. When forecasting interest rates, an IA should consider: ( )

    a) monetary policy changes.

    b) fiscal policy changes.

    c) inflation.

    d) all of the above.

45. Which of the following situations does NOT represent a bull signal? ( )

    a) A decrease in the advance-decline line.

    b) New highs are increasing.

    c) Stock prices break through their moving average line from below.

    d) A bottom head-and-shoulders formation.

46. A young, healthy, single individual professional with medium investment knowledge, high risk tolerance, a moderate tax rate, and a long-term horizon should have the following type of asset mix: ( )

    a) little amount of cash, large amount of fixed income, moderate amount of equities

    b) moderate amount of cash, large amount of fixed income, little amount of equities

    c) little amount of cash, moderate amount of fixed income, large amount of equities

    d) large amount of cash, moderate amount of fixed income, little amount of equities

47. What are the suggested rules of thumb for the preferred dividend coverage ratio? ( )

    a) above 2.5 for both industrials and utilities

    b) above 2.0 for industrials and 3.0 for utilities

    c) above 3.0 for industrials and 2.0 for utilities

    d) there are no rules of thumb for this ratio

48. The key disclosure forms for a segregated fund include: ( )

    a) Simple prospectuses, client statements, information folders, and financial statements.

    b) Application forms, contracts, information folders, financial statements, and client statements.

    c) Application forms, contracts, information folders, financial statements, client statements, and summary fact statements.

    d) Application forms, contracts, and financial statements.

Refer to the following information to answer Questions 49-50:

Assume Helen invested a lump sum of $200,000 in a front-end load segregated fund, with a 100% maturity guarantee after 10 years. Treat the value of any maturity guarantees as capital gains income.

( )   49. What are the tax consequences if Helen wishes to redeem her $200,000 deposit after 10 years, when the market value of her holdings is $195,000?

   a) She can claim a capital loss of $5,000 against any income earned.

   b) A capital gain of $5,000 is taxable in the year of redemption.

   c) There are no taxes payable on the transaction.

   d) none of the above

( )   50. What are the tax consequences if Helen resets her deposit after 5 years, locking in the gain in market value to $220,000. At the end of the additional 10 years, she liquidates her holdings, which have a market value of $210,000?

   a) She can defer the capital gains payable for five years to the end of her initial 10-year contract.

   b) A capital gain of $20,000 is taxable in the year the contract is reset.

   c) No capital gain liability is triggered at the time of redemption.

   d) A capital gain of $20,000 is taxable in the year of redemption.

( )   51. The combination of securities in a portfolio is determined using the following guideline:

   a) The investor's primary objectives determine the asset allocation strategy; the investor's secondary objectives determine specific securities that are selected.

   b) The investor's primary objectives determine the specific securities that are selected; the investor's secondary objectives determine the asset allocation strategy.

   c) neither (a) nor (b)

   d) both (a) and (b) depending on the investor's level of risk tolerance

( )   52. The securities industry's Code of Ethics is based upon the principles of:

   a) fairness and trust

   b) integrity, justice, honesty, responsibility, and reliability

   c) the financial advisor's code of ethics

   d) both (a) and (b)

53. The regulatory body responsible for monitoring the capital adequacy of insurance companies is the _____ .   ( )

    a) insurance companies act

    b) OSFI

    c) provincial securities commission

    d) CLHIA

54. Insurance companies that sell segregated funds: ( )

    a) must disclose third-party credit ratings to prospective segregated fund purchasers

    b) can include third-party credit ratings in marketing materials

    c) neither (a) nor (b)

    d) both (a) and (b)

55. What are the two components of a trust relationship between advisor and client?   ( )

    a) knowledge and integrity

    b) competence and integrity

    c) honesty and competence

    d) knowledge and disclosure

56. What is the main danger in comparing mutual fund performance?   ( )

    a) The funds may have two different investment objectives.

    b) Historical returns provide no guarantee of future returns.

    c) A fund's asset allocation may not be taken into consideration.

    d) Comparisons with stock market indices may not account for dividend reinvestment.

57. What are two reasons why mutual fund managers would use derivative securities in managing their portfolios?   ( )

    a) To reduce risk and assist in market entry and exit.

    b) To speculate and reduce the amount of money leaving the fund.

    c) To provide greater diversification and reduce risk.

    d) To take advantage of volatile securities and assist in entry and exit of the market.

Refer to the following information to answer Questions 58-59:

An investor obtains the following market prices for a call option on ABC Company's common shares that are currently trading at $8.00 per share. The exercise price on the call option is $10 and the call premium is $1.50.

( )   58. What is the time value premium for ABC Company's call option?

     a) $1.50

     b) $0

     c) $8.00

     d) $2.00

( )   59. What is the net profit (ignoring transactions costs) for an investor who purchases one contract if they hold the option to the expiration date at which time the share price is $12?

     a) $400

     b) $200

     c) $50

     d) none of the above

( )   60. When interest rates are rising, the prices of REITs usually_____ ; however, they do provide a good hedge during _____ periods.

     a) increase; inflationary

     b) decrease; deflationary

     c) remain unchanged; deflationary

     d) decrease; inflationary

Refer to the following information to answer Questions 61-62:

Atlantic Fund Company is offering a new mutual fund to investors. The new fund's net asset value per unit is $12 plus a 3.5% up-front sales charge.

( )   61. What is the offering price for Atlantic Fund Company's new mutual fund?

     a) $11.58

     b) $12.42

     c) $12.44

     d) none of the above

62. What is the sales charge as a percentage of the net amount invested by purchasers?   ( )

    a) 3.50%

    b) 3.67%

    c) 3.84%

    d) none of the above

63. The main disadvantages of mutual funds include: ( )

    a) lack of liquidity, they are unsuitable for short-term investments, and there are few types of funds available

    b) they are not suitable for both short-term investments and emergency reserves, plus professional management is not perfect in building mutual fund portfolios

    c) they are not eligible for margin accounts, few purchase plans are available, and they are not accepted as loan collateral

    d) high management fees, they are not suitable for emergency reserves, and are not eligible for margin accounts

64. What is the fully diluted EPS for a company that has net earnings of $10 million, and has 1 million shares outstanding, if the company has 200,000 convertible preferred shares outstanding, each of which is convertible into one common share. The preferred shares receive an annual dividend of $5.   ( )

    a) $10.00

    b) $9.00

    c) $8.33

    d) none of the above

65. A fixed-dollar withdrawal plan: ( )

    a) withdraws a specified percentage of the investor's mutual fund portfolio each year

    b) withdraws a specified amount of the investor's mutual fund portfolio over a predetermined time period

    c) withdraws a specified dollar amount determined by the mutual fund investor on a monthly or quarterly basis

    d) withdraws a specified dollar amount determined by the mutual fund holder each year

( )   66. You purchase a stock for $26 and hold it for five years. The annual dividend per share for this stock is $2.50. If you sell the stock at the end of the fifth year for $24, what is your return on this stock?

    a) -7.7%

    b) 8.1%

    c) 40.4%

    d) none of the above

( )   67. A "growth" manager would invest in stocks with relatively _____ P/E ratios and _____ dividend yields.

    a) high; high

    b) high; low

    c) low; low

    d) low; high

( )   68. What effect would a rise in the T-Bill rate have on both call and put option prices?

    a) call prices would decrease; put prices would increase

    b) call prices would increase; put prices would decrease

    c) call prices would not change; put prices would decrease

    d) none of the above

( )   69. According to the "Life Cycle Theory," a person aged 52 years old would focus on:

    a) preserving capital and income

    b) growth and tax minimization

    c) income and liquidity

    d) safety and liquidity

( )   70. Which of the following is not a style related to fixed income managers?

    a) credit quality

    b) spread traders

    c) exchange rate anticipators

    d) all of the above are fixed income manager styles

( )   71. RRIFs differ from RRSPs because:

    a) RRIFs shelter income earned within the plan.

    b) RRIFs may hold stocks, bonds, mutual funds and T-bills.

    c) RRIFs require minimum annual withdrawals.

    d) RRIFs may be self-directed.

72. What is the main objective(s) of equity mutual funds?   (   )

    a) search for capital gains and be willing to forego broad diversification benefits in hope of achieving above average returns

    b) capital gains

    c) to provide diversification with a combination of income, safety and capital appreciation

    d) income and safety of principal

73. The following factors should be considered when establishing investment objectives except: (   )

    a) ethical considerations

    b) inflation

    c) risk

    d) liquidity

74. When there is falling inflation, P/E levels will _____ as the discount rate _____ .   (   )

    a) increase; decreases

    b) decrease; increases

    c) remain unchanged; remains unchanged

    d) none of the above

75. The Elliot Wave Theory suggests that the stock market moves up in a series of _____ waves, and down in a series of _____ waves.   (   )

    a) three; three

    b) five; five

    c) three; five

    d) five; three

76. An investor purchases a newly issued unit for $25. This unit is composed of 1 preferred share and 1 common share. At the time of issue, the preferred share traded for $9 and the common for $18. What is the adjusted cost base of each if the investor decided to sell both shares?   (   )

    a) preferred is $8.33 while common is $16.67.

    b) preferred is $9.00 while common is $18.00.

    c) preferred is $9.72 while common is $19.44.

    d) none of the above

( )   77. A client has approached you with the following information:

Security	Expected Return	Market Value
ABC Co.	9%	$200,000
DEF Co.	10%	$220,000
GHI Co.	12%	$430,000

If the client holds the given market values of the above securities in their portfolio, what is the return the investor can expect?

a) 10.33%

b) 10.78%

c) 11%

d) none of the above

( )   78. MNO Co. has shares selling in the market for $11.50. If the last dividend paid was $1.26, and the expected growth of dividends is 5%, what return do investors require?

a) 10.96%

b) 11.50%

c) 15.96%

d) 16.50%

( )   79. Based on the Dividend Discount Model and all else remaining constant, correctly complete the following statement. A firm's P/E ratio will increase if:

a) the growth rate decreases.

b) the firm decreases its payout ratio.

c) the discount rate rises.

d) inflation expectations decline.

( )   80. An investor is in the 40% tax bracket (combined federal and provincial tax rate), and receives $140 in dividends from a Canadian corporation. How much tax must be paid on the dividend?

a) $56.00

b) $51.34

c) $46.67

d) none of the above

81. An investor's portfolio had a beginning market value of $470,000. Since then the investor has deposited $40,000 and has withdrawn $20,000. The end-of-period market value is $500,000. What is this investor's total return?   (   )

    a) 2.1%

    b) 6.4%

    c) 10.4%

    d) none of the above

82. In which stage of the industry life cycle will you see higher dividend yields?   (   )

    a) Emerging

    b) Rapid Growth

    c) Mature Industries

    d) Declining Industries

83. Which of the following factors directly affect security prices?   (   )

    I. Unemployment

    II. Fiscal Policies

    III. Monetary Policy

    IV. Flow of Funds

    V. Inflation

    a) all of the above

    b) none of the above

    c) I, II, III, V

    d) II, III, IV, V

84. _____ investment funds usually provide higher returns than _____ funds, but lower returns than _____ funds.   (   )

    a) Money market; mortgage; dividend

    b) Balanced; equity; specialty

    c) Balanced; bond; dividend

    d) Balanced; real estate; specialty

85. What is the effective after-tax cost of a $6,000 investment in a LSVCC by an investor in a 40% marginal tax bracket, if she contributes them to her RRSP? Assume the LSVCC qualifies for the maximum federal tax credit, and an equal provincial tax credit.   (   )

    a) $1,800

    b) $2,100

    c) $4,500

    d) none of the above

( )   86. The following restrictions apply to most mutual funds:

a) cannot own more than 10% of a company's total securities

b) cannot own more than 10% of a company's voting stock

c) both (a) and (b)

d) neither (a) nor (b)

( )   87. What is the beta of a stock that has an expected return of 10%, if the market expected return is 12%, and the T bill rate is 7%, according to CAPM?

a) 0.60

b) 1.00

c) 1.67

d) none of the above

( )   88. What is the market risk premium in the question above?

a) 2%

b) 3%

c) 5%

d) insufficient information

( )   89. Which of the following statements regarding mutual fund regulation is (are) true?

I. The distribution of mutual funds is regulated by the MFDA.

II. The funds themselves are regulated by the IDA.

III. Both the distribution of mutual funds, as well as the funds themselves are regulated by the provincial securities commissions.

IV. The MFDA and the IDA are both SROs.

a) I, II

b) I, IV

c) II, IV

d) III

( )   90. Closed-end funds have the following disadvantages except:

a) they may be sold short

b) they are subject to stock exchange requirements

c) deferred sales charges do not usually decline through time

d) they often do not provide for automatic reinvestment of distributions

91. REITs and royalty trusts are examples of _____ .   (   )

   a) unit investment trusts.

   b) income trusts.

   c) MBSs.

   d) none of the above

92. Segregated fund must satisfy the following requirements, except: (   )

   a) The initial term of the segregated fund must be at least 10 years.

   b) The amount of the maturity guarantee payable at the end of the term
      must be at least 75%.

   c) There can be no guarantee of any amounts payable on redemption of
      the contract before death or the maturity date.

   d) none of the above

93. Segregated funds provide investors with the following advantage(s) except: (   )

   a) protection from creditors

   b) maturity guarantees

   c) probate bypass

   d) CDIC protection

94. _____ are products that are similar to segregated funds that   (   )
   are offered by mutual fund companies.

   a) Portfolio funds

   b) Wrap funds

   c) Protected funds

   d) none of the above

95. The following are primary ethical values in the Code of Ethics estab-   (   )
   lished by the securities industry, except for:

   a) Registrants must hold client information in strict confidence.

   b) Registrants must use proper care and exercise independent profession-
      al judgement.

   c) Registrants must act quickly to ensure that all client accounts are settled
      by the required date.

   d) Registrants must act in accordance with applicable Securities Act(s).

( )   96. Which of the following statements best describes a fiduciary relationship?

      a) They are agent-principal relationships where the principal is vulnerable and the agent has greater expertise or authority.

      b) They are agent-principal relationships where the agent is vulnerable and the principal has greater expertise or authority.

      c) They are agent-principal relationships where the principal needs the moral and ethical guidance of the agent.

      d) They are agency principal relationships where the agent needs the moral and ethical guidance of the principal.

( )   97. The inclusion of reset dates for segregated funds implies that:

      a) investors can "lock-in" capital gains without affecting their maturity guarantee in any other way.

      b) there will be a greater chance of payments being made under maturity guarantees.

      c) both (a) and (b)

      d) neither (a) nor (b)

( )   98. Segregated funds are not protected from creditors if:

      a) the client was legally insolvent when the contract was purchased

      b) the contract was purchased within two years of bankruptcy

      c) both (a) and (b)

      d) neither (a) nor (b)

Refer to the following information to answer Questions 99-100:

Margaret is a 25-year old dot.com entrepreneur. She just sold her business and "netted" $5 million after all tax considerations. She has no plans to re-enter the workforce in the near future, and would like to enjoy life and live off her windfall, indefinitely if possible. She has never contributed to an RRSP or a company pension plan.

( )   99. Margaret's primary investment objective(s) should focus on _____ while relevant secondary objectives should include _____.

      a) growth and income; tax minimization

      b) tax minimization; growth

      c) preservation of capital and income; tax minimization

      d) liquidity; growth

( )   100. The most appropriate investment mix for Margaret from the following would be:

      a) 20% cash, 50% fixed-income, 30% equities

      b) 10% cash, 30% fixed-income, 60% equities

      c) 40% cash, 50% fixed-income, 10% equities

      d) 30% cash, 50% fixed-income, 20% equities

EXAM I
CSC PRACTICE EXAMINATION

ANSWERS

Answers to CSC Practice Examination #1

Please note that the page references below refer to the chapter and page number(s) in the CSC textbook where you will find the information.

Question	Answer		Level of Difficulty	Chapter
1.	B	pg. 1-12, 1-13	E	
2.	C	pg. 5-46	E	5
3.	B	pg. 1-54	M	1
4.	A	pg. 4-20, 4-21, 4-27	E	4
5.	B	pg. 2-23, 2-24	M	2
6.	D	pg. 2-28	D	2
7.	B	pg. 4-14	M	4
8.	B	pg. 2-1, 2-2	M	2
9.	D	pg. 5-37 to 5-40	D	5
10.	C	pg. 5-45	M	5
11.	B	pg. 6-37	M	6
12.	A	pg. 3-34	E	3
13.	B	pg. 3-8	M	3
14.	A	pg. 1-13	E	1
15.	B	50% margin = $0.50 \times \$2 \times 100 \times 10 = \$1,000$	M	6
16.	C	Max. loan = $0.40 \times \$1,800 = \$720$ Deposit = $\$1000 - \$720 = \$280$	D	6
17.	C	Deposit = $0.50 \times \$5 \times 1000 = \$2,500$	D	6
18.	A	Profit = $(\$5 - \$4) \times 1000 = \$1,000$	M	6
19.	D	pg. 3-24 to 3-26	M	3
20.	D	pg. 4-14	M	4
21.	B	pg. 2-10, 2-11	E	2
22.	C	pg. 4-15	E	4
23.	C	pg. 5-36	M	5
24.	A	pg. 6-47	M	6
25.	B	pg. 6-48	M	6
26.	D	pg. 1-40, 1-41	M	1
27.	D	pg. 1-1, 1-2, 1-7, 1-8	M	1
28.	C	pg. 2-14, 2-15	M	2
29.	B	$\$7m \times \{[1 - (1/1.08)^6]/0.08\} + 100m \times [1/(1.08)^6] = \$95.38m$	D	5
30.	A	pg. 5-17 to 5-21, 5-39	D	5

Question	Answer	Level of Difficulty	Chapter
31.	A Price at yr.1 = \$100 since yield = coupon rate Return = $(100 - 105 + 7)/105$ = 1.90%	D	5
32.	A $\$7m \times (120/365) = \$2.301m$	D	5
33.	A $(40 - 18.5 \times 2)/(18.5 \times 2) = 8.11\%$	D	6
34.	C $(2/40) = 5\%$	D	6
35.	A Common share yield = $(0.45/18.5)$ = 2.43% Payback = $8.1/(5 - 2.43) = 3.16$ years	D	6
36.	D pg. 5-12	M	5
37.	D pg. 5-24, 5-25	M	5
38.	B $(1000 \times 12 \times 0.30)$ + $(1000 \times 1.8 \times 0.60) = \$4,680$	D	6
39.	B Stock X: Max. loan = $0.70 \times \$12,750$ = \$8,925 Previous loan: $\$12,000 - 3,600$ = \$8,400 Excess: $\$8,925 - \$8,400 = \$525$ Stock Y: Max. loan = 0 Repay previous loan $\$1,800 - \$1,080$ = \$720 (deposit required) Total deposit = $\$720 - \$525 = \$195$	D	6
40.	D pg. 3-5	M	3
41.	C pg. 3-11	M	3
42.	B $[(100 - 99.45)/99.45] \times (365/190)$ = 1.06%	D	5
43.	A Bond sells at face value so yield to maturity = coupon rate	M	5
44.	D pg. 5-14	M	5
45.	D pg. 3-24	M	3
46.	D pg. 3-2, 3-3	D	3
47.	C pg. 6-47	M	6
48.	C pg. 4-27	E	4
49.	C pg. 2-29	D	2
50.	C pg. 1-6, 1-7	M	1
51.	D pg. 6-42	D	6

Question	Answer	Level of Difficulty	Chapter
52.	C pg. 4-10, 4-11	M	4
53.	C pg. 6-19	M	6
54.	C pg. 5-14	D	5
55.	D pg. 1-12, 1-13	M	1
56.	A $0.30 \times [500 \times \$22] = \$3,300$	M	6
57.	B $25 \times 500 \times 1.30 = 16,250$ $16,250 - 3,300 - 11,000 = 1,950$	D	6
58.	C pg. 2-4, 2-5	M	2
59.	C pg. 2-39	M	2
60.	D pg. 5-36	M	5
61.	D pg. 2-20 to 2-22	M	2
62.	D pg. 2-4	M	2
63.	A pg. 4-15, 4-16	M	4
64.	A pg. 5-5	M	5
65.	C Purchase Price = $1,005 +$ $(40/365 \times \$60) = \$1,011.58$	D	5
66.	B pg. 3-10, 3-11	M	3
67.	C pg. 3-1, 3-2	M	3
68.	C pg. 2-24	M	2
69.	B pg. 2-34	M	2
70.	C pg. 5-36	M	5
71.	C Yield $= [6 + (100 - 120)/20] /$ $[(100 + 120)/2] = (6 - 1)/110$ $= 4.55\%$	D	5
72.	B pg. 3-39	M	3
73.	D pg. 3-30 to 3-33	M	3
74.	B pg. 6-24	M	6
75.	C pg. 5-37 to 5-40	M	5
76.	C pg. 3-19, 3-20	M	3
77.	A $[80,000 - (80,000 \times 0.10) -$ $(72,000 \times 0.10)] \times 0.10 = \$6,480$	D	4
78.	C $(80,000 - 10,000) / 7 = \$10,000$	M	4
79.	A pg. 3-9	D	3
80.	C $800,000/4 = 0.2$ million, pg. 6-26	E	6
81.	C pg. 5-35	M	5
82.	D pg. 6-28, 6-29	M	6

Question	Answer	Level of Difficulty	Chapter
83.	C pg. 3-12	M	3
84.	A pg. 3-16	D	3
85.	C pg. 6-24	D	6
86.	B pg. 5-37, 5-38	M	5
87.	B pg. 5-45	M	5
88.	A pg. 5-17, 5-20	M	5
89.	D pg. 4-19, 4-34	M	4
90.	B pg. 4-18, 4-19	M	4
91.	B pg. 4-31, 4-32	D	4
92.	A pg. 5-50	M	5
93.	D pg. 1-59, 1-60	D	1
94.	A Price = $(0.06 \times \$20) / 0.08 = \$15$	D	6
95.	C pg. 6-19 to 6-23	M	6
96.	C pg. 4-14	M	4
97.	A pg. 4-25, 4-26	M	4
98.	B pg. 4-27, 4-28	M	4
99.	A pg. 6-17	M	61
100.	C pg. 6-48	M	6

EXAM 2

CSC PRACTICE EXAMINATION

ANSWERS

Answers to CSC Practice Examination #2

Please note that the page references below refer to the chapter and page number(s) in the CSC textbook where you will find the information.

Question	Answer	Level of Difficulty	Chapter
1.	B pg. 9-2 to 9-6	E	9
2.	B II, IV, V, VI pg. 10-4 to 10-8	D	10
3.	B I, III, VII pg. 10-4 to 10-8	D	10
4.	D IV = Max (20 − 22, 0) = 0; TV= 3 − 0 = 3	M	9
5.	D 20 / 3 = 6.67	M	9
6.	A pg. 7-36	E	7
7.	C 60 = NAV / (1 − .05), so NAV = 60 × 0.95 = \$57.00	M	7
8.	A pg. 7-61	M	7
9.	B pg. 9-6, 9-7	M	9
10.	C pg. 9-19, 9-20	M	9
11.	C pg. 10-64	E	10
12.	D pg. 12-38	D	12
13.	D pg. 10-59 to 10-61	E	10
14.	A pg. 12-44, 12-45	M	12
15.	A pg. 9-29	M	9
16.	C pg. 12-8	E	12
17.	C pg. 7-67	E	7
18.	A Maximum is the lower of \$13,500 or 0.18 × \$70,000 = \$12,600; so 12,600 − 8,000 = \$4,600	M	11
19.	C (50 − 45) / (5 + 1) = \$0.83	M	9
20.	C (49.50 − 45) / 5 = \$0.90	M	9
21.	A (500,000 / 5) × \$45 = \$4,500,000	D	9
22.	B (544,200 − 220,200) / 500,400 = 0.65	M	10
23.	B (88,900 + 9,000 + 40,100) / (147,800 + 5,400 + 83,500) × 100 = 58.3%	D	10
24.	A (525,200 − 158,300) / 125,658 = \$2.92		
25.	A pg. 7-67, 7-68	M	7
26.	A pg. 12-8	M	12
27.	B pg. 11-20	M	11
28.	B pg. 7-29	M	7

Question	Answer		Level of Difficulty	Chapter
29.	B	$1.25 / (.12 - 0.055) = \$19.23$	M	10
30.	A	$(0.75 / 2.25) / (.15 - .03) = 2.78$ times	D	10
31.	C	pg. 10-15, 10-16	M	10
32.	D	pg. 12-14	E	12
33.	D	The profitability ratios give conflicting signals	M	10
34.	C	The ROT for current/quick are 2.0/1.0 for both utilities and industrials; therefore II is the only correct answer	M	10
35.	B	The ROT for debt-to-equity and interest coverage are 1.5 and 2.0 for utilities and 0.5 and 3.0 for industrials; therefore II and III are correct	D	10
36.	A	$[(\$22.40 \times 400) + (\$24.60 \times 300)] / 700 = \$23.34$	M	11
37.	B	$(100 \times \$8) - (100 \times \$6.5) = \$150$ superficial loss pg. 11-23, 11-24	M	11
38.	C	pg. 12-18	E	12
39.	C	pg. 12-30	E	12
40.	A	pg. 10-17, 10-18	E	10
41.	B	$(22 + 21 + 22 + 20 + 22) / 5 = \$21.40$	M	10
42.	A	$(21 + 22 + 20 + 22 + 20) / 5 = \$21.00$	M	10
43.	D	pg. 12-46	M	12
44.	D	pg. 12-50 to 12-51	M	12
45.	A	pg. 10-65 to 10-72	M	10
46.	C	pg. 12-40	M	12
47.	C	pg. 10-36	M	10
48.	C	pg. 8-48	M	8
49.	C	pg. 8-40, 8-41 The capital gain of \$5,000 on the maturity guarantee is offset by the capital loss of \$5,000	M	8
50.	D	pg.8-41	D	8
51.	A	pg. 13-11	M	13
52.	D	pg. 13-3	M	13

Question	Answer	Level of Difficulty	Chapter
53.	B pg. 8-13	M	8
54.	B pg. 8-33	M	8
55.	B pg. 13-5, 13-6	E	13
56.	B pg. 7-56	M	7
57.	A pg. 7-13	M	7
58.	A TV = 1.50 − 0 = 1.50	M	9
59.	C Profit = (12 - 10) × 100 − 150 = \$50	D	9
60.	D pg. 7-62, 7-63	M	7
61.	C 12 / (1 − .035) = 12.44	M	7
62.	B 0.44 / 12.00 = 3.67%	M	7
63.	B pg. 7-4	M	7
64.	C Basic EPS = (10m − 1m) / 1m = \$9.00; Fully diluted EPS = 10m / (1m + 0.2m) = \$8.33	D	10
65.	C pg. 7-31	M	7
66.	C [24 + (5 × 2.50) − 26] / 26 = 40.4%	D	12
67.	B pg. 12-28	M	12
68.	B pg. 9-22	D	9
69.	B pg. 11-7, 11-8	M	11
70.	C pg.12-30	E	12
71.	C pg. 11-30	M	11
72.	B pg. 7-38	M	7
73.	A pg. 12-18 to 12-21	M	12
74.	A pg. 10-54	M	10
75.	D pg. 10-71	M	10
76.	A Preferred = (9/27 × 25) = \$8.33; Common = (18/27 × 25) = \$16.67	M	11
77.	B (.09 × 200,000/850,000) + (.10 × 220,000/850,000) + (.12 × 430,000/850,000) = 10.78%	M	12
78.	D [1.26(1.05) / 11.50] + 0.05 = 16.5%	D	10
79.	D pg. 10-52, 10-53	M	10
80.	C (140 × 1.25 × 0.4) − (140 × 1.25 × 0.1333) = \$46.67	D	11
81.	C [(500,000 − (470,000 + 40,000 − 20,000)] / [470,000 + (40,000 − 20,000) / 2] = 10 / 480 = 2.1%	D	12

Question	Answer	Level of Difficulty	Chapter
82.	C pg. 10-15	M	10
83.	D pg. 10-4 to 10-11	M	10
84.	C pg. 7-41	M	7
85.	B The maximum federal credit = $0.15 \times \$5,000$ (limit for credit) = \$750; provincial credit = \$750; net after-tax contribution to RRSP = $6,000 - 750 - 750 - (6,000 \times 0.40)$ = \$2,100	D	7
86.	C pg. 7-12, 7-13	M	7
87.	A $10 = 7 + beta \times (12 - 7)$; So, beta = $(10 - 7) / 5 = 0.60$	D	12
88.	C pg. 12-17	M	12
89.	B pg. 7-18	M	7
90.	A pg. 7-57, 7-58	M	7
91.	B pg. 7-62 to 7-64	M	7
92.	D pg. 8-10, 8-13	M	8
93.	D pg. 8-10, 8-11	M	8
94.	C pg. 8-17	M	8
95.	C pg. 13-3	M	13
96.	A pg. 13-7	M	13
97.	B pg. 8-27, 8-28 A is wrong because it will also extend the term of the maturity guarantee	M	8
98.	A pg. 8-4, 8-5	M	8
99.	A pg. 13-9 to 13-15	M	13
100.	B pg. 13-9 to 13-15 A, C, and D are overly conservative and also entail higher taxes on interest income	M	13